Seed

Book II

Charged

Joshua David

Cover art by Christian Bentulan.

ISBN-13: 978-1-0878-7706-8

DEDICATION

For my boys,
may they someday smile at the memory of their dada
clicking keys as they slept,
trying to make their world a little bit brighter.

CONTENTS

1

I SPREAD THE GOOD NEWS. Beyond other choices I've made, both noble and destructive, that is still my calling. Jess remains my north star. How, then, did I bring the sparse remnants of our world to the brink of annihilation? How could war be born of such pure intentions? I'm still human, despite my alien composition. I try to move with the whispers of better angels when I can hear them, but we all slip and stumble. I am not innocent. When challenged with the choices that define me, sometimes I hear only whispers from the darkness. Good news can be hard to find even when it's in your own hand.

Do you know of Jess? Have you heard the good news? Too few have. That's my fault, too. I'll explain who she is, or was, as best I can with what time I have left. Jess saved me, and you, whether you know it or not. She stood against Seed and took the place of all of us as it tried to strike its final blow. Her life laid down was enough to halt the inevitable, but it is unclear if her victory can endure. The wickedness that first lit the fuse of judgment has been invited, even forced, back into our reality. I fear Jess had only so much to give.

Even after being shown a higher path, our future is more uncertain than ever. I'm slowly accepting that uncertainty itself is the one rule that can't be broken. If you knew Jess's kindness and boundless compassion, you would think that she might guide us through this unsteady wilderness from wherever she resides, but I have come to understand that she won't help us in that way. Belief lives in uncertainty. Faith needs space. Choices, even those of life and death, wouldn't matter as much if they were pressed too hard by one side or another. Jess wouldn't want the way ahead to be crowded and choked of its freedom, even if it was a beautiful spirit like hers that created limits. I see her reluctance to present herself more forcefully as a gift, but that piece of gratitude is the most difficult to form.

If you read to understand the war between east and west to prepare yourself for what horrors likely lie beyond the conflict, I'm afraid the most dangerous decisions will remain shrouded in doubt even after my recitation of events. I can tell you what I did and why, what we all did to save humanity from itself, but our small corner of existence is so big now that I both fear and know that my tale alone won't be enough. In the end, you must prepare yourself like we all should have before any of this madness began: with morality ahead of strategy. Listen to Jess if you can hear her.

Bloodshed thrived long before I existed and will live long after I have gone, but I stoked this particular fire. Looking at the painful aftermath, and staring at a silvery reflection of a terrifying future, I am now forced to contemplate every decision that culminated in tragedy. Where did I go wrong? What can be done to save what is left?

2

It began on a barstool. I was spreading the good news and toasting to my more valorous parts. The few inhabitants of a town called Cedar in southern Utah were enthralled. They seemed interested, anyway. They were nervous, too. I hadn't traveled so far for purely a social visit and a chance to tell my tale of Jess; I had been led to the town by reports of Dweller activity in the area. People needed help.

Outside the bar, a squad of well-armed Dwellers gathered, trying to conceal their approach among the broken buildings and the foliage reclaiming the structures. They, too, had been led to the town by reports, but theirs had something to do with me. I had spent months hunting them down and was beginning to get a reputation.

I would give them a chance, of course. They could hear my message and choose to take a higher road than robbing and raping and eating the pioneers who ventured into the wastes to try to make new homes and lives for themselves, or I would beat them to death. Sometimes I'd toss them off something tall. Sometimes I'd twist the rifles they used to terrorize their victims around their necks until something important would pop. You get the idea. I felt like it was a pretty fair deal, considering. I was good either way.

I sat and I preached as the Dwellers approached, delivering my tale of Jess with nuance and charm derived from numerous recitations. I was having as nice of a time as I could while wandering the wastes and new settlements in search of people to save. One of the couples who'd gathered to greet me and tell me of their recent woes even had a daughter not much older than me. Forget good news; this was great news! She looked pretty good by pioneer standards. I couldn't tell, though, if she liked me because she liked me or because I was the purported half-Seed meat-shield that would stand between her and the aforementioned robbing and raping and eating. Again, I was good either way. I layered as much allure into my story as I could and sent it inconspicuously her way.

Jess was nowhere to be found, if you're wondering. I spoke to her constantly, hoping she could hear me. I received nothing in return. Not a word. I searched my heart for her inspiration as often as I could make myself meditate on better ideas than policing the wastes. For a time, I felt like I found her there. I felt some sense of guidance. But, as of late, nothing. I was beginning to think the entire exercise was nothing more than exaggerated mourning. My sense of her was perhaps a function of denial, a feeling left inside after loving someone so much. But the sentiment was fading. I felt increasingly alone.

I was upset by her absence, if I'm telling the truth. And I was further upset about being upset about it. It was ridiculous to expect her to be there, the more I pondered the impossibility. She was unquestionably special. Magnificent and special and beautiful beyond compare, but she was dead. The voice I heard after she departed was only an echo in my mind from a spirit imbued with such spectacular power. Any fantasies I entertained about what form of her companionship might be possible after her departure seemed increasingly silly as time passed. I could be a believer in the potential she had sacrificed to give us and in all that she taught us but I couldn't be silly. I found it embarrassing to cling to the absurd notion of such a long-distance relationship.

They were almost upon us. I counted nine by the twitches of my audience's eyes and the reflections in the glass around me. I could hear some of their movements, the shaking of their gear. I think I began to smell them, but the wastes were fraught with odd odors, so it was hard to discern. My senses, I was learning, were heightened after my involuntary infusion of alien. I couldn't tell if they were improved or just returned to an earlier and more perfect state. Either way, I could hear a steel magazine brush tactical nylon mesh fifty yards away. My adversaries weren't as sneaky as they thought, especially toting heavy gear to what would be another comical effort to kill me.

When I heard footsteps on the concrete outside, it was go-time. "Get down!" I abruptly commanded to my audience. They scattered and dove to the ground like they'd been aching to do for some time. I knew they were displeased by my tactics, by making them wait. I could see them restraining their objections while I spoke. But I had a larger plan in mind. Jess's example still filled me with spirit, so I couldn't simply end the violent filth that stalked the townsfolk. I had to give them a choice, which inevitably came with risks.

A shadow crossed in front of the floor-to-ceiling window closest to the door. It clutched the shadow of an M16. My newest adversary thought he was about to burst heroically through the door and fill us all with lead. He was in for a rough evening.

I shot across the room at a speed none had seen since Seed was pacified. With one fist through the window, I had my first target in a chokehold from behind before the glass hit the ground. I snatched the rifle from his hands and smashed it into the floor, shattering it to pieces. Through the panicked gurgles making their way up his esophagus, I understood that my new friend was already beginning to have a change of heart.

I took out my knife and held it to his throat. That was just for dramatic effect. I could have taken his head off sans tools, but I had a dramatic message to deliver. "Drop your weapons!" I shouted at the others. "This isn't going to end how you hoped, but there is still a way to leave here alive if you show yourselves and surrender."

A second Dweller had approached the entrance from the opposite direction and stopped when I grabbed his comrade. I could see him through the glass as I stood near the opened door. I wondered what he was thinking. Of the remaining eight, he had the best angle on me. Would he relent or attack? He had been ordered here, sent by one of the ruthless commanders who had sprung up while Seed reigned and had grown even more powerful after its departure. But was this particular Dweller loyal enough or afraid enough of his boss to tangle with Sal after what he had likely heard and what he had just seen? How much power did his warlord wield?

He shot me! Can you believe that? There I was trying to save him from himself, and he shot me for it. This was the reception I was becoming accustomed to after so long hunting down the scum... or spreading the good news – whatever you might like to call my acts. Gratitude for my mercy was rare. If a Dweller did choose to leave a life of villainy behind for a more honorable existence, it was usually after an unpleasant encounter and under some duress. The whole process was really starting to rub me the wrong way. All work and no appreciation was beginning to make Sal a dull boy.

I knew the bullet was coming when Stupid raised the rifle. That gave me a head start. I wasn't faster than Seed was, as far as I knew. I never saw a host dodge a bullet, anyway. The Angels always had an advantage with ballistics. But I was still getting faster with practice. By the time the barrel was pointed at my head, I was already moving out of the trajectory and raising my previously knife-wielding hand to stop the projectile. A bullet travels ahead of its sound, a nuisance I never noticed before becoming otherworldly, so I couldn't hear it coming. But the instant that lead began to tear through the fleshy outer of my grip, I tried to grasp the painful object as it flew by and splattered my blood. I just missed. I put enough pressure on the round to warp its path, though. It smacked hard into the floor just behind me. I hadn't caught one yet, but neither was I done training.

I yelled in pain. The hole in my hand would heal soon enough but it hurt every time. Then I yelled at Stupid, "Are you kidding me! I'm trying to give you a chance, Stupid!"

I was pissed. I was so tired of my job, spouting what seemed like nonsense at the ingrates. It seemed impossible that they would ever understand. How could they, really? How could they be out stealing and murdering, then beaten unconscious or otherwise violently subdued, then be ready to hear a cool story about a beautiful woman who had died to save them from what they had helped the world become? There was not a fruitful way to make that jarring transition work, or I hadn't found it if there was.

I took my frustrations out on Stupid. He tried to kill me, so an eye for an eye, etc. I threw my shaking, terrified first target a good twenty feet across the room. He hit the wall hard enough to knock him out cold. Then I shot off after my would-be murderer. He got off another round as I approached but was way off target. I seized the weapon out of his hands and hit him in the head with it, a bit too hard judging by the folding inward of the side of his melon and the blood and goo that painted the glass beside him. I don't think that's what I was trying to do, but I wasn't too worried about it. The dark liquid flowing from his broken cranium probably meant that a hundred future pioneers wouldn't be touched by his evil hands. The execution was good news in its own way.

Then came the serious gunfire. The remaining Dwellers abandoned tactics and foreplay. It was time to go loud and kill everyone. Bullets crashed everywhere around me, breaking the glass façade of the bar. One caught me in the leg but didn't slow me down much. I raced through the newly opened window to check on my audience. They had all taken cover as best they could. Being a pioneer in what was supposed to be a beautifully restarted world was a harrowing existence. Nature wasn't any friendlier than it always had been, and the Dweller threat was widespread and pervasive. There wasn't a single new village I'd visited that hadn't had a few encounters. Pioneers had to know how to fight. Mine were doing well enough. But the sight of them under heavy fire dispelled any notion I had of making friends with our murderers. The Dwellers wanted blood. They would see blood.

I had left my miraculous blade by the bar. I truly hoped that I wouldn't need it. But I'd had enough of playing nice that day. It was the pointlessness of it all that infuriated me the most. Why menace the innocent? Why live like parasites on the backs of others instead of creating an honorable life with the boundless opportunity recently opened in the world? The answer kept smacking me in the face while I tried to spread a message of peace and love and morality: they were Dwellers, people low enough to find comfort in the shadow of a monster like Seed. Maybe they were never meant to follow a spirit like Jess.

Time to go to work, yet again. I grabbed the blade and picked up a table to shield myself from the incoming fire. An aggressive trio of Dwellers was advancing toward the building, guns blazing. Not a smart move to be out in the open when righteous fury is in motion. With the table leading the charge, I sprinted toward the middle scumbag as fast as I could. Forty-eight mph was my personal land speed record so far, but neither was I done training. The table shattered when I hit him, sending his broken body flying backward. Along the way, I hit the target on my right with the blade. His two halves were shocked to be separated while still stacked atop each other. He wouldn't be causing anyone any more harm while he thought his last disjointed and terrified thoughts. I figured I'd take a round or two from my third target before I got to him, but he chose a different path. After seeing the gruesome show, he was oscar mic as quick as his puny legs would carry him. The others followed suit, still shooting haphazardly, trying to murder me even in retreat.

I had a choice to make: let them live to murder another day or not. I chose not. When I got back to the bar to check on everyone, I was covered in blood.

As I entered, I saw my first Dweller still unconscious on the floor. I had forgotten about that one. As I walked over to him, the townsfolk almost in unison called out, "No!" They were sweet, worried about a guy who ten minutes ago would have done unspeakable things to each and every one of them. I smiled at their disapproval. They were good people.

"I wasn't going to kill him," I said with a chuckle as I made my way back to the bar. Then I thought about whether I was lying or not. I picked up the bottle of scotch I'd been sipping before all the commotion and took a nice long drink. Sadly, the heavenly nectar wouldn't do a thing to ease my conflicted soul. Invincibility had come with a terrible, unbearable, awful price: I couldn't get drunk no matter how hard I tried. And believe me, I tried. I rested my forehead on the bar as I clutched the bottle. What was I doing? What had I become?

When the remaining Dweller regained consciousness, I asked him as politely as I could to join me for a drink. He shuffled to the seat next to me as every eye in the bar leered at him. As he sat, I put my hand on his shoulder, slathering a bit of his friends' blood on his shirt. He trembled as he looked at me. I smiled as friendly a smile as I could force through tired teeth, then began the interrogation. "No good news for you, sir." He had no idea what I was talking about. "I'm afraid you only get 'or else.' You will tell me every detail about your encampment, your forces, and your leader, or else I will tear an appendage off your body and shove it in a place you wouldn't believe it can fit."

He talked, and I proved once again that I hadn't lost any of my charm.

3

I saw choices in three directions. I could go home, to Jess's temple, or I could chase after the bandits who hid in the hills and hunted the innocent. Rest and be with family, try to learn something more about humanity's relationship with the Visitor, or dispense more good news mixed with my brand of justice.

Home had blossomed into as beautiful a place as can sprout in a bleak desert. Since quietly relocating Jess's remains to what had become her final resting place, I had been back to Nellis a handful of times. Each time saw dazzling developments. The race to remake life was moving at breakneck speed. The gates were open wide. More and more people were traveling in and out of the refuge. With more people came more structures, more ideas, and more ways to connect humanity. Projects entailing technologies gathered from the widening corners of our small world were always in the works.

James and Mary presided over the percolating oasis as its natural leaders, one concerned with keeping what was left of humanity safe, the other inspiring them to take insane risks if they could find in themselves the requisite belief. And Grover still asserted himself into the mix, using his political prowess to negotiate between the two conflicting sentiments when necessary. He was always happy to remind them that he was the President of the United States, after all. He'd remind anyone who'd listen, really.

My first trip away from Nellis to Jess's home took far longer than expected. I planned to be gone for a few days at most. I'd drop off my unusual package without delay and circle back to look for Pete. I didn't so much as make it past the next valley to the east when I bumped into people - real people, not the dwelling and eating other people kind. They had been hiding in ancient caves in what they called the Valley of Fire. The name seemed redundant with every valley around Vegas sweltering miserably in the ceaselessly burning sun.

My new friends had been hiding and keeping themselves alive on their own for many years. One couple in the small group even had a small child. It was amazing that simple stealth had been enough to survive the apocalypse and the Dwellers that accompanied the evil. But even my solitude-hardened new companions were now on the run. The Dwellers had become legion in the vast wilderness of the southwest, probably following the shadow of Seed as it descended upon Jess toward the end. The vile swarm was predictably ticked off when their god suddenly went flaccid. I was told that the Dwellers were out for answers and vengeance, seemingly trying to rekindle the hate and violence of their master with sacrifices and mayhem.

I directed the refugees to Nellis, of course, but I couldn't leave their escape to chance. I waited a good while for the Dwellers to catch up. They didn't receive the good news I had so hoped to share on my inaugural excursion. After hearing the grim tales of their intended prey, I decided they weren't my target audience. Instead, I delighted in the surprise of each of my victims as they attacked a creature that more resembled their lost deity the more they shot and cleaved. I found their final screams comical, but I admit that my sense of humor may have been somewhat tainted by a lifetime of loss and war.

So began my plight. Two steps forward, then a journey back into the wild looking for trouble. The routine of trying to save people while trying to save people kept me lost, farther and farther away from home for longer and longer.

When I did make it back, the visits increasingly stirred two emotions that were not mixing well within my increasingly lonely soul: joy and angst. Though I cherished every word exchanged with James and Mary and loved mingling with new and old friends, especially my Angels, something made me feel out of place in my own home. I think it was the new couple more than anything – my adoptive parents, as it was turned out. They loved me so much. I was showered with their attention and affection. Nothing was wrong with that. But there was something in the volume that betrayed the pure sentiment. They were both loving me as though I were two children, and that was beginning to wear. Pete was gone. Jess was gone. I remained. Though the tragedy was as simple as it was painful, our strange circumstances made it seem as though both Pete and Jess should be standing right next to me in whatever form might be possible. They pressed upon me the importance of my missions so fervently that I felt as though they thought me capable of bringing them back if I only worked harder or with more faith. Everything seemed possible in light of our victory. The grand blessing came with the burden of living up to its magnitude.

Maybe I was overthinking it. Maybe Mary was just that nice, and James seemed nicer than he had been for many years because I was done deliberately and constantly pissing him off all the time. I don't know. Maybe it was more my conscience screaming out for me to do more with my gift than I was. It was quite a gift, and I was using it mostly to beat up the bad guys, a helpful but cheap exercise.

Either way, something wasn't sitting right. Being close to my family heightened rather than alleviated the sense. Did I discuss my way out of that conundrum with the wisest two people on the planet? No. I beat up more bad guys and continued failing at my missions to bring back Pete or make my way closer to Jess.

Which leads me to my second choice: visit Jess. If her spirit lived on, it was the easiest to find in her castle. It really was a castle. I'm not oversimplifying or overstating. She literally built a castle. She was something like thirteen years old when she ran from her hospital in Vegas with her first followers. It made sense that a young girl would build a fairytale if she had the power. Jess had power in spades.

When I first approached, I could barely believe my eyes, even after everything I had seen Jess do. I thought I might wander the dazzling canyons of Zion for some time before I found the right spot. Mary had given me specific directions, but most of the towering red monoliths looked about the same, so taking a right at the thousand-foot sunset-colored spire wasn't as specific as it first sounded. I wasn't lost for long. Peaking above the natural pinnacles were silver redoubts and a towering bastion shining in the setting sun. It was a castle.

Jess had nestled her structure into a canyon carved by a tributary of the Virgin River, which was brilliant. The fortification was fed by a stream of clean water and was bolstered by the surrounding rock. Seed would have had a hard time negotiating the terrain even before the ramparts went up, and food would often come toward the inhabitants for a drink rather than be hunted through the wilderness.

The innermost structures were smaller, a village of sorts, the beginning of her dream. The first blocks were made of stone, not Visitor, which seemed out of place at first. But then I remembered her words: that the Visitor was made to copy its surroundings. Asking for another of something was like asking a bird to fly. So, her first requests were simpler: please make more of these modest blocks so we might have a roof over our heads.

As Jess grew, so did her dream along with her ability to negotiate with the Visitor. She negotiated walls, one concentric ring after another, three layers deep, in some places hundreds of feet high, with at least fifty yards in between the rings. Then came a great hall, which was so large that it crossed two circular sections of defenses, a magnificent place for her growing followers to gather. Many homes sprang up among the larger structures over the years to house new arrivals. Then came more grand halls to house various activities in addition to the people. Libraries were the oldest. More advanced centers of learning and experimentation followed as the knowledge contained in the village expanded.

I marveled at the gateway when I approached. I was expecting an actual gate, maybe a drawbridge, something both whimsical and so imposing that Seed couldn't climb it or break it. Instead, two immense but relatively normal doors stood cracked open in the wall that seemed to touch the sky when standing before it. Why would she have open doors? She was brave, no doubt, but not stupid. She might risk herself but never those she protected, certainly never so flagrantly.

The two doors were a few feet apart. I looked around for something or someone that might explain the situation. Nothing. It was quiet except for a gentle, cool breeze swirling in the rust-colored canyon. I peeked inside each door. The sun was setting behind me, so mostly darkness lay behind them. Okay, she left the door open. Weird, but okay. But which one? The hallways behind seemed to lead in different directions and neither toward the center of the complex. Then I saw an inscription in the wall between the two: CHOOSE THE RIGHT PATH.

I could feel her standing right next to me. I even looked. Nothing there, but the breeze held hints of her laughter.

Fine, my love. It's the one on the right. Hilarious. But a fifty-fifty chance of invasion? If a host approached, or a hundred, she left the odds of attack at a coin toss. It seemed sloppy until I entered the darkening tunnel. Two more doors. Then two more. It was a maze.

I counted nine sets of doors before I made it through. I always went right, hoping that I was deciphering her riddle – which I was never very good at. Up and down stairs as the loops of the maze circled and crossed each other. I was feeling my way through the darkness toward the end. With the long series of choices in place, if a mindless host would have entered, or even a mob, they would have had less than a one in a thousand chance of making it inside. A person, on the other hand, could walk right in if they followed her simple instruction. She was so dazzling and odd in her beautiful way. She left the door open and closed at the same time.

When I finally entered, I wished I had taken a left. Seed stood howling in my path as my eyes adjusted to both the candlelight on the other side of the room and the most horrifying sight I could have possibly seen. Not a wandering host. Not the benign Visitor. Seed stood before me, readying itself to rip me to shreds.

My knees buckled. I was nauseous. I had believed in her so much that I thought we had won, really won. But here lived evil again, screaming at me as it had for what seemed like my whole life. When it lunged, I barely put up a fight. I wasn't sure that I wanted to stick around a planet if it was still infected with Seed after what we'd already sacrificed to purge the monster.

Seed screeched and howled as it swiped at me again and again. I fought back with only enough speed and force to blunt the attacks. My mind was dizzy. Everything we did was for nothing?

Then came a small voice from somewhere behind the thing trying to kill me. "Stop it! Stop it right now!" She was yelling in our direction, but the quick shouts sounded like she was yelling at a dog to stop barking. She wasn't afraid; she was annoyed. I was being murdered, and someone wanted the bloodshed to quiet down a little. Why did I always feel upside down when I encountered any piece of Jess?

At her calls, the beast surprisingly relented. "I am so sorry," she said, embarrassed. "But you are early," she said somewhat accusatorily.

"You are, no doubt, acquainted with Jess," I grumbled as I began to piece the situation together.

"Obviously," she quipped, "who do you think built this place? Santa?" And she was a touch rude. Definitely an acquaintance. "Who are you?" she finished, like her incongruous question logically followed.

"You know that I'm late but you don't know who I am. You're like a student of hers, aren't you? Tell me I'm wrong!" I was back to being mildly aggravated, a more normal mood.

"Yes..."

"And this is your guardian."

"You could call him that, I guess." She looked at her friend with a puzzled expression but nodded in agreement. "He guards the door, sometimes, so... Anyway, I'm Faye. Who are you?"

"I'm Sal," I sighed.

"Nice to meet you, Sal," she said hurrying the conversation along. "Is Jess with you?"

I couldn't entirely hold back the tears. "You could say that."

"Oh, dear," she replied. She was saddened by the news but still in a strange hurry. "Well, that makes more sense then."

"How's that?" Aggravation was giving way to accepting the confusion always twirling in Jess's wake.

"Some strange things have been happening here. I suspected, honestly, but hoped for the best, you know?" With that, she walked up to me and hugged me. It was a tight and long squeeze. She held the embrace compassionately and looked up at me for my response before letting go. "Are you okay?"

She had green, tender eyes. Freckles dotted her smooth skin. I would have found her attractive if she was a few notches less annoying.

I hugged back. "Not really."

We stood for some time in that embrace, which felt odd but nice after the way my journey had gone. When we both relaxed after our strange meeting, I let go. "You want to come in and see the place?" she asked with a friendlier tone. "Of course, you do!" she answered her own question, building up to being back in a hurry. "Lots of cool stuff in this place. I'll give you the tour."

I was feeling calm enough to let my curiosity stir about my miraculous surroundings when the guardian stepped forward again. This time it grunted as it approached me and held out its arms in a way that appeared as though it was trying to hug me in turn.

I jumped back. "Oh, you gotta be kidding me!" Another grunt. It stopped in its tracks and looked to Faye for guidance.

"Yeah, he's a hugger. Probably gets it from me," Faye said with half a smile and half a scrunched-up face, admitting that maybe it wasn't the best idea to be hugging an alien corpse or whatever it was. "You just saw the mean side of him. He's really very friendly when he's not keeping out the possessed or those other people who are almost as bad."

"Dwellers."

"You call them Dwellers? What's that about?"

A fascinating tour and friendly conversation followed, my first recitation of the good news beyond my home. Faye gave me an earful as well. We had a lot to talk about.

Dwellers lead me to my final choice: hunt down those remaining so the people around Cedar could live in peace, at least as much as I could temporarily provide.

Which would you have chosen? I thought about Jess and tried to feel some sense of direction, but there was nothing to be found in my heart. I thought about James and Mary, and how happy they'd be to have me home – overly happy. I thought about Faye and a castle that turned out to be more of a university than anything else. I wondered where I was needed most.

I went after the bad guys. Among other options, why not give something of myself for my neighbors? I don't know if that was wrong, but now, looking at a nightmare hovering over a graveyard, part of me wishes I would have stepped left instead of right.

4

Spying the sprawling structure that housed my latest audience/targets, I longed for a better version of the play about to be performed for what felt like the hundredth time. I wished an odd wish: that there was more than just one uniquely gifted soul like me to spread the good news. Resilient as I was, I still needed backup.

I thought of asking some Angels to accompany me on my excursions, but most of them were scattered across the blossoming landscape, looking to find or rebuild lost lives. A few remained on base, but they were needed more for security there than protecting the invincible out here. Even a handful of green riflemen would have been handy, though an inexperienced squad clunking around in Atlases still wouldn't solve the tactical situation in front of me.

The Dwellers were holed-up in a building that looked too big to be real: a distribution center east of St. George that had to be half a mile from end to end. What I needed for a successful incursion was another me, someone to flank the hostiles so I didn't have to blaze down the warpath alone, a holy but unhappy beacon for everyone's gunfire. Kicking over the first domino so hard always made such a mess that a polite series of events culminating in a welcomed recitation of the good news was highly unlikely.

Dwellers were everywhere, more than I'd seen in one place since Vegas. They were behaving more civilized and organized than normal, too. Armed guards stood at every accessible door. A few patrols circled the perimeter. This was going to turn ugly in a hurry if I didn't come up with a more delicate plan than my usual approach.

What would Jess do? Kneeling behind one of the hundreds of semi-trucks still parked in eternal expectancy outside the building, I closed my eyes and touched my chest in the place I felt her the most. Just a word, Jess, and I'll listen, I thought. Nothing in return, as usual. I wasn't quite ready to give up, though. I slowed my mind and focused for a moment only on her, on how beautiful and weird and mesmerizing she was. I tried to hear her voice in my memories. Which oddly cheerful or unexpectedly angry words of her's best matched my situation?

My psyche slipped back to kicking the crap out of the first Dwellers we met together. That was a good memory, in a way. I did really well in that fight, much better than expected. But that couldn't be the answer I sought. She was angry at me when I heroically fought that bunch. Then she gave herself up to people who were out to kill her just for the chance to change some hearts. Could that be my answer?

I didn't like the plan. And I didn't like not knowing who it came from. Did I just decide to give up without a fight, or was it my lost love that made the call in the present but from the past? Maybe I was going crazy wandering the world alone, again. Maybe memories are more than tracks laid in grey matter. I didn't have time to sort it all out, though an arrangement more definitive needed to be decided upon in our impossible relationship. My feet were already moving me closer to an entrance.

I moved out from the cover of the trucks very slowly with my hands raised. I waited until they saw me before I moved farther.

"Stop right there!" one shouted. I inched slowly forward, not to antagonize but so we didn't have to shout. "Stop!" he commanded again.

"Okay, stopping!" I called back, trying to remove any sarcasm. "I'm surrendering, so you can relax."

"Get on the ground!" were my next orders as two approached with rifles pointed at my chest.

"Yeah, that part's not going to happen, but I'm still not here to fight." I smiled and tried to emphasize the emptiness of my raised hands. "I came to talk."

The one who'd been shouting at me stopped farther away than I could reach, and his partner circled wide to flank me. Good moves for what were supposed to be blood-thirsty amateurs. I was impressed and unnerved.

The flanker saw the sword on my back and started to tremble. He screamed to his partner, "It's him!"

"Yes, it's me," I tried to interrupt, "but, again, just here to..."

The one in front of me fired his weapon in the air. The alarm was rung, and the first domino was kicked over harder than I was hoping for. I could hear yelling all over the area. Footsteps crisscrossed everywhere. I was soon surrounded.

"Everyone feel better now?" I asked, trying to lighten the mood and show them I wasn't as rattled as the fifty murderers around me. I scanned around and behind me. Lots of rifles. This predicament was going to hurt if, or when, it went south. Among the rifles, I saw a few odd pistols, too. Square-faced and thicker than usual. I knew every sidearm in the book. These weren't in the book. I was confident, however, they'd hurt just as much.

"I'm going to tell you one last time," barked my first assailant. "Get on the ground and toss that weapon away, or you're going to die here!"

"Sorry, never going to happen, friend. I don't lie down. I don't disarm. And I will speak. I will say what I came here to say with you as my guide or as a corpse under my boot. If you know who I am, then you already know it doesn't matter much to me either way." I was beginning to lose my cool, like always. They were making me fail at the only thing that might bring me closer to Jess, and the frustration was getting so bad that I was starting to see little black spots in my vision that could only be cured by ripping one of the idiots limb from limb. "So, please," I said through clenched teeth, "be kind and calm. Escort me inside like the guest that I am."

Confused silence and shaky guns encircled me. I spun a very slow circle to see each of them directly, to look them in their eyes and watch their decisions. If I saw so much as a knuckle whiten, I was going to paint the semi-trucks red.

Then she spoke. It was her! In a whisper, seemingly from far away, but it was her. "Sal," drifted her soft breath, "look up."

"Jess!" I cried to nowhere in particular. I looked up. In the sky above, I didn't see the beautiful apparition for which I yearned. I saw a jet. How weird. Somebody was flying a jet, and it looked like it was headed in the direction of Nellis. "What the f..."

This wasn't the first time I'd been hit with a stun gun, so I knew the drill. But this one packed a new punch. I saw blue lightning coming at me, on me, everywhere, then I didn't see anything at all.

5

Nellis was bustling with life that day. Most of the dozen gates were open wide. People were arriving for safety, supplies, information, or just the company the sanctuary provided. People were leaving after being refreshed, on their way to what might be a new place for a new future or back to an established home. It was a hub for humanity, a place where few wanted to live but everyone wanted to be.

James was gardening, of all things. Not much could survive in the hellish climate, but watermelons oddly sprouted in the endless sun if enough water was supplied. He acted, with some sincerity, as though he disliked the activity. He was needed elsewhere, of course. The heavy burden of the base's security still rested on his capable shoulders. He should have been inspecting patrols, checking up on equipment repairs, or helping coordinate the defenses of off-site settlements, but he had other orders. Mary said that he needed a hobby, that the military and the rest of the world could wait while he relaxed and exhaled. She took to gardening soon after her arrival, so James followed in the pastime, even organizing her plot and planning future generations with a bit more structure. Secretly, I think he enjoyed the peace.

Grover was giving a tour and happened by James bent over in the dirt. Grover still loved nothing more than the sound of his own voice, so he took it upon himself to welcome and provide an orientation to all newcomers. Most visitors were bemused meeting the President of the United States after there were no states, but some took him seriously. A few called him Mr. President and shook his hand after their tour, which fueled Grover more than food or water ever could. Grover wanted to introduce his group to the brave and famous General Hardt as he passed by, so he spoke loud enough for James to hear, "And this is General Hardt, the commander of our military and man who led the final charge against Seed. James, would you like to…"

"No, I would not, Grover!" James shouted without looking. He thought of a place in the garden that could use some Grover-shaped fertilizer. "Does it look like I'm doing that right now?"

Mary appeared, as she often did when conflict arose. She had been inside the RV that she called home when she heard Grover's polished inflection intrude. She could see the train wreck coming a mile away. "James," was all she had to say in a disappointed tone to deflate his antagonism.

"Fine," he replied as he stood and brushed dirt from his clothes.

"Oh, Mary!" Grover said as she emerged. "Everyone, this is Mary, Jess's mother." He bowed as he gestured in Mary's direction. He was filled past overflow with ego but in Mary's presence he couldn't help but dispense with his practiced persona and show real respect. The exact amount Jess had sacrificed to save them all was still a matter of internal debate; what Mary had sacrificed was glaring and appreciated by anyone who knew her story.

Mary waved a kind wave in the small crowd's direction. James approached with an obligatory but not insincere smile. "Hello, everyone," he said as he neared. It seemed to everyone like he was about to say more when a flicker of light in the sky caught his eye. He stopped in his tracks and squinted at the horizon.

Grover looked to James for the rest of his welcoming speech, but James was frozen. "Commander, is everything…"

"Shut up!" James snapped before he could finish. It was a suppressed reflex whenever Grover opened his mouth, but if James was rude out loud, it meant he was upset.

"James?" Mary called from behind. "Is everything…"

James only had orders. "Mary, run to the command center! Do it now and go below! Grover, get these people inside. Use the armory. Move!" he shouted as he began running to the command center himself. Panicked looks only lasted a moment, then everyone ran.

James kept shouting as he raced across the base. He zigzagged between buildings to warn everyone he could while making his way. By the time he got to Jack's, the commotion was spreading ahead of him. Jack appeared from a doorway, beer still in his hand. "What's going on, James?" he asked unconcerned and with only the slightest slur in his coarse speech.

"Incoming!"

"Incoming?" Jack looked around. "What in the heck are you…"

"Incoming, damn it! Incoming!" James repeated as he passed in a hurry. "Get those people out of there and somewhere more secure. You have one minute, two tops." Then he was gone between the buildings as he ran toward the mountain.

Phil, an Angel and one of James's captains, met James at the entrance to the command center. "Sir?"

"Do we have eyes on it?" James asked, out of breath.

"Eyes on what, sir?"

"Jet," James replied, pointing at the aircraft while resting the other hand on his knee.

"No, sir."

"Get everyone you can inside. You have sixty seconds and not one more. Then shut the blast doors."

Inside, they waited. All eyes were on the monitors in the conference room. Alice was long gone, so everything had to be operated manually, which was hardly better than being blind. Finally, a camera on the wall locked onto the approaching jet.

Mary was unimpressed. "James, it's just a plane. Isn't that kind of a good thing, considering?"

"We don't know what it is," James replied, glued to the screens. "But Bone bombers don't usually carry friendly passengers; they carry munitions."

A bomb dropped. Gasps filled the room. As soon as its payload was loosed, the jet banked hard to return east along its same flight path. Mary moved under James's arm and squeezed him as the two watched the object fall. Mary shut her eyes when it was about to hit. James kept watching.

Then, nothing. Everyone looked at each other. Was the explosion yet to come? "James," Mary asked now that it seemed as though incineration had been postponed, "who would do this?"

"That's a good question. There are a few candidates," James answered into the silent room still waiting for an explosion. "The war was bigger than Seed when it started. Someone might still be fighting. We could be a target just for existing on the wrong dirt."

Still, nothing. The group was becoming restless. Waiting for death was exhausting in a strange way. Phil interrupted the suspense, "Sir, most ordnance is set to detonate long before impact."

"I know!" James answered, annoyed at first. "I know," he said again as he put his hand on Phil's shoulder. "Gear up. There are a few functioning Atlases on the sublevels. We need to go take a look."

"Sir, I'll recon and report back."

"I'm coming with you."

As three Atlases approached the impact site, Phil once again thought to keep his commander, along with his favorite bartender, back from the threat. But the three heard crying ahead before he could speak. They all ran toward the danger.

A small, old house on the base, one built for airmen long ago, had been hit. Half the roof had collapsed, and the rest of the structure didn't look stable. The three Atlases tore at the walls and debris muffling the crying, soon uncovering a woman pinned under a fallen support beam. She was injured but alive and holding her baby, sheltering him from the crushing weight with her own body. Both cried for help. "Get them out!" James shouted as he carefully lifted the beam with the strength of the Atlas.

Once freed, the mother coughed and pleaded, "My husband..." She coughed again. "Still inside."

"I'll get him," James answered.

Phil, carrying a tiny baby in the Atlas's hulking metal arms, tried to object. "Sir, I can do it. The bomb, Sir."

"Get them to safety," James ordered as he began making his way toward the rear of the house. As he dug through rubble to what looked like a bedroom, he found both his targets, one crushing the other. He'd have to move the bomb to get to the father.

The choice forced a second thought. He was risking everyone on base to try to save someone who looked to be in bad shape if not worse. He paused as he contemplated the long path which formed his strange life, a line of decisions he'd carved behind him to reach where he was standing at that moment. He wondered if he ought to not roll the dice once more. Maybe he should retreat the way he came.

Phil raced both mother and child to the infirmary. Jack was waiting forty yards away from the impact. Having unloaded his payload, he was watching for James to emerge or a ball of fire to swallow him whole. He chuckled when he saw a bomb fly back into the sky. It flew far enough to land beyond the wall. James appeared from the wreckage with another body on his shoulder. It was too mangled to be alive.

As James approached with slow, heavy footsteps, Jack asked, "Why hit us like this? It makes no sense."

"I don't know," James said as he looked back at the destroyed home and shook his head in sadness and disbelief. "But to hell with that garden."

6

I awoke in a jail cell. What kind of twisted freak builds a dingy jail inside a dark warehouse in the middle of nowhere? I was about to find out.

Disoriented, lying on my stomach, I ran my hand along the filth covering the ground. I stretched to touch the bars of the makeshift prison. The mismatched columns of rectangular steel had been repurposed from all kinds of equipment in the warehouse. It was crap craftmanship, but the Dwellers were really trying. I gave them an E for effort and laughed at their folly. Did they truly believe they could hold me in a flimsy cage? I laughed more at the charade and the bloodbath in the works. As soon as I could feel all my appendages again, things were going to get messy.

As I squirmed and giggled irrationally on the floor, men outside my cell hastily stood and readied their weapons. They weren't all pointed at me, though. I looked to my left and right. More cells. More people. The others looked like they'd been in for a while. They were cowering before their captors and stealing quick looks at me. I wondered if they knew who I was and hoped for salvation. I wasn't sure how I could save them all.

It was a good tactic to keep me pinned not with the junky bars but with their lives, good and infuriating. As I clumsily made it to my hands and knees, I started to see some of those special black spots of rage in my still-blurry vision. Whoever set all this up was not dying quickly. Neither were their friends. Neither were their pets.

"He's up!" one shouted into the darkness behind him when he saw me struggle to rise. The warehouse behind him was mostly lost to the night. Only a few candles and lanterns were lit. Their dim flickers were no match for the staggering size of the enclosure.

I squinted into the darkness for my target. Who would soon scream their last breath? I was sure the Dweller chieftain was about to appear, some dirty lunatic that missed his old overlord, some murderous scumbag who was just a touch more violent than the rest or who possessed just a few more IQ points with which to control the others. I was sure he'd be wearing a necklace of ears or something equally vile. I made it to kneeling by the time he arrived.

Just when you think there is absolutely, positively no way to be more irritated, the universe throws you a curveball to remind you that there are no limits. A pair of combat boots approached. They were polished. Fairly neat fatigues housed the rest of his tall frame. And around his neck was something even more infuriating than a necklace of flesh trophies: dog tags. This chieftain had once played for the home team. I couldn't quickly think of a way to dispatch him with proper justice. A Dweller, well, you can think of ways to execute one of those in a style befitting his crimes. But how should a traitor die?

"If you move, they'll shoot you along with the others," he said in calm and low tones as he approached, "but I'm guessin' you figured that out already." He laughed at his attempt at a joke and at what I supposed he thought was his tactical superiority. He pulled up a stepstool to use as a chair close to my bars. I thought about snatching his neck and pulling his body through the spaces between the bars that it couldn't possibly fit. "Yeah, you got everyone here on edge, Sal of Nellis," he said as he leaned in to get a better look at me. "Not me, though. I'm not buying it."

Most of the tingling in my feet and fingers was gone. Half-alien killing machine nearly operational, but this particular lunatic had my attention, so much so that I welcomed the banter before the screaming. What was a neat and seemingly capable soldier doing with this bunch? "What did you hit me with," I asked before we got to the meatier parts of what needed to be said.

"Oh, that!" he said with some glee. "Honestly, I'm surprised you survived. That's a close-range energy weapon we used from time to time on Seed." He stood and grabbed the device off the belt of his comrade. "He had the thing cranked to its highest setting when he shot you," he said as he chuckled in my direction. Then he turned back to the Dweller and shouted hard enough to spit in the guy's face, "Which I specifically ordered him not to do!" He returned his focus to me, smiling and casual. "I'll deal with that later."

"You used it on Seed?" I asked with genuine confusion. "I thought you guys were all buddies."

"Well," he exhaled slowly as he sat again, "that was before, in a different time and place. You have to adapt to your surroundings to overcome." He sat and thought for a moment about something that troubled him. "You know what I mean?" he finally asked as the moment passed.

"It was sometime later that you decided to start kissing Seed's butt and hanging out with cannibals?" I was rude but genuine. I really wanted to know.

Everyone was still and silent. The chieftain looked at me with a cold, dead stare I hadn't seen in some time. He looked through me more than at me. I thought for sure he was about to make his move. I figured I could take out the chieftain along with half the scum in my first charge, then rescue as many people as I could. It was a painful plan, though. I couldn't see how many were captured and how many Dwellers surrounded us. I would be walking out alive even if riddled with bullets, but it didn't feel right to be so reckless with innocent lives. I didn't place them in danger but I felt that their danger was now my responsibility.

Finally, Chieftain burst into laughter. When his laughter slowed enough to speak, he called back to his men, "Can you believe this guy?" He let out a long sigh but kept smiling. "I don't know what to do with you, Sal. I want to keep you around just for the entertainment."

"Yeah, I'm all kinds of sunshine at a party like this," I replied as I stood and cracked my neck to loosen the stiffness from being electrocuted and time on the concrete floor. "Would you like a demonstration?"

More laughter. His men were smart enough to take a few steps back, but the giddy chieftain was only amused. "What are you going to do, Sal?" he said with a smile. "You going to break this steel like the top of a tank?" He laughed even harder. "You going to strike me down like the devil I am with your magic sword?"

I was utterly disarmed. He was mocking me. Not for effect, really mocking me. He thought I was a fraud. He had heard or read the good news that I had been so enthusiastically sharing with his gang but he didn't believe it. I felt flabbergasted. I had been called many things by the Dwellers, often with their last curses, but never once a fraud.

When I didn't immediately respond, he stood to look me in the eye. "Yeah, I didn't think so. But it was a pretty good story." He was grinning again, happy to be holding all the cards. "I'll make you a deal, Sal. It wasn't my original plan, but I'll let you live. I'll let these people live, too, as a sign of my goodwill. You can join my admittedly ragtag bunch here, under my command. They could use someone with experience when I leave, and I could use an emissary to Nellis when the time is right. All I ask in return is that you tell these men the truth. I'm curious as well about how Seed changed. That's a pretty good deal, son, considering all the trouble you've caused." He looked at me with sincere concern for my reply. I think he really thought I would join him. I think he really wanted me to. I was still far too confused to come up with an adequate response. As I stood in quiet bewilderment, he turned to walk away. "You think about it, Sal of Nellis," he called behind him as he marched into the shadows. "You think about it."

The slick psychopath who built a dingy jail inside a dark warehouse in the middle of nowhere was right. I needed to think about some things. I called out to him before he entirely disappeared into the darkness, "What's your mission? What are your orders?"

"Classified," he called back to me, "but, you know, fighting the war, saving the world. That kind of stuff." He was laughing again as he drifted out of sight. "Beat up a tank," I heard him whisper in a chuckle in the darkness.

I turned to the back of my cell to ponder my weird day. I looked to my left and right again at my fellow captives. How was I going to get them all out? "It's going to be okay," I said quietly, not sure if I was lying. When I inspected the back wall of my cage, I had to laugh again. Nothing. The last quarter of my box was only the thin steel of the wall of the warehouse. I could have busted out of this clink before my transfusion of alien. The chieftain wasn't bluffing: he honestly didn't think I had it in me to break free. He thought I made the whole thing up: the tank, the sword, Jess, everything. But they had my sword. I brought a magic sword to the party and I still wasn't a VIP.

I spun back around to my unsteady guard. "Hey, man, I'm not asking you to give it to me, so don't get twitchy on me. But where is the blade I came in with?"

The rifle rose higher to point at my head and trembled. "I didn't take it!" he responded in a quiet shout.

"Of course not. Didn't say you did, so relax. But where is it? I feel like we might be having a different conversation if…"

"Someone else took it. That's what I'm telling you. One of the new guys snatched it and ran off, so don't bother trying to get it. It's gone."

That explained some things, I guessed. I turned back toward the thin barrier stopping me from seeing the world beyond. I could probably just run through it. I hadn't tried that particular feat, but I was pretty sure I could manage. Then maybe double back for my cellmates when the search party came after me? I couldn't be sure they wouldn't kill the other captives out of anger or spite. I sat back down on the dusty concrete. I was so sick of my job.

"Hey," I said to my fellow inmates, "you guys want to do something weird with me?" I reached my hands out toward them. They didn't move a muscle, terrified of the guns still pointed in their direction. "Come on, I swear it will make you feel a little better."

"What are you doing!" the guard shouted.

I didn't look back. "You touch that trigger and that gun is going somewhere you won't believe it can fit. So, shhh."

Back to my prayer. Ok, here we go. Eyes shut. Head down. "Please, whoever or whatever might be listening… Look, I'm really trying here. Can I please get a little help or direction?" I whispered into the darkness. Worst prayer ever.

Unsurprisingly, no response was forthcoming. All I could think of was Jess when I shut my eyes and waited. She had spoken to me, I thought, or I couldn't quite remember the order of things around the time of my electrocution. But she told me to look up, and I saw a jet headed toward Nellis. I needed to check on that monumental revelation but had other problems. "Where are you, Jess?" I murmured while still hoping for some kind of answer.

I put my hands on my face to hold back the sadness. I missed her more than anything.

I was spreading the good news, but look where it had gotten me: a jail populated by my least favorite people. The façade of my reality was as grim as ever. It wasn't supposed to be like this. Things were supposed to be better after sacrificing everything to rid the world of evil.

But I wasn't ready to give up. I was getting closer to giving in to my worst tendencies, but not there yet. I thought of all the smiles and kisses. They sustained me. My crappy façade was a necessary envelope for choices. Nothing more. A reflection of who I had been, maybe. Maybe the message was already present if I could decipher the line of sparkling memories of her.

"Get your boss!" I shouted to the guard. I'd take one more stab at this, belief manifest, then I was leaving one way or the other. My choice would be as pure as I could conceive: tell Jess's story. If that didn't work, to hell with it.

"Get Reptile," my guard shouted at some Dwellers passing by in the darkness behind him.

"Oh, you gotta be kidding me," I sighed as I shook my head at the guard. "Reptile?" I could feel my fuse shortening before he arrived.

"And he's made his decision!" Reptile said confidently when he appeared again. "What's it going to be, killer?"

"You want to know what happened," I said concealing the volcano of frustration building toward the thing called Reptile. I couldn't not ask. "Okay, first, why 'Reptile?'" I asked while rubbing my nearly-exploding forehead.

"That's my name, son. Well, it's Ripley. Reptile's a callsign. And these idiots love it, so…"

"Really, you need to stop calling me 'son,'" I interrupted. If I heard it again, I thought I might lose it. "Please," I shoved through clenched teach.

"Fine, boy," he laughed a little before becoming agitated himself. "You got somethin' to tell me?"

"Yes, I do." I tried to force a smile on my face. "Look, I'm harmless, right? So, what's with all the rifles and hostages? You're hedging, which says you're either scared or just screwing with me. We can't make a deal without trust. Just tell everyone to stand down and I'll tell you what happened to Seed, please."

Reptile laughed and shook his head. He looked to be truly appreciative of my odd entertainment. He seemed out of place entirely, as a matter of fact. But I didn't have time to both tell my story and get his. I had a plane to catch.

"Fine," he said acting exasperated. "Alright, boys," he called out, "lower your weapons and listen up. I think this is going to be good." He sat back on his stool, way too close to the killing machine. A group of his men drew closer, waiting for a new version of the good news.

"Okay," I said with my hands raised in the air. I took a few steps forward to my cell's bars. "First," I said as I put one finger on the inside of one bar, "I'm not the one who did anything to Seed." I put another finger on the inside of the bar next to the first. "The same person who did this to me was the one responsible." As gently and slowly as I could, I bent both bars to the side and stepped through the new opening.

Those rifles were back on me in a hurry. "What the..." Reptile whispered in amazement.

"Easy! Easy, everyone," I cut in as I moved toward their boss. They weren't taking it easy. I could see my guard's fingertip whiten from pressure. He was about to fire.

Caught one! Yes! Finally, doing something right. I held the nearly undamaged bullet in my nearly bloodless hand. Yes! I tossed it gently back to my guard.

Reptile was about to congratulate me on the achievement, no doubt, as he began to hiss. But I snatched him by the throat and lifted him a foot into the air. "Tell them to drop their weapons and take a few steps back unless you want to see what your insides look like." I winked. I think he was becoming a believer. I spun his whole body around with a subtle lift inside my raised grip. "Tell them," I ordered while staying just behind my new meat-shield.

"Drop your weapons!" he shouted. Squeals of his fear echoed inside the building. Guns began hitting the floor.

"Good, Reptile," I said as I put him down gently. "Now, did you really lose my hotblade? I'm fond of it, as you can imagine since you read my book."

Shock replaced any other emotion trying to surface in the chieftain. "It was taken. I am so sorry."

"Oh, I'm not the one to ask for forgiveness. Be glad about that. I'm all out of patience for people like you. But my love wouldn't give up on you, not so long as you tried to follow her example. You understand me, don't you?"

"I think so."

"Well, read it again if you missed something. Now, you'll let these people go. You'll lead your regiment away from here after you explain to them the absolute truth behind every word I wrote. You'll make it your new mission to help the people trying to settle in this area in every way you can. And if I ever hear a tale of Reptile or his men doing anything other than practicing kindness and mercy, I will find you and I will keep you alive as long as I can while I leave the good news at the door. We clear?"

"Crystal."

"That's a good Reptile. Now, do you have a functioning vehicle? There's somewhere I need to be."

"Yeah," Reptile happily responded, glad to be off the hook for the time being. "That's why we stopped here, for the fuel. It's getting tougher to treat chemically but we're…"

"Whatever. Where are the keys, pop? I need to borrow the car."

7

Nellis was on lockdown the next morning, its disposition mimicking its commander's. James was furious at everyone and everything, which is another way of saying himself. He felt foolish and lazy for dropping his guard and failing to keep his soldiers battle-ready. He knew better. Though seemingly placid compared to the turmoil of Seed, James understood that the world was still shattered, therefore dangerous. Under calm scenery always slithered threats. Since he and his community had withstood the end of an age, survivors more capable than a Dweller or a drifter should have been expected. Behind the veil of the hum and beyond the reach of their limited sight, anything wicked might have gathered strength. Instead of training and preparation, watermelons.

"James," Grover complained from the comfort of his chair in the command center, "you're telling me to direct people to leave and you're directing me to get messages out to people to come back. You're the tactician, obviously, but I'm lost."

Mary thought to punctuate the protest. "He's right, James. And we haven't decided why we're doing either. We're running away from and running toward something we don't yet understand."

James looked to Phil for any salt he might want to shove in the wound. Phil was too smart to speak. He raised his hands in deferment. "Jack?" James asked as his gaze scanned the mostly-empty conference table. Most people with any leadership ability had long left the facility.

"I get it. Innocents out. Fighters in. We're getting ready for something we don't understand, but ready." Jack was already bored with all the fear and commotion. He would have preferred practicing his usual craft, but people were scared, thus otherwise occupied. No one was drinking.

James glared at Grover and Mary. The loud lecture headed their way was cut short by Kate, who'd remained on base as lead tech officer. There wasn't much tech to tinker with beyond Nellis's walls, so she stayed where she could be most useful. She burst into the room, out of breath. "Please tell me some good news, Kate," James begged.

"Big problem," she said between deep breaths. "Big, big problem. I was working on modulating the power we're sending out to our settlements to try to facilitate communication. I picked up the pace, you know, because we need to get the word out. I went to Alice's mainframe to grab a few things I thought might help and I was blocked by a new door, or wall, or something."

No one had any idea what the smart lady was saying. "What kind of new door, dear?" Mary asked, puzzled. Alice's room was still Jess's domicile, as far as anyone could comprehend the situation. Mary sensed a message.

"It's silver. I think it's Seed metal. There's just a wall of the stuff where the door was."

James looked to the ceiling and shut his eyes. "Oh, this just gets better." The someone-living-in-the-basement dilemma had yet to be demystified. It chose to fester when everything topside was bordering on panic. "Phil."

"On it," Phil replied.

"Jack," James began.

"I'm not worried about Jess down there," he cut in. "She can take care of herself."

Mary was finally entirely in agreement with someone in the room. "Thank you, Jack." She emphasized "Jack" to let James know what little gratitude was headed his direction.

"Well, that's fine, Jack," James replied through exasperation. "Because I want you to go to California."

"Ah, you want me to round up those fighters."

"Exactly. They'll listen to you. They'll follow you."

"Well, no one's thirsty, anyway. I'll plan out a trip." He put his hand for a moment on Mary's shoulder as he stood. "Mary," he asked, "can you keep this place from spinning off the planet if I'm gone?"

"I'll do my best with what I have to work with." She glared at James, in whom she found a disappointing lack of faith. "Godspeed, Jack."

Jack laughed as he jabbed James in the chest on his way toward the door. "We'll be alright, big guy. We been through worse."

Grover wasn't done complaining at the thought of bringing more people back to the base after he had been ordered to turn them away. "James, those men aren't going to leave a family out there if they have one. They'll bring them here, a place from which you are trying to evacuate families."

"Grover," James began with irritation replacing exasperation, "I swear to..."

Mary put her foot down, though she wasn't sure of what direction to take, either. "Enough of this! Let's check on Jess while we calmly work out what it is we're trying to accomplish in response to being somewhat attacked."

James wasn't done commanding. "We're trying to put a war installation back on a war footing, Mary. We're trying to prevent further loss of life. We're trying to not get bombed out of existence on the next pass," he loudly lectured.

"Enough," she repeated in a whisper. James fell silent. The true commander had spoken. The three began to make their way to catch up with Phil and Kate.

8

I made a friend. What a refreshing experience. The scattered townsfolk I helped defend against Dwellers were always appreciative and welcoming, but being buddies with the blood-soaked alien guy was usually an arms-length exercise. And, honestly, I wasn't great company. Pining for lost love and always preaching about morality's power to ward off evil weren't the most magnetic traits, soaked in blood or not.

Joe was waiting for me on the interstate. As I approached in the Reptile's shiny Humvee, he held my blade high over his head. He was walking toward Vegas and looked like a hitchhiker more than a Dweller. I wondered how he knew which way I'd go, but it turned out that Joe was brighter than the average bandit. I tried to thank him as I stopped alongside him and rolled down the window, but his apologies proceeded my gratitude.

"I'm so sorry I took it," he began, cowering now that we were face to face. "I didn't know what else to do. Reptile loves technology, and thinking about him getting his hands on this had me worried. I just wanted to get it far away from there. Maybe I should have stayed, though, and helped."

"It's alright," I assured him. "It worked out, so your instincts were right. But how'd you know I was headed this way."

"I didn't," he said as he gently and respectfully passed the blade through the open window. "But I read your message, your good news or whatever." He started to chuckle at the name but quickly suppressed the expression from surfacing. He didn't know how I'd take his light attitude or in what mood he might find me. "Anyway, I saw that plane and how you looked at it. It seemed to be traveling this direction, so I figured."

I was impressed. He was a believer, at least to some degree. He wanted to help and took action, an action that would have assured a horrible death if the Dwellers had caught up to him before I did. A follower of Jess in the ranks of the Dwellers was good news in itself. Thankfully, her grace was bubbling in the world beyond my bloody sword.

"Well, thank you. I appreciate you taking the risk. I am worried about that plane and I am headed to Nellis, in fact. Where you headed?"

"Just away from them. I didn't want to be there in the first place but didn't have many options. If they catch me... Well, you know what they'll do."

"Welcome aboard, if you'd like to come along," I said as I gestured to get in.

He hesitated. I wondered if I was that bad of company. "Are you sure?" he asked. "I'm a Dweller, like you say. I wasn't before but I guess I just was."

"All is forgiven." I was happy it wasn't the prospect of my lousy company. "Hop in."

Once he was situated and we were underway, I asked, "What do you mean that you weren't before? What were you?"

It turned out that Joe was never a Dweller of any kind, which made me question my odd mission in the wastes all the more. He had stumbled into their ranks after Seed had gone. I wondered how many others who might have tasted my justice had been swept up in the growing but fractured force after Seed relented. Joe wanted to survive so he took up arms out of desperation and under duress. Had I met him under different circumstances… I cringed at the thought.

I chalked our meeting up to Providence the more Joe spoke of his past. He had good insight into Reptile and some new intel on how humanity had managed against Seed far beyond our desert valley. He was a fresh-out-of-school computer scientist when Judgment fell, working his first job as a contractor for the DOD on the east coast. When everything hit the fan and splattered all over everyone everywhere, he was shipped off to NORAD along with a group of valuable personnel. He stayed there for years in an installation not entirely different than my home, but Seed eventually found its way inside their mountain fortress. Joe escaped the attack and lived in the Rockies, hiding from cabin to cabin with a small band of survivors. When Seed finally stopped hunting them through the snowy peaks, the group cautiously went their separate ways. Joe headed home to Utah. He had family in the area and knew of an enormous and well-defended NSA facility near Salt Lake where he had interned. He hoped to find some lost faces there. Instead, he found Reptile.

I was glad for the company. A relatively normal person was a find. A relatively normal, highly-educated engineer who believed in Jess and wanted to help the cause? That was like finding a leprechaun riding a unicorn. I felt like we became good friends while we traveled together to Nellis. I told him all about what might become his new home: the good people, my parents, the President, and Jack's. I made it out to be a lovely place, just a tad glossier than it actually was. I wanted the leprechaun and his unicorn to stick around.

I didn't tell him that a tank would fire on us as we approached his prospective residence. If I would have known, I may have left that part out.

9

We were rolling fast as we rounded the last corner before entering the valley. Once Nellis was in sight, I took us off the highway and down an access road north of the base. Most of the path had been reclaimed by the drifting sand, but I didn't let loose terrain slow me down. My odd composition had retired any worry about trivialities like car accidents. I needed to steer clear of high-voltage electrocution, however. I might ask Jess about that clause in the contract if she could be bothered for an actual answer. Regardless, traffic was light that afternoon. It always was. People were hard to come by after Judgment. With only minimal concern for my mortal passenger to lighten my lead foot, we raced across the bleak landscape with reckless abandon.

As we entered the darkness of the char surrounding the base, I noticed the northernmost gate was shut. That wasn't entirely out of order. The few gates on the northern perimeter weren't used much. But it was open when I left. Then the next was locked down. And the next. Dread began to sink in as we finally found an open entrance. Something was wrong. The jet was not part of an electrified delusion, and it hadn't brought good news.

As I turned us toward the opening, I saw an odd obstacle: just behind the massive doors waited an M1A2 Abrams. It was flanked by an Atlas. A rifle and tank barrel were both locking on to our position. I barely had time to touch the brakes before the tank fired.

The round screamed just ahead of our vehicle and smashed into the dirt thirty feet ahead of us. We came to a sliding halt as I frantically tried to not roll the truck as we plowed through the black dust.

Joe was terrified. I was mad. "Sit tight. I'll figure this out," I said as I left the cab.

I walked toward the tank waving my hands in the air and shouting. The noisy flailing was as well as I could communicate from a distance, "Stop shooting, idiots!" My actual words were far more profane.

The tank aimed again, this time right at me. Really mad. So tired of inhospitable arrivals. "Shoot me and see what happens!" I screamed. I was still more than a hundred yards away, so I didn't think they could hear, but I wanted to give whoever it was a chance to stand down. If I was shot one more time that week, the cheese might have slipped off my cracker.

Lifting his hand to shield his eyes from the sun, the Atlased soldier finally recognized me. He smacked the armor of the tank twice to get the attention of the occupants. The big gun relented and pointed at the dirt.

I circled back for Joe once we were no longer about to be obliterated. As we drove slowly toward the entrance, the tank backed farther into the base to open a more welcoming path. Inside the Atlas, I found a familiar Angel. "What in the world are you guys doing out here?" I asked, not restraining my irritation.

"Calm down, kid," Bart shot back with an unimpressed smirk. Bart had helped train me for years as I spent every ounce of my energy learning to kill Seed. Having witnessed every embarrassing mistake along the way, he was perpetually unimpressed by my antics. I loved him for it. How I longed for stoicism and callus reactions after all the drama usually encircling my exploits. "We got bombed while you were out there preachin' or whatever it is you do while the rest of us work." Ah, and insults. I missed insults from friends while I was away. "We're taking a defensive posture and not welcoming speeding delinquents with the same enthusiasm."

Any anger evaporated. I was home.

After an awkward hug with an Atlas, I looked around the base. Nothing seemed out of place. "Bombed, huh? Whoever bombed us did a crap job." I smiled at Bart and waited for at least a grin.

"There was one casualty," he soberly replied. My joke wasn't funny.

"Where's my dad?" I asked with a grimace.

"Throne room."

"Copy," I said as I started back toward the Humvee. "Anyone we know?"

"We know everyone."

We made our way slowly and cautiously to the command center. I caught a few waves as I drove by, but everyone seemed too busy or too stressed for a proper greeting. Some were packing to leave. Some were unpacking to stay. Many were gearing up at the armory. I had no idea what was going on.

I wasn't alone. "Thank God!" Mary exclaimed as she saw me peek into the conference room. James saw me but lost me to a rush of hugs and questions. "How are you? How is it going out there? Where have you been?"

From inside an intense squeeze, I tried to respond. "Well, I was in Utah. In the past few days, I was shot, electrocuted, imprisoned, and shot again."

"Not well, then," Mary replied as she released her embrace and forced a smile under a scrunched nose.

I'd seen that same scrunch a dozen times on a similarly beautiful face. I was so happy to be home, yet already hurting from the familiarity.

James left his chair to greet me in turn. "Glad you're back, son. We need you. Did you hear?"

"Bombed, but that makes no sense. People around here have a tough time getting clean water. Who's flying jets and attacking bases these days?"

"You partly answered your own question." I guess I had. They weren't locals. "It's really good to have you back."

Mary interrupted another embrace. "I don't see how that answers anything. But maybe you can talk some sense into your father about how we're dealing with this. I'm not having much luck."

"Impossible, Mom. He's far more sensible than I am."

She frowned and shook her head. "Yes, you're both very handsome and impressed by your own jokes. Now, we really need to get you caught up on everything. But first, more hugs this way. We miss you when you go."

I could hear Grover talking, as always, as he made his way down the hallway to the conference room. "Do I smell Grover?" I asked vaguely as he entered.

"Hilarious, Sal. Nice to have you home," he said hurriedly as he fumbled with notebooks in his arms. Then he stopped for a moment to lecture me. "You know, you might remember…"

"That you're the President of the…"

"That I helped you when it mattered most," he cut in indignantly.

"You mean that time you gave a hotblade to two zombies who were trying to kill me?" I thought it was a good comeback until the silence in the room reminded me that one of those zombies was my brother, a brother I had yet to bring home. The painful tension that swiftly sucked the oxygen out of the room was exactly why I often stayed away. I walked over to the President to shake his hand and hopefully end the awkward quiet. I didn't look back to see the pain I was sure had clouded James's expression. "I do appreciate it, Grover. It just doesn't feel right to not give your majesty a hard time."

"Hilarious. Do you already know about what happened?" he asked.

"Bombed."

"No, what happened downstairs."

"What happened downstairs?" I asked with quick and sharp focus on anything that might have to do with Jess.

"Grover!" Mary chastised. It was obviously news the two had wanted to share privately.

"Seriously, guys, what happened downstairs?" I couldn't think of a reason they'd withhold.

"Nothing too concerning," Mary fumbled for the right words. "Jess walled herself in down there. Maybe a response to what's happening up here."

"Wait," James tried to say as I made my way toward the stairs. I knew he didn't really think I'd stick around for a briefing if Jess was somehow nearby. One index finger in the air denoted my complete lack of concern for the entire rest of the world if in the next moment I might be closer to her.

The basement arrived in a flash. The rest of my crew had to worry about fatigue and oxygen and other mundane necessities. I had a moment alone to examine the obstacle. I thought I might be able to make my way closer to her core before I discovered the new wall but found myself blocked at the first door off of the stairs. A smooth surface of Visitor occupied the otherwise normal entrance, so smooth that I could see my reflection. I looked like I had been shot, electrocuted, imprisoned, etc., worse for wear even though I couldn't wear out. I should have showered before my date.

I felt around the façade for an opening or weakness, but the shield was complete. Maybe around. If you're not cheating, you're not trying, or so I've heard. I made my way to an adjacent room on the sub-level. The walls dividing the main spaces were either steel and concrete or slightly friendlier cinderblock and concrete, but I figured I could bust through without too much pain. I was wrong. When I made my first strike, I hit something harder than anything I'd ever felt. The friendly cinderblock was smashed to pieces with only a light splash of my blood, but Jess's wall remained on the other side without so much as a dent.

I walked slowly back toward the stairs as a few bones in my hand shuffled painfully back into place. How could I reach her if I wasn't allowed in? Why wasn't I, of all people, allowed in? I was shaking my still-contorted fist and muttering anger under my breath as I passed by the first doorway again.

She was there, as clear and bright as day, seemingly just a few steps behind the translucent shell! "Jess!" I screamed when I saw her. I ran to greet her and awaited some reply, but she hadn't heard me. "Jess," I said again. She wasn't looking at me either. She was looking down as though she was working out a puzzle, her slender finger touching her perfect chin in contemplation. "Jess!" I screamed again as loudly as I could. Nothing. To heck with bones, I hit the shell again. The pain screamed up my arm and clouded my vision. Smarter people don't break their hand twice in the same minute. I looked down at the damage. Not pretty.

When I looked back, she was standing right in front of me, just behind her shell. She was looking outward toward the stairs. Had she heard me? Maybe the thud of my mangled fist? "Jess," I said again as I positioned myself directly in her view. She couldn't see me but she was looking for something. She couldn't hear me but seemed like she was listening. I put my hand gently against the barrier as I stood in shock and frustration. She squinted and moved her head from side to side, still looking, looking right through me. After a moment, she lifted her hand and touched it to where mine rested. Finally, we were connecting in some way.

"What is going on down here, Sal!" James shouted as he rounded the last landing of stairs above.

"Dad!" I shouted back. "She's here!"

When I looked back to the barrier, she was gone. Only my shabby reflection remained.

"We heard some kind of crashes on the way down. Shook the whole stairwell. Are you ok?"

"No," I whispered with my hands and forehead resting on the shell. "I'm not ok at all." I felt for the moment like I was watching her casket sink into the ground again. Mourning twisted itself into nausea.

"What happened?" Mary asked as she followed down the steps.

"She was here, Mary. She was right here in front of me. I looked away, and she was gone."

"Oh, dear," she sighed as she wrapped her arms around me. "James, let me handle this one. You go finish up with Grover. We'll be along shortly."

James squeezed my shoulder silently and started back up the stairs.

I don't know why I always tried to hide my tears from Mary. She always knew. "Come sit," she said softly as she took a seat on the last step. "We've been here before, you and I. Haven't we?"

"Yes, ma'am," I replied with a grin and a tear as I sat. Another lecture was headed my way. I wanted to hear it. I wanted more to make sense. I was so tired of being lost. "She was looking for me, I think," I blurted out before an avalanche of logic crushed my little dream, "or looking for something."

"Of course, she was, Sal. Do you know why?" I didn't. I tossed my hands up in exasperation. Mary saw the almost-repaired mess of my hand. "Oh dear," she said again with a kind smile toward her dumb but passionate pupil. "Do you know what I see when I look at this strange wall?" she asked rhetorically. "I see just what I need to see. I am reassured that Jess lives on, something I know but like to be reminded of in this physical world. I love seeing her will still expressed. That's the end of it for me."

"You might want to stick around. She was really just here."

"I know, sweetie. I know she was here for you, but that's not the point. Do you know what your father sees when he looks at this wall? He sees that Jess is scared, just like him. He sees Jess defending herself from a terrible threat, just like he should do for everyone around him. That's the end of this for him. I think you see Jess trying to find you because you are trying to find her. But maybe something is in the way, something keeping you apart. I'm afraid you know more about that part than I do."

I didn't have the slightest idea of how to reply. I thought to argue over Jess truly being in front of me not moments before but I knew better. "Well, I think death is our first problem." I wasn't trying to be cruel, but my thoughts were sloppy after being disheartened by so many months of nothing but frustration.

Mary laughed, thank God. "That is quite the obstacle, isn't it?" she joked and chuckled. "But you just saw her. Strange as it might be, I don't think that's your first issue."

"Jess said something weird and beautiful, once... Constantly, really." I laughed at all the weirdness and beauty that comprised our brief relationship. "Love is immortal and death is only a horizon."

"And a horizon is nothing save for the limit of our sight," Mary finished. "She liked that one. And she loved you." I got another hug. "You're getting it."

"I guess I'm not supposed to sit down here forever and ever, right?"

"See." Mary was smiling and standing and waiting for me to catch up.

I stood alongside her. "Fine, but I did see her in that wall." I had to protest a little. I was leaving Jess again.

10

When Mary and I arrived topside, everyone in the conference room kept to their conversations and politely ignored the fact that I had just endured a gut-wrenching experience. Bart, Phil, Kate, and Jack had joined the group. It looked like James was about to deliver instructions.

I sat quietly next to Jack. He mussed my hair like I was ten years old. That was my greeting. "You enjoying the red-alert pucker-factor around here?" he grumbled in a whisper and smiled.

I tossed his hand off me. "I'm not enjoying anything, Jack."

"Somebody needs a drink."

"Doesn't help." The admission made me feel even worse.

"Nonsense."

"Okay," James began a little louder than the quiet chatter. "Jack's prepped for his trip, but we need another two envoys. We've got essential personnel scattered south and north of here as well." James thought about the directions for a moment and then looked to me. "Sal, you just got back from Utah. Bump into anyone with training on your excursion?"

"Did I ever," I mumbled while still dreaming of Jess.

"Would you like to enlighten us?" James asked impatiently.

"What?" I responded, facing back toward reality. "Oh, I met an ex-military, or current-military... I don't know. Anyway, someone with training had infiltrated and assumed command over a weird bunch of Dwellers outside of St. George. He was shaping them into some kind of an organized force, but it wasn't clear why."

"Did he have any useful intel? Was he from a base?"

"Sorry, I don't know. I was in a hurry, and he didn't seem like he was playing for our team. He was cruel and smart and just strange. He had read my report ahead of time but didn't believe it. He was holding hostages to try to keep me under control, so I just helped him act a bit more appropriately before I took off."

James wasn't happy with my tardy report. "Well, this is promising, Sal. You may have noticed that we've been attacked recently and..."

"No, it wasn't this guy," I cut in. "I'm sure of it. He was scrounging for gas. No way he's got sophisticated tech."

"Ok," James continued curiously, "so what was his deal? Military and commanding Dwellers doesn't jive."

"He said he was fighting the war and trying to save the world, but the guy was a real snake. I didn't believe it. His name is Reptile, if that tells you anything."

"Ah," James replied thoughtfully like he'd figured something out, "was he real evasive about what you did ask? Kinda slimy?"

"Yep."

"And he was telling the others what to do but wasn't participating. Seemed like he was acting apart from the original group. More of a whisperer behind the scenes."

"That's him exactly," I replied, impressed by the insight.

"I think you met a spook, son. I wasn't entirely disappointed that they were all gone. Of course, he didn't say where he was from. Even if he had, it probably would have been a lie." James nodded in affirmation of his conclusion. "That's interesting, though."

"A spook like a spy, James?" Grover asked. "I don't understand. What is there to spy on anymore?"

"Us, I suppose." James thought on the matter. "But spies aren't really like the spies in old movies. They're more often about blending into their surroundings and quietly influencing events on the ground behind enemy lines. Special Ops more often than not. But this one sounds like no Angel. Sal, I think you should try to make contact again. Do you think you could? I'm sure he has more information if you can squeeze him. We're flying pretty blind here, and you enjoy squeezing people."

"Yeah, I could clean up, resupply, and be oscar mic pretty quick. As a matter of fact, I brought back a present for Kate that could be useful. One of the Reptile's crew had an engineering background and was kind enough to defect. He might know where the snake is headed."

"Good. And be careful. He's as dangerous and crafty as they come if I'm right. You can be misguided even if you can't be hurt."

"Will do." I started planning my hasty trip in my head when I thought back to the bomb. I still didn't know where I might be ultimately headed if reprisal was in order. "Wait, what forensics do we have on the bomb that hit us? Maybe I should plan a longer trip."

"Well," James answered with some irritation at the question and his lack of an answer, "we don't have any. I don't have a bomb squad. I barely have any squad. Hence this meeting."

"Dangerous ordnance is still just sitting on base?" That was too sloppy for James's standards.

"Not exactly," Jack answered with a chuckle. "He threw it away!" He laughed more as he leaned back in his chair.

"Well, someone should take a..." I thought about the situation for a second. "Crap, I'm the bomb squad, aren't I?" Jack winked and mussed my hair again at the idea of watching me ride a ball of fire across the desert.

11

I didn't think I would ever be back in an Atlas. What would be the point? Wearing thin sheets of steel and carbon overlaying a few steel bars was more nuisance than armor. But when I tried to charge ahead to defuse a bomb that I knew nothing about, my parents insisted on "minimal protection," as if it would help. If the warhead blew, I'd just be painfully picking Atlas parts out of my body. But I obeyed, missing the freedom that came along with being a renegade.

As I suited up, a mob gathered in a wide circle around the bomb. The few Angels around suited up as well to futilely stand watch over something they couldn't control. Some medics waited near a Humvee to retrieve what would be left of me if things went south. Then there was the general audience. A pack of spectators gathered at a seemingly safe distance though they had no idea what a safe distance was. But they wanted to see the show; safety be damned. As I clunked by in the Atlas and surveyed the crass crowd, one of those darker whispers inside me hoped my target was a nuke. Deep into the onlookers, much closer than they should have been, I found Jack and Grover in lawn chairs. Jack had brought along a six-pack and a colorful beach umbrella. The two toasted my arrival and the coming explosion. C'mon nuke.

"Be careful," Mary called out as I moved away from the crowd.

"Whatever," I mumbled under the clanking of the armor. I wasn't in the right frame of mind to be the bomb squad. Those guys, from what I understood, needed pure focus tipped with nerves of steel. I was an unstable explosive in search of another.

As I neared the twice-smashed heap of metal that was once a terrifying bomb, I surmised that I wouldn't be choosing whether to cut the blue wire or the red wire. Everything was destroyed. If something wanted to explode, it would have got on with it already. Gasps emanated from my audience as I began tearing off pieces of the outer shell with little care, sending the fragments haphazardly into the air.

Nothing was inside, at least to my uneducated eyes, that might convey something about its origin. I had no idea what I was dissecting. The husk looked like empty scrap more than anything. On to the nose cone, where the scary stuff was supposed to be. I sloppily tore that plating off, too. I thought about plugging my ears, but I couldn't operate on the device and plug both at the same time. Then I saw the dreaded payload. My week was getting weirder and weirder.

I picked up the whole bomb. The back half mostly fell off in the dirt, but I carried the important stuff toward the crowd. Some stood dumbfounded. Some began running away. They suspected the cheese had finally slipped off the cracker. I enjoyed the terror of the gawkers. While others ran, James stood statuesque as I approached. Typical. I passed by him and went straight for the lawn chairs. More of the crowd yelled and fled. Good pandemonium. Grover started screaming a wonderful, high-pitched squeal. He stumbled in the black dirt as he ran away. Jack kept sipping. Typical. After tossing what was left of our intruder at his feet and climbing out of the stupid Atlas, I took Grover's spot and beer.

"Well?" Jack asked as we sat and sipped.

"It's a note in a big bottle, Jack. I figured you're best qualified to do the honors."

"Huh," he noted curiously as he leaned forward in his short chair and over his distended belly.

James caught up to the scene after trying to calm the fleeing spectators, earnest as always. "What are you doing?" he asked accusatorily.

"The bomb squad requires refreshment and expert analysis. Here I sit with an expert on combustibles." I wasn't in the mood to be any kind of squad.

"Stop screwing around," he ordered. "What's…"

"Ha, it is a note in a bottle!" Jack was delighted by the odd message he fished out of the nose. "Says whoever kicked Seed's butt needs to report to these coordinates. My coordinates are rusty but I think that's around DC."

James snatched the note and read:

We have calculated that the change in Seed emanated from this vicinity. If someone or a group is responsible or has information about the change, report to these coordinates as soon as possible. Your insight is requested by the DOD. 38.87N 77.01W

The typed note was signed with overly-festive teal ink and with an unmistakably feminine flair: -Eve

"We were bombed by some chick at the Department of Defense?" James asked to no one in particular. He shook his head in disbelief.

We sipped leisurely while the boss contemplated. I already knew what was coming. I would be obliged to protest, but my wheels were already spinning about the cute loops in the signature.

James continued as he thought, "They couldn't get a message through the hum. They couldn't risk a cross-country courier with all these lunatics running around. Most pilots are long dead and most aircraft are rusting away. So, they loaded a piloting program onto a bomber with enough range to get here and back. Maybe back. That was some kind of makeshift drone that hit us. That's why it hit the base and not out in the field where it should have been. Nothing navigates perfectly without GPS and constant updates."

"I say we send Grover," I said between drinks. "He's the diplomatic type." Cute loops or no, a cross-country trip sounded miserable the more I thought about it. A hundred miles through the local ruins and their crazed inhabitants was depressing enough.

"Be serious, Sal. He'd get eaten alive out there."

"Bonus?" Even James chuckled at the thought but quickly acted the commander again.

"I could send a special unit that could make the trip but that would leave us close to defenseless. Though I don't think the DOD is trying to murder us, this message still says that the world contains serious people with serious capabilities in addition to all the lunatics running wild."

There it was. I was on recon. Having just disposed of the local threat, I was now conscripted to dispose of the distant one. "I'll have to walk unless you've got a plane that flies itself. Nothing terrestrial will hold that much gas and still move through who knows what kind of terrain."

"We could put you on an ICBM. Bomb 'em back," Jack interrupted, hardly withholding his amusement.

"You know how bad that would hurt? Plus, I've recently been educated about the limits of this gift. I don't know…"

"Ugh," Jack groaned as he stood and chugged the last of his bottle, "everyone's so uptight around here. I'm going to California. Wait," he paused as he thought through the buzz, "I am still going to California, right?"

"Yes, please," James replied. "Nothing has happened here that says we don't still need to put this facility back in order."

"Good," Jack sighed as he walked away. I was pretty sure that was our goodbye.

"Well," James said as he lent me a hand to stand, "we need to work out transportation."

"I'm not sure I've accepted the mission."

"I'm not sure I was asking." James smiled a condescending smile and patted me on the shoulder.

12

Looking back, and up at an ambivalent sky blotted by doom, maybe I should have stayed home. No, I don't want to travel two thousand miles because a note told me to. That was an option. No, I don't want to leave my home undefended. No, I don't want to challenge more Dwellers and be forced to pound them into the dirt so they leave the few nice folks out there alone. I already have enough blood on my hands for two lifetimes. No, I don't want a mission, any mission, no matter how seemingly urgent. I'm tired of emergencies. I just want to be still. Okay? I want to be left alone long enough to figure out what I'm supposed to do before I start doing it as hard as I must.

But that's not the way things work. Is it? Time sticks you like a knife in the back regardless of what ledge lies before you. It's always time to do, never time to reflect.

I slept in the basement that evening, telling no one where I had gone. I slept surprisingly well on the concrete floor snuggling an alien wall. I'd hoped, of course, Jess would make contact. Under the circumstances, I wanted her advice nearly as much as her love. More about my activities was feeling wrong, like the machine that was my life had lost a crucial component but had clunked along regardless of the malady, all the way to the foot of her enclosure.

Alone and in total darkness, I didn't expect to be awoken by anything other than my tireless body wanting to rise when I didn't. "Sal," Mary called from a flight above. "There have been some developments up here I think you'll want to see."

She knew where I was even when I was hiding, perhaps because I was hiding. "Don't you want to know if I've been chatting with Jess?" I was annoyed at being poked, so I felt like poking back.

More footsteps. Here it came: another lesson.

She was more aggravated than I expected, but the disposition of the student can dictate the mood of the teacher. "We have other things to do, so I'll make this quick," she began hastily. "Do you want to know why I can interact with Jess as much as I like but you have a hard time? Let's just skip right to the end, for once. Do you want to know why she can't see you when she looks?"

"Ah…" I wanted more time to be offended at the hurtful remark, but the lesson carried on.

"Look into the reflection," she ordered as she rounded the steps. "Look. What do you see?"

I looked. Still worse for wear. "I just see my reflection where I'd like to see a different face." It was a sincere answer but somehow wrong, of course.

"See, you can't avoid speaking the truth even while you're trying to escape it." She'd already lost me. "It's like your subconscious is talking to us both." Totally lost. "You can't see her because you're trying to see the woman you met in the desert, but she's moved on. You're still stuck here, haunted by the past instead of grateful for it, and dreading the future instead of grateful for it. She's not. She's making choices. She's influencing us. And that's so amazing that I have a hard time understanding why you don't fall on your knees and thank God you live in the present that you do. If you did, you'd have an easier time finding her. The face would be different. Understand?"

"Find her in a place no one can touch..." My mind drifted to something she'd said to me once but returned quickly to the lingering insults just leveled against me. "The same God that stood by and watched His whole planet be flooded by demons?" I meant it, at least in part. And, poke.

"The God who gave you James and Pete and Jess. The God who gave you the opportunity to rid your own personal world of demons."

"Gave me Jess for all of a few hours, then dragged me along to suffer and watch her die." Mary's disgusted expression said that the lesson was over. I'm pretty sure I failed the quiz. Mary turned and shook her head in frustration as she went back the way she came.

I stared into the reflection. She was right, of course. I knew I was all screwed up before Mary had said a word. I knew Jess would agree. I just didn't want to say it out loud, or, God forbid, ask for help.

Timid, tired, and confused, I snuck into the conference room hoping to find it empty. It was full of life and noise. James was presiding over a briefing from Kate, who was as enthusiastic as I'd ever seen her. Joe sat at her side as she spoke and flashed images across the matrix of screens. He was occasionally called upon to fill in a technical gap here or there.

James flashed me a nasty look as I approached. It said, "What did you do to upset Mary?" I made up my mind that moment to leave again. Cross-country this time. The new couple had tossed one straw too many upon my back. I couldn't deal with them both criticizing my demeanor. No one at home, it appeared, appreciated my pain. No company at all for my misery.

"Sal," Kate said as I sat, "I think you're going to love this!"

"I could use some good news," I replied as I awaited the gist of the latest discovery.

"We've, Joe and I, have got great news for your trip. Great news for the whole world, really!" She laughed her nerdy, nervous laugh while I chewed on the fact that they, too, had already concluded I was leaving.

How convenient. "How's infinite power sound?"

That sounded pretty awesome. "What? How'd you manage that?" I asked with appropriate skepticism.

"Oh, we didn't," she responded, humbled by even the notion that she could solve a puzzle so monumental. "No, Seed did, or the Visitor. You know what I mean."

Seed did have that one figured out. It never tired, no matter how much we fought. But we had never figured out how it had figured it out. "Ok, I'm all ears. What are we putting in the gas tank? Seed goop in the gas tank?" I wondered for a sickening instant if I was referring to myself. Stupid subconscious.

"Sword gas tank!" she said with glee. "Joe showed me how to suspend the Visitor material with an array of magnets. We'd never thought to try that, even though maybe we should have after the grenades we built together. Anyway, along with some air arc cutting techniques I've refined over the past few months of experiments, we successfully separated a hilt from a blade. We were never able to make much more than a scratch no matter what we did to those things, but Joe had it all figured out. He just never had a functioning device cloned from pure visitor to work with, so not much luck on his end either. But with a powerful enough energy field, it's like the Visitor forgets what it was trying to copy or what it was trying to be. So, while it was suspended and severed, I reworked the connection to something other than the blade mechanism, and bingo! A battery that seems to think it's still feeding the hotblade with energy but doesn't try to complete the physical form. Isn't that amazing!"

Scientists are so enamored with their craft. It's hard not to love them, even when you're in a bad mood.

"It is amazing, Kate." I looked over to see the sour look I knew would be on Mary's face. Yes, it was an amazing present to live in. Yes, I should have been grateful to whatever entity powered the moment, to whatever had provided all those moments with Jess, but I wasn't going to say it. I looked back at Kate. "That's really good work. You, too, Joe. I knew you were going to fit in.

"So," I began as I scanned the rest of the dazzled faces around the table, "now we just need to piece some heavy-duty electric motors to something with wheels, then I'm outta here to meet our man-slaughtering new friends at the DOD."

"Done!" Kate cut in. Your bike was an obvious candidate. It's outside."

"Wow! Okay," I said as I looked around at the faces I'd soon be leaving, "any special messages for our counterparts if I make it that far?"

"I'll field that one," James replied with authority. "Kate, Joe, everyone, thank you. This is stunning progress. We'll work through more of the possibilities when we meet again. Dismissed."

Everyone gathered their things and made a few more gestures of congratulations toward the techs as they made their way for the door. Mary kissed James on the forehead and left as well. We were soon alone in the quiet, empty room.

A warm smile crossed James's face before he began. I wasn't, apparently, being yelled at for my lousy demeanor. "I want to tell you something I think will help both here and where you're going. I know you're having a tough time."

"I'm just…"

"It's okay. Everyone can see it, and you should know that no one can blame you. You have every right to handle your burden how you see fit. None of us carry it, only you."

"That doesn't stop all the helpful advice."

James put up his hands to deflect my juvenile disrespect but the strange smile kept creeping across his face. He usually wasn't so content while lecturing me. "Do you think I saved you, all those years ago?"

The question caught me off guard, but there was only one answer. "Yes, and I appreciate it."

"You're wrong." Off guard again. James kept smiling as he continued, "You saved me. I should have told you that already. I've let you think otherwise because of selfishness or maybe as a lifeline to try to keep you under control. But I see the error now.

"The truth is that my team and I were headed in a very different direction when we came across you and your mom, a direction that would have seen an entirely different outcome than this one. I saw you guys running across that bloody, broken city and I immediately understood what Jess was trying to explain when I spoke with her. She had, in her special way, impressed upon me the importance of moral choices regardless of circumstances. Anyway, my squad had been directed to move toward our next mission objective when you crossed our path. Survivors were fleeing everywhere, so seeing you wasn't unusual. Then we noticed that monster on your trail, and something clicked inside me. My men thought I was nuts to disobey orders and risk a direct engagement over only two people, but I knew exactly what I was supposed to do. I knew it completely, right down to my bones. We pulled you out of that house, a few moments too late, but we got you. You were so scared, so sad. You put your shaking arms around me when we all finally stopped running. Do you remember that? I felt that squeeze and knew I was finally on the right track after so long spinning my wheels in gore and defeat. So, I just kept going down that road, the road you revealed. Now, look at us. You saved me, then you saved us all."

"I don't know what to say. Thank you?"

"Ha," James laughed, "thank you! But now I want you to see your path ahead in the same light. If I were you, I think I'd feel just the way you do. I think I'd do just what you do. But I want you to be better than me, Son. See what I see as an old man who's seen some things. Those people you help and the people you might help on this trip, try to see how they're helping you. They give you the chance to be better. That's a path to a future you couldn't have without them. I still don't know what I believe in after all this, but I believe that."

"You've been spending a lot of time with Mary." True gratitude and genuine connection were still sticky emotions.

"I knew you were going to say that!" he exclaimed, chuckling again. "But, yes, I have. C'mon, my boy. I think you've got a present outside."

13

As we stepped into the blinding sunlight from the shade of the underground fortress, the first thing my adjusting eyes saw was the wall. Some techs were working on one of the cannons still pointing lifelessly at the dirt. I thought for a moment about how the now dormant fortification had meant so much to my life. It was the only successful bulwark against the nightmares beyond. It had saved my butt more times than I could count. And it was the encircling wall of a prison, a strangling force that choked my freedom and will to fight for years that felt like ages. I didn't know what it meant that we might need it again, but the sight of its revival was unsettling. Whatever the wall was to be, it was an injustice to still need protection after seeing the nightmares finally recede.

My daydream about cosmic justice was interrupted by Kate's perky expression. "Tah dah!" she said too loudly considering how close she was to my face. Then she laughed her nervous laugh at her awkwardness. I believe I heard a snort. Loveable, but getting on my nerves like everyone else.

My bike looked great, a shiny relic of freedom. Sadly, the range of that freedom had always been limited. Not wanting to carry a shiny, 1000 lb. paperweight across the desert on my back, I hadn't touched it for months. I ran my hand over the chassis and examined the modifications. Surprisingly little was changed, only a hastily rigged metal cube welded in place of a graphene battery network. It didn't look as miraculous as its purported function. "The hilt of a Seedy hotblade is in the box? How much power is it putting out?"

"That's the craziest part!" Again, too loud. "We don't know!"

"Well, you can test…"

"Of course, we did that, Sal. But that's the thing. We never hit a limit on the meters. We'd have to put a real draw on it to see what it can do, something we already know sucks a known quantity of juice, but we didn't have the time. So, for all we know, you're only limited by the strength of the connection to the source."

Many had gathered around to see the new toy. They waited for my outpouring of gratefulness. "Thank you, Kate. Thank you, Joe," I offered with missing enthusiasm. Quiet stares made me want to start packing.

James interrupted the uncomfortable scene. "Okay, back to it, everyone. We've got a base to put back together." As dusty footsteps carried off the crowd, James turned to me. I think I concealed the wince in anticipation of my overdue lecture. Still, none was forthcoming.

"Tell me what you need."

Nothing was the answer but didn't seem right. I didn't even need the bike. I was already an overpowered agent of evil eradication, only now with a distant target on my list. Someone had to pay for the life taken from our home though no one was keen to say it. "Not much," I finally answered, avoiding the unpleasant details surrounding the trip. "Just minimal gear and similar instructions, then I'm gone," I said with slightly more enthusiasm than I should have.

James smiled his not quite condescending smile, one I'd seen a thousand times. "Find out everything you can. Help everyone you can. Report back to me soon and in one piece. Those are my instructions, Son. And say a proper goodbye to Mary before you go. You know she only wants the best for you."

I disobeyed the most important part of those orders. I geared up quickly and made it a short goodbye at the gate. No apology was forthcoming. I told myself it was about a lack of time, that another convoluted and penetrating round with Mary would only bog me down, but I was ducking something else. Jess didn't get a farewell, either. If she wanted to block me out of her sanctum, that was her call. Not like we were spending much quality time together, anyway.

Later that morning, after a few hugs with quick and obligatory nice words, Bart waived for the tank to back away from the gate so I could pass. I figured a quick fist bump would convey enough sentiment to my old training officer, but he had something else on his mind, the thing no one was keen to say. "What did they tell you to do out there?" Bart asked in a hushed voice while awkwardly shaking my extended fist in a drawn-out gesture.

"Recon. See what's what. A long but simple assignment."

"Simple, my ass," the hush grew louder. I acted surprised but I knew what he meant. "Those two…" Bart looked back to Mary and James and smiled but he was withholding anger. Then he exhaled and released his grip. He gathered himself. "Those two are presiding over something beautiful here," he said in a more regular manner. "But your dad ain't really runnin' the show here anymore. You know that, right?"

"I…"

"Yeah, you do. Just listen to me. This place is a miracle. I'm not immune to that. But this little island isn't the whole world. I don't think the natural order of things will ever change out there."

For a moment, I thought Bart just wanted to warn me of danger. That was nice. Unnecessary, but nice. "I'll keep my eyes…"

"That's not what I'm saying, kid." He looked into my eyes to make sure I'd get the message. "I'm saying this place only exists for the same reason nice places always have, because some mean bastard was somewhere far away putting his boot through someone's face, a worse someone who wanted to take it all away or knock it all down. I'm saying whatever they told you, whatever your girlfriend told you, whatever you believe in now, maybe all that stuff don't fly too far outside of this one special place."

I was mildly offended but also in complete agreement. The wastes were a mess. I was about to go deeper than ever. A smile and a hug for everyone I met might not be the right prescription for making it home or keeping it safe.

Bart wanted to punctuate his already clear advice. "Whatever else you're trying to be, remember you're still a soldier. You find trouble out there, you burn it to the ground and don't look back. That's how something like this place survives."

I couldn't help but grin. Finally, someone was speaking my language instead of gibberish or optimism. Maybe that's redundant.

"Copy that, old friend." I finally got my fist bump, then I was on my way.

14

Alone at last, I sped down the dusty highway away from home. My first order of business was obvious: recklessly test the maximum velocity of my renovated ride. The needle on the speedometer touched 118 before the intermittent slides across the flows of dirt drifting over the disappearing road became concerning. But there was no end to the throttle. The chunk of alien goo previously stuffed into the handle of a blade was enough to rocket me across the landscape at blistering speeds without end.

I marveled at the power of the cosmic material, the same material that murdered most of my world, that shredded my mother before my eyes, that now fueled my engine and my heart. The list of alien feats was adorned with revolting marvels to behold. "The Visitor," Jess had called it. The words didn't seem as correct when they weren't flowing from her full lips. Typical visits don't invoke so much blood nor end in reanimation. The term was too innocuous for something so evil and profound. I'd happily complain about the clerical misnomer but I guessed she wouldn't listen. She was busy hiding behind a wall of her Visitor for reasons she didn't bother to communicate.

I could see the warehouse that had recently been my prison as I crossed the northern outskirts of St. George. The structure wasn't too far out of my way for a visit of my own. If Reptile was being a cooperative convert, all the better for everyone. If not, he wouldn't see mercy twice. Either way, he was going to answer some questions for my dad. No more spooky sidesteps.

The place was abandoned. A handful of vehicles were missing outside. I hadn't taken inventory during my short stay, but the interior looked picked clean of anything useful. That was impressive in a way. Dwellers never moved methodically nor with speed. Theirs was a sloppier affair when it came time to do anything.

But the snake I sought wasn't a casual Dweller. He was something more. Perhaps he was a spy, whatever that meant nowadays. Where had he slithered? I hiked around the perimeter of the enormous compound until I found a set of fresh tracks.

He wouldn't! Would he? He couldn't possibly be so stupid and want to die so messily. But there they were: a series of conspicuous ruts heading in the direction of my favorite castle. My body was aflame in hate. If Reptile had so much as muddied a rug on that holy ground... Well, I think you know.

Ignoring reckless slides across loose terrain, I raced through the red canyons. When I saw the parade of the Reptile's vehicles parked haphazardly outside the wall, I stopped caring about answers to James's questions. The gang of murderous, parasitical scum was already inside, a trespass more offensive than I could withstand. My blade was out and humming as I entered the right door.

Sadly, I was stripped of some of my precious rage on the convoluted entry. Right door. Right door. Right turn. Up the stairs. Left turn. Down the stairs. Right door.

When I finally entered, I was almost attacked, but I wasn't in the mood to horse around. "Raar!" screamed the guard.

"Down, boy! Where are the outsiders?" When the previously fearsome host grunted a confused grunt with what I swear was a hint of a shoulder shrug, I chewed on the obvious question. "And why didn't you destroy the outsiders? You literally have only one job here."

A disappointed grunt. Can you believe I felt bad for making him feel bad about himself? Nothing was going how I had planned. "Come on," I offered in apology. "Let's find 'em together. You can kill some, too."

A more threatening and purposeful grunt. We were on the move together through the compound. We burst from the outer ring into the first open courtyard. The sun was hanging low, making the silvery construction of the walls and tower shine. The homes and buildings in between the defensive structures stood brightly in the shadows, gathering the reflections from above. People mingled here and there with no alarm. I was the odd man out, not Reptile and his dirty gang.

Rushing for vengeance, I spotted a disappointingly calm and familiar face: a Dweller from the warehouse sitting on a porch and playing a board game with a local. As I approached, he was more confused than frightened. "What are you doing here!" I shouted louder than the situation required.

"I was told to wait out here, kinda for security… I think. But nothing was going on, so…"

With a fiery blade limp towards the dirt, I rubbed my forehead in frustration. "Where is Reptile?"

"Oh, he's inside, with… Faye? I think that's her name. She wanted his help with some medical…"

"Okay, shut up." I stomped along my confused, angry path to the inner ring of the compound. As I walked away, I noticed the local resident gesture a big shoulder shrug to his opponent. Dwellers had invaded Jess's temple and I was the one disturbing the peace.

My blade was back where it belonged, safely sheathed, as the guardian and I moved more slowly and with more dignity as we scouted the massive, innermost structure. Classes were being taught in happy rooms bubbling with chatter and laughter, into which we quickly poked our puzzled heads. Libraries were being organized. In a side room off a wide, crescent-shaped hallway, a young girl was having her teeth worked on by someone doing their darnedest to be a dentist. No theft, rape, torture, or murder to be found. How bizarre.

Reptile had decided to live up to his end of the bargain, at least for now. He appeared to be guilty only of beginning his new crusade in a direction I didn't appreciate.

I finally bumped into a small group passing by who recognized me and my confusion. "Oh, Sal!" one offered with a hug. They were always hugging. Creepily nice. "You look like you're looking for something."

"You have no idea."

My guide wasn't sure how to respond so continued kindly helping. "Okay, well, Faye took a new group to the hospital. Is that what you're after?"

"Yes, thank you," I mumbled over a tight jaw as I walked away. My guardian got in another hug. So creepy. Jess was a waterfall of joy, peace, and friendship flowing through the hearts of everyone who lived in her home, even the possessed. The grave hadn't slowed her down one bit.

"Sal!" Faye yelled when we finally found her. Reptile was leisurely lounging nearby on an old school stool, something a doctor used to sit on when he gave you news about your eventually fatal illness. A group of his Dwellers stood in a loose ring around the scene as well, watching Faye do something with a guardian she had strapped to a chair in the middle of the room. I knew I couldn't avoid the hug.

"Hi, Faye," I gasped through a squeeze.

"Did you come to find your friends? How are you?"

"They're not exactly…" I gave Reptile the old stink eye to put him on notice when I was interrupted before a real answer.

"Hey! I'm glad you're here. We were doing brain scans, and yours is really the prize pony," she said beaming with excitement.

"You and this crew were just practicing medicine, huh?" I was adjusting to the aggravation of the odd situation.

"Yeah!" she answered with escalating enthusiasm. "Your friend, Ripley, knows all kinds of crazy stuff about the Visitor and how it interacts with people. Isn't that amazing? I'm so glad you sent him here."

"I did not send him here." I recalled recent fantasies about ripping his arms off his body, though he did appear to be playing nicely. The closer I was to Jess, and standing in her towering tomb was about as close as I could get, the more nothing made any sense at all. I was always disarmed when she was near.

"Oh," Faye interrupted my thousand-yard stare in Reptile's direction. "Well, I think you're going to like what he showed us. Get in the chair!"

Reptile had yet to say a single word. He had barely moved in his relaxed position. If I had burst into a different room to dismember a different person, hysterical and panicked responses, one way or the other, would have erupted. Not Reptile. He was as cold as ice, calculating his words and moves in still silence from behind a grin that was either heartwarming and friendly or a mask he wore while he quietly unsheathed a dagger behind his back. At least I could see it now. James had opened my eyes just enough.

"What are you going to do to me?" I asked as I obediently made my way toward the chair that required straps for some reason.

"We're going to see what's wrong with your brain, killer," Reptile finally spoke with a big, toothy smile.

Faye laughed. "That would take a while!" A few of the others, a mix of Dweller and acolyte, chuckled along.

I was strapped down as a three-armed plastic claw descended from the ceiling, each prong tipped with a metal hexagon plate pointed toward my skull. I turned toward the comedian and got to the point, "What are you doing here?"

"Face forward," and a little shove to my chin came from Faye.

"I wanted to see it with my own eyes. You were quite a demonstration, but I guess I needed a little more proof. Can you blame me for being skeptical?" Reptile replied.

I couldn't judge his expression out of the corner of my eye. The machine began to spin the arms around my head with increasing speed as the plates drew closer.

"I can blame you for bringing your people to a place where they don't..."

"Face forward! Be still!" Faye observed on a nearby computer screen that I was screwing up the scan.

"Easy, killer. Like I said, I read your book. Isn't this where you'd want us to be, in the halls of the one who gave her life for everyone?"

I couldn't see his eyes, so it was tough to determine his sincerity. "My dad says you're a spook, someone not to be trusted."

"Your father is a wise man."

That didn't answer anything. I bet myself he'd answer more directly if one of those arms was slowly crunching and tearing its way out of its socket, but my usual approach didn't seem appropriate. "That doesn't answer the question; does it, Reptile?" I figured I'd have to dance his dance to find out anything with a bunch of do-gooder witnesses around.

"I think it does. Besides, what does it matter what I was yesterday if now we're on the same team?"

We were not on the same team. Were we? Dang it if he wasn't already screwing with me. "If we're all friends now, then tell me about your mission and where you're from."

I couldn't see it but I knew that grin was back. "It really is classified, killer. And I take my orders very seriously. Everyone knowing everything just isn't how our business works, is it?"

"Classified by who? Everyone who played by those rules is dead."

"And what does that tell you, Sal of Nellis? The old command structure must not be entirely gone. But I must admit that I haven't been updated in some time. Regardless, I keep following my directives until I hear otherwise."

The spinning arms slowed and retracted. Faye was busy typing while a colorful image of my brain began to take shape on her monitor. I didn't have more to offer the slippery Reptile other than coercion, which would have to wait. "I'm headed away from here on a classified mission of my own. Would you do me the professional courtesy of at least telling me what you can? I don't know much about what's been going on outside my sandbox."

Reptile was pleased he'd checkmated me into normal conversation. He perked up in his seat to face me more directly as I did the same. I kept in mind that the straps were just for show when a monster like me was the patient. "I'd be happy to, especially if you'd do me the courtesy of telling me what happened to that treasonous little ingrate, Joseph, and your special sword which I rightfully confiscated."

"I never found that blade and I don't know your ingrate." I did my best to lie but I knew I was outclassed at the moment. Hopefully, he bought it.

"That's too bad," Reptile sighed, seeming genuinely disappointed. "My superiors love technology, and I have a special protocol for deserters. Well, I guess it's my turn," he carried on without missing a beat. It seemed like he bought it. "Obviously, I can't tell you my specific instructions, but you seem like a good enough kid outside of all the needless damage you've caused my organization. I'll fill in a few holes for you. First, I suggest you gather more intel on your targets and think harder on your strategy before you make a move against someone. Now, I know what you think of your Dwellers and your Seed. You see enemies and pour your heart and soul into defeating them. That's truly admirable. I like to think I used to be just like you. But after you've been around awhile, kid, you start to see the shades of gray. You see that the good side has its own issues and the bad side often has a rationale for their violence. You start to make judgment calls based on best possible outcomes instead of victory and defeat.

"A common understanding in my business is that it's often a good idea to become friends with the enemy of your enemy, regardless of who that might be. Why throw good American meat into the grinder when maybe someone a little further down the gray scale will happily take their place. That's where I come in. You can curse me for associating with the people you despise, but if you saw the big picture, you might thank me for my extended time behind enemy lines."

Still, he'd said nothing. I was withholding, too, so I couldn't be too upset with my intel opponent. "But you didn't befriend the enemy of an enemy. You buddied up with a buddy."

"Shades of gray, son. And I will add that you and your special girlfriend upended the whole game before my plans came to fruition. That's not a bad thing, not at all. You made a positive difference, so I'll tell you one more thing: since you don't yet know every enemy out there, some of your recent activity has been misguided by blissful ignorance. There are forces in this world that would keep you awake at night if you knew what they were capable of. Now, don't get your panties in a twist at this part, because I'm trying to help you. You think you're the top of the food chain because of your special relationship with the dark side, but you're not. Even with everything you can do, you're out of your league if you're about to step onto the big stage."

"Noted," I said with a nod. I believed him. And of my many charming character flaws, flaming hubris is not one. "Enlighten me, then. What's so scary out there that it causes the shadowy Reptile to lose sleep?"

Faye burst into the interrogation, of which I wasn't sure who was the subject and who was the investigator. "Done! This is unbelievable! Ripley, you were exactly right. There is no field disruption in Sal's brain when he moves or thinks, but everything structural is similar to our guardians."

"What now?" I asked as I hopped off the chair and made my way to the screen. I'd forgotten I was in the middle of a medical procedure. Reptile stood and followed just behind me.

"Let's both pray you never find out," came a low whisper over my shoulder. Now he was whispering in my ear, maybe what he had wanted all along.

"See this last scan, Sal." Faye pointed at an image from the previous guinea pig. "This is what Ripley was talking about. We've been banging our heads on desks for years around here trying to figure out the exact mechanism by which Seed controls its victims. We knew it locked out whole sections of the brain because we could follow the organic electrical impulses in the neurons as they fired and hit invisible walls when they tried to crisscross the important cognitive and memory centers. That's one of the reasons people act like they do with the Visitor inside them. They can't remember anything. No language, no sense of self, nothing. Every idea that tries to bubble up gets shut down before it can act on anything physical in the body."

"Isn't the brain physical?" I had almost no idea the mad scientist was saying.

"Eh, one of those gray areas." Faye snickered at her eavesdropping. "Anyway, what we could never discern was how the parasite caused unaffected parts of the body to move by way of the victim's brain. We knew it did because we could watch that, too. But there was never a physical link, even with twists and spikes of that stuff in the victim's head. But, bang! There it is!"

I was looking at rainbow-colored spaghetti overlaying a picture of a skull and squidgy gray matter. "Um."

"Right there!" Faye just couldn't believe we weren't seeing it. "Here's you. No bending or alteration of the electromagnetic field around and inside your head. Here's our friend. When he thinks or moves, the hum is contorted. So, it's not broadcasting a signal through or to the brain. That's why we never found it. It's using the signal that's already present to heat up neurons to provide the electrons that power the biological signals. The parasite is not really doing much in there. It's more like an antenna."

"Okay." I was already lost in the explanation.

Reptile thought to elicit more information, though. "What does that mean, darlin'?"

"Gosh, I don't know," she said puzzled but excited. Jess would have been proud. Puzzled and excited was how she spent most of her time. I could feel her there, cheering her pupil and the possibilities. I tried not to shun the silly thought. She was around us, somewhere, in one form or another. Of all the people influencing the events in the room, she was still atop the list.

I took my turn. "What now?"

"Well, I guess now we try again to unlock the Visitor's corresponding code so we can try to find an off-switch for the antenna and finally heal these people. That's what Jess was trying to do when she went off to find you." Faye looked away from the computer with sad eyes. "Sorry, Sal, I don't mean to imply…"

"It's fine, Faye. What code?"

Her sad eyes turned to quiet disappointment. I guess I was supposed to already understand the enigma. "The code! The only code that matters. Well, two, actually." She turned back to the screen and was back to problem-solving. "We've got a rough map of how the Visitor interacts with people via their DNA, though that makes little sense in itself, but we've got nothing on the Visitor's DNA, for lack of a better word. This stuff lives and operates like nothing anybody's ever seen. And until we know its basic instructions or patterns, we're dead in the water if we're trying to find out how one code talks to the other. That's probably what we'll need if we ever hope to flip the right switch."

Describing the Visitor as alive took me aback considering Seed was crawling around inside me. "Seed is alive?"

Faye was bored with the question before it left my mouth. "Obviously. It eats. It replicates itself. It's capable of all kinds of activities that terrestrial parasites only wish they could pull off."

Reptile was still dwelling on the first part of the crazy nonsense. "You all sequenced human DNA to try to undo this process? How did you pull that off? And what do you mean DNA itself makes little sense?"

"Yeah, Jess sent her guardians up north to the college not long after she made this place to get the right equipment. We sequenced a bunch of victims to try to see if there was a marker for who Seed merged with and who it didn't. But the whole endeavor was a dead end, and not just because we only had the one code. The more you look at DNA for any reason, even for just a basic understanding of how it operates, the less it makes sense. That makes it tough to imagine any kind of remedy based on something you'll probably never understand."

"How do you mean, darlin'? People have been tinkering with DNA for a long time." I could see Reptile compiling the notes in his head for a report to somebody interested in the subject.

Faye turned back to us. The answer appeared to weigh on her. She had the silent attention of everyone in the room. "Okay, I'll try to explain. Those all-important neurons we have been looking at are just cells, right?" Nods. "Well, they're built of proteins, mostly, and every one of those proteins is a copy of unzipped DNA. So, that makes sense. A living spirit needs a physical structure for reasons not entirely understood, so it keeps a blueprint of the building blocks it needs in every cell. A bit redundant for the otherwise cruel efficiency of nature, but let's say that particular redundancy squeaked by all the natural selection nonsense.

"The real problem arrives when you have a handle on that basic process and then begin to delineate why it's happening so that you can manipulate the molecular system. Sure, there are copies of vital proteins encoded in each strand. And you can imagine that part of the code, let's call it, somehow forms instructions on what to do with the little proteins once they're created. That's already a bit of a stretch considering the alternatively rudimentary function of protein synthesis, but let's go with it because it seems to be implicit in the mechanism. Now, what reads that code? That's where the otherwise sensible model begins to fall apart. A code is encrypted information by definition, meaning it is not the physical thing, or in this case process, it represents. It needs a cipher to be of any use. But there is no cipher. Nothing encircling DNA is anything even close to a mechanism that could interpret complex instructions somehow encoded in a series of nitrogen-based molecules.

"For the longest time, people just seemed to think that the code read itself. They put it in countless books that made their way here. But it's just so stupid. How could an otherwise inanimate ribbon built of utterly inanimate molecules ever pull off a feat like reading itself? I know grown people with perfectly functioning biological supercomputers filling up their frontal lobes that can't read a book because they haven't built up the ciphers in their neural patterns. DNA is infinitely more complicated than anything ever written, and the going theory is that it reads itself without any adequate system in place to read anything and without any parallel associations to decode the molecular data. Doesn't make any sense. Zero. Like I said, dead end. How could we hope to wield such a mysterious tool to help people when we don't understand its most basic function?"

Quiet looks scanned adjacent faces. Nope, no one had the slightest idea what the sweet scientist had just carefully explained. I took away from the lecture that people didn't really know why life was alive in the first place. I liked it better when I just had an evil metal worm in my head helping me move my limbs. Now, I didn't know which of us was more alive or if either of us was.

I was unquestionably still standing in Jess's temple. Bewilderment crushed every mind that dared enter.

"And don't even get me started on epigenetics!" Faye suddenly called out too loudly for the proximity of her audience. "And if I have to talk about Helicase or any of its impossibly brilliant counterparts, I'm going to need a drink!"

I couldn't tell if Reptile followed the lesson any better than the rest of us, but boy was he interested. That maniacal grin was gone. Every contrived expression or gesture was gone. He looked innocent for a moment like he'd just seen his first puppy. "Faye, forgive me for my continuing ignorance, but knowing what you know and knowing what you don't know, do you still think if you found Seed's DNA, or similar information, you could actually reverse the process?"

"Mmm," Faye contorted her freckled face while she considered the question. "I can't really say. That was the goal, of course. Thanks to you, we're a big step closer. We know how Seed is talking to the victim. We know from old academia a good amount about the physical processes of the victim's thoughts and memories. If we knew what code Seed was operating on, we could perhaps understand the language that linked the two. Then we could either try to manipulate Seed to change its behavior or alter the victim in a way that would make them more resilient to Seed's control. I would say we would be that close, but, in the end, none of this ever really worked. Jess and her unique spirit proved to be the only thing that could alter the process to any degree. That said, I have to believe that she would want us to believe there was a way. Everything physical was just a puzzle of spiritual influences to her. Maybe that's the real reason DNA seems suspicious and we've never found anything similar in Seed: because physical phenomena are only necessary manifestations of spirit. Working on a problem, though, is itself believing we can solve it. Would we be blessed for that belief? No one can say until we try."

Now spirits were mixing with DNA and aliens. I was getting a headache. Reptile seemed as satisfied as he was going to be. He stood up straight, pulled his shirt tight, and put the blank grin back on his stony face. "Thank you so much for that, Faye. Illuminating. I'm so glad we stopped by and made your acquaintance. Is there anything we can do for you or your people before we go, maybe something to help with your research?"

She was eating out of his hand. All the spook talk hadn't slowed her trust. He was smooth; I had to give him that. "No, we're fine here, Ripley," she responded with a smile while she reached out and held his hands. "What about you? Anything we can do to help you on your super-secret mission? You're welcome to stay longer if you like. There's so much more here to learn than biology."

"Oh, that's very kind, darlin'. I truly hope to take you up on that offer when we don't have other business." He held out his arms for a last hug. "This is the custom, I believe." The two shared a quick embrace, then Reptile turned toward me.

"Try to hug me and see what happens," I growled in reflex. My day had not gone how I had hoped.

"Of course not, killer." He smiled and held out his hand. "Friends?"

"Associates." We shook on it.

15

I saw her in the night.

Faye escorted me to my room after we waved goodbye to Reptile and company. That pack of weirdos headed back the way they came. I guessed back to the warehouse. To do what, I hadn't found out. But I wasn't interested in discovering their plans nor in an amicable farewell. I only wanted to make sure they were gone. As the plume of dust from the convoy snaked its way into the canyons, Faye asked, "How long will you stay?"

"Just tonight."

"Wish you'd stay longer. You'd be a big help around here. And it seems like you could use being here."

"I could and I will, but I have somewhere I have to go."

"Classified?" she asked sarcastically and with a raised brow.

"You have the requisite clearance, Faye. I'm headed to…"

"Am I a spy now!" She made a few excited karate chops harmlessly into the air in front of her.

"A terrifying one."

"I could teach you a thing or two," she said as she stepped away with a sneer. "Come on, tough guy. I'll show you where you should stay."

I hadn't seen Jess's room before I was shown the door. It was on the second floor of the main complex. I suppose you could call it the keep, a noble rise of myriad rooms and corridors supporting one of the towers. This part of the castle was older, a combination of conjured stone with smooth metal filling the gaps where the intricacies of masonry had become too complex. Conduits clung low to the ground and climbed where necessary to touch a light. Jess was a solid carpenter, considering her detached upbringing, but a lousy electrician. The makeshift wiring looked like it arrived after construction.

"Are you sure it's okay? I feel weird using her room," I asked before I turned the knob.

"If it's anyone's room now, it's yours," Faye replied with a shrug. "You guys made a lasting bond, short as it was." I got a sideways hug to ease the hurt. "Plus, this place if filling up, which is wonderful. But nobody else wants the spot either out of reverence, even though Jess wouldn't approve. I think it's meant to be yours."

I meandered for a moment inside. There wasn't nearly as much of her there as I both wished for and dreaded. Books here and there. A great view of the patchwork of sprawling courtyards below. A desk with a pen but no paper. A bed for one. It felt empty and cold. She was gone, and I was lost inside her tiny abode.

I lay atop the sheets with my clothes on, looking up at the ceiling and wondering if I was in the right spot. Was there a right spot for something like me?

I couldn't help but think of Jess, being surrounded by her legacy. How she would have loved the home she created. I could hear children playing through the open window. Few noises are as heartening as the pitch of those giggles, even to hardened hearts like mine. Voices occasionally rose above the breeze and calm chatter, usually ending in laughter. Jokes were always a few decibels more boisterous than casual conversation. What would she be doing on a cool evening like this if I hadn't taken her by the hand and led her across the desert to her death? She'd be mingling, I thought. She'd bounce from face to face exploring everyone's activities. She'd interject her sweet madness. She'd help if she could, then be gone a few beats too short, off to the next spot to soak up the glow of people on the same path. And she'd pray. She'd do lots of that. Not the pleading, aggravated garbage that I ejected when I tried. She'd be thankful and ask God to let the peaceful community stand for as long as it could.

I felt her fingers in mine, interlaced with a squeeze. She was hovering over my sleepy eyes, beaming a smile brighter than any other. I lurched up like lightning. "Jess!" I tried to exclaim, but she knew it was coming. Her delicate finger crossed my lips before I could shout. She was excited, beckoning me along to see something amazing. That was always her job, for some reason: to invite me forward to see something I couldn't without her.

She glided toward the window. It was dark outside. The voices had faded. Smoke from a few chimneys shrouded the grounds. What was I supposed to see this time? I didn't care. I looked at her and moved to hold her. Her hands gently touched my cheeks as I gazed into the depths of her eyes. For once, I didn't want to move a muscle. I wanted to savor. Then a shove at my cheek. She forced me to look farther into the distance. In the blackness of the night, a storm had gathered, blotting out the stars, leaving the earth below as dark as the heavens above. Lightning crackled in the distance but it didn't look typical. Wide, blue bolts crashed with more intensity than white lightning. It lingered longer than a flash, blazing against the ground as it carved jagged paths in our direction. It was an unnatural horizon, an approaching threat.

I took her hand in mine again and squeezed her entwined grip. Whatever was coming for us, it would have to get through me. And nothing was getting through me. I would not fail her again.

I was gripping the sheets with enough force to pulverize the material. Stupid dreams. I sat up in a rush for the second time. The storm was

63

gone. The night was calm. I was alone, again, or still. I wiped the sweat from my forehead and looked out of the window. I had dozed late into the night. The village below was sleeping. Stars lit the maze beneath and the canyons beyond. Just a stupid dream, but I could still feel the impression of her fingers locked between mine.

Faye had said this happened to followers from time to time. On one of my visits, she blurted out that she had spoken with Jess. Half of me was stunned, wanting to hear every syllable Jess had imparted; the other half wanted to tell Faye where to stick her cruel fantasies. After some negotiation between Faye and my attitude problem, I was told that many had seen Jess. Some reported feeling a presence at a time they thought was more than coincidental. Some said they had full conversations as though Jess was in the room with them. But they were all believers, each in love with her in their own way. For some reason, I couldn't trust the other people sitting in the same boat. "The place is haunted?" I sarcastically asked.

After everything I'd seen, you might think I'd be less of a fool. You'd be wrong.

"She spoke to you through a computer before she spoke to any of us," Faye had indignantly replied. She had a point. Maybe the whole world was haunted by spirit. Then again, maybe that was as silly as it sounded.

My heart was still racing as I lay back down. I was sure I wouldn't sleep again, staring up at the ceiling and pondering the dream. At first light, I would go. Another dizzying visit had left me in a mood to move on without goodbyes.

I'd hoped for a silent departure as the first rays of twilight touched my window. I quietly gathered my few worldly items and snuck down the hallway, then the stairs. No one saw me move through the courtyards. When I came upon the sometimes-ferocious guardian of the door, I patted his shoulder and whispered, "Good morning and good job." His cold, silvery eyes hardly seemed to notice me. Leaving, I supposed, was not as stimulating as arriving.

"Hey, Sal!" one of the community's residents, Davis, surprised me as I exited the maze. The hunters of the village had gathered beyond the wall. I had chatted with members of the group from time to time but never seen them in action.

I was greeting them with what names I could remember when I was disturbed by one member of the team. They'd brought along a female host. I wasn't sure how to greet her in turn. "That's Lucy," Davis spoke up. "She's better at this than any of us. Really, I don't think we even need to go, other than to hunt people."

"Good morning, Lucy," I managed with a smile. No reply. "What do you mean 'hunt people?'"

"We're hunting souls as well as meat," Davis chuckled. "We take wide circles away from here not because we need to but in hopes of finding more survivors. You want to come along?"

"A rain check. I've got a really long haul ahead…"

"Nah, you look like you could use some of the tranquil excitement of a hunt. Come on, we'll head your way. Won't slow you down."

"Okay, east then." Then I saw a face even stranger than Lucy's among the group, one that had been slightly obscured by the hood of her jacket. "Wait, I know you," I reported as I tried to place the features.

"Yes, you do," she happily replied with a wide smile. "You saved me."

That was it. She was in the Dweller's jail alongside me. It was dark then and her face had been concealed with dirt and worry, but it was her. "That's great that you made it here." I was relieved Reptile had let them go without further harassment, then curious. "How did you make it here?"

She paused for a moment before Davis answered for her, in a hurry because I told him to be. "She's New Girl. Came in with that group of yours. Says she's deadly with a bow. We're looking forward to seeing if she's legit," Davis said as he and the others piled into the back of an old Chevy pickup.

"I'm okay," she said bashfully as she hurried along with the group.

I shrugged it off, guessing she stuck with Reptile just long enough to make it somewhere better. You do what you have to.

16

The valley sang in the first chimes of sunlight. I couldn't hear the tune, though. I wanted to move on, to accomplish my mission. Then I could return to a place where I felt out of touch and to a job I hated. Though that made little sense, I remained fixated. I had an objective. I kept my eyes on the prize and hardly noticed the grandeur of nature slapping me across the face.

We left the truck and my bike in a tiny ghost town along the river. I suppose all towns qualify as ghost towns now.

The group of hunters slipped quietly into the woods and snaked along the water looking for prey, sticking close to brush for concealment but never disturbing a branch that might crack. They kept their light panting from the swift motion low and their footsteps quick but soft. Without a signal, the squad would occasionally pause to listen and look.

They were a solid, well-trained unit, one that had done this a thousand times. The new girl was folding in almost seamlessly. I was doing my best to keep up. I could have shot ahead, but the force would have loudly broken the fluidity of the procession. I had to watch my heavy steps. Davis had been correct, though: moving with the team and focusing on something other than impending danger or cosmic riddles did bring a modicum of peace.

A pause. Davis motioned toward the water. Two does stood near the edge of the river. Davis motioned again, waving us off the targets, then pointed to the brush. A four-point buck stood high, smelling the air. With a flick of his hand, Davis designated the new girl to advance and take the shot.

She moved like a whisper while the rest of us looked on quietly from the orange and yellow leaves still clinging to the trees. She drew the bow as the buck took a cautious step forward. One more step and she would have a clear shot.

As we waited, Davis moved next to me and tapped my shoulder. He pointed back toward the road. "There's our real target." He winked. Through the dense foliage blocking the distant street, I saw movement but couldn't tell what it was.

New Girl released the shot, but I think Davis's movement or comment distracted her. The projectile was going to hit the animal but miss the mark. We'd have to chase a bloody, wounded beast with an arrow sticking out of its shoulder across the valley before we were done.

I exploded after the arrow. Why not just stop the mistake in flight? I arrived a half-second too late. The buck dropped down on its front ankles from the pain and shock of the impact. With a quick grunt to express the agony followed by heavy breathing, he tried to stand again to run.

I made the tough call, but couldn't execute it before Lucy caught up. I grabbed for the neck to hold the beast down but was failing against the strength of terror and pain. I could apply immeasurable pressure with the Visitor fortifying my might but I couldn't weigh any more than I did. The buck could easily ragdoll me into the woods and I'd have nothing to say about it if I couldn't hang on. Unexpectedly, Lucy helped hold him down. She looked into my eyes for the obvious answer, I think. I reached for the neck. With a twist and a snap, it was over. Our quarry went limp. Lucy gently brushed its cheek as it lay in front of us, dead or dying.

Hosts still made me feel uneasy. They weren't trying to kill me anymore, which was nice, but their behavior was so strange. They were always curious, always moving or looking. And some, like Lucy, had regained a tiny fraction of their humanity. I had asked Faye how she trained her Pitbull to stand by the door of the castle. She replied, "Neuroplasticity." She may as well have replied, "Blue elephants," but she did go on to explain that even with a horrific intruder inside it, the human brain would try like crazy to reconnect itself to the body any way it could. Some hosts, she said, were further along the process with help and encouragement. I didn't say it, even though Jess had shouted it from somewhere deep in my mind, but I noticed that what she was describing was immaterial love healing a physical body.

They were still creepy.

"Good save, brother!" Davis exclaimed as he caught up. "You, too, Lucy. Good work. See, I told you that you guys didn't need the rest of us."

"You guys," he said like ol' Lucy and I were the same kind of creature. He made a valid observation, and I didn't like it.

"What were you pointing at that caused this, Davis?"

"Oh, right." He didn't pause at my accusation. He couldn't care less if I judged him. "Up there." He pointed again. "Somebody walking by the road."

I was done with Davis's happy squad and otherwise wasting time. I raced up to the road alone. We had found a wanderer. I could tell long before I caught up, though, that it was another host. Its gate was rhythmic and calm as it proceeded down the road, its head looking from side to side to take in the view. It wasn't scared. Humans had to worry more. They were twitchy and cautious.

"Hello," I said as I stood in its path. It gazed at me for a moment, hardly exuding a reaction, and walked around me to continue ahead.

I was back on my bike before the others made their way to the road. I stopped out of courtesy but wasn't in the mood to chat. "It's another patient for Dr. Faye," I said to Davis as I rolled to a stop. "Thank you for the hunt, everyone. It was a nice morning."

"You're welcome, Sal." A hug rushed me before I could dodge it. Then another. Oh, they just didn't stop. I held out my fist for a bump when I got to Lucy. Nothing. "Take care of yourself out there. Come and see us when you can."

"Will do." I was thinking not.

17

No one to fight. Nothing to do but ride and ride. Ride away from home. Ride away from Judgment. The flowing howl of the wind in my face and the slow spin of the graceful scenery were welcome as my new companions. They had nothing to say, nothing to ask of me. Gifts without a catch. I soaked them in, inhaling the solitude I craved and allowing it to nourish nerves long frayed.

It didn't work. For a while, maybe. But boredom is an invitation. I enjoyed the ride, twisting the throttle enough to keep things interesting as the tires skimmed the sparse asphalt struggling to cling to the earth while the empty world slowly shrugged it off. I admired the landscape blowing by. The colors of the receding season were breathtaking and hummed all the brighter, perhaps, without people around to jostle their natural transition. I appreciated the peace until I realized I wasn't so much enjoying it as I was grasping for it. I was shoving my thoughts deeper into the radiant scenery as I rode, herding them away from darker frontiers. I didn't want to remember all that had happened, what I lost, the wickedness that remained, and the job that I hated. I emphatically didn't want to think about my encounter with Jess only hours before. Undisturbed confusion concerning her message was easier than trying to understand. Before I made the Rockies, though, all I could think about was the soaring magnitude of my bewildering predicament. The splendor of my surroundings faded away as cold stress spilled over from rising uncertainty.

A storm was coming, she had said or implied, whatever the dead do to us in our dreams. What was I supposed to do about it? Punch lightning? I couldn't tame a sloppy infestation as incompetent as the Dwellers. If things were about to get worse, I'd already lost. I wondered if the storm had something to do with Nellis and its predicament with the newly intrusive Department of Defense. I wondered if I was wondering too hard about a stupid dream.

The chill in the mountains offered some relief. Finally, something real to worry about. I stopped in the woods for a break and grabbed the only jacket I brought out of one of my hefty saddlebags. You don't think about thick coats when you live in Vegas. The sun was still high and warmed me enough, but I had to consider what the evening would be like. Could I freeze to death? Would the Visitor permit me to die at all, let alone from negligent apparel?

I looked around for one of those cabins in which Joe hid for years while he ducked Seed among the shadows of the looming peaks. There was nothing visible from my vantage. Life was erased, save for the lone narrator. No smoking chimneys to chase. No sounds to follow. Just me and the trees.

I made it out of the snowy summits before dark but knew I wouldn't make it too much farther. I had hoped for a friendly face to appear in Denver, but it was a disaster. Wherever any bulk of humanity had tried to cling, war was inescapable. I raced through the ruins as fast as I could while dodging unnatural potholes born of a bomb.

Kansas was my last hope. It seemed, though, that there was nothing in Kansas before there was nothing everywhere else. I had never seen so much nothing. I didn't bother hoping for a friendly face; I just scanned the vast expanses stretching out from the sides of the highway for a decent spot to camp.

My eyes caught something unusual. I slowed. The sky was darkening so the view was difficult to make out. It was a farm. Everywhere was a farm but this one held sparks of precious life. There was motion around a mill. Something stirred ahead of a plow in the field. Lights were on. I'd found people! And Dwellers never had the motivation to grow food to sustain themselves, so the chances of these folks trying to eat me were appreciably low.

I rolled slowly down the highway toward the farm. The darkness of the night swelled the shadows so I still couldn't decipher much detail, but it looked like a functioning home. I was excited to meet someone other than my usual audience. Maybe I could spread the good news without anyone screaming or bleeding. I was in a pretty good mood, for me, as I rounded the corner of the property and ventured down the old dirt road that ran to the house.

There was something odd about that spinning mill, though. The main gear was turning but the blades meant to catch the wind were too broken to produce much pressure. The breeze was calm, too. A quiet, still night had descended onto the plains. I squinted and made out people and a pulley system attached to the emaciated building. The residents must have rigged something to allow manual labor to be applied, and the poor farmers were out in the night laboring away. Finally, something I'd be good at. I'd lend a hand.

"Hello," I yelled in as friendly a tone as I could manufacture. I waved a greeting at the group of people pushing against the protruding pegs of a makeshift wheel. They didn't respond. "Hello?" I said again when I was close enough to be easily heard.

Finally, I drew sufficiently near to see the prison for what it was. There were chains around those people. The inmates were shuffling lethargically in the only direction they could move. Some sicko had set up a penal plantation. I could see more details of the shuffling group ahead of the plow in the distance, too. More people. More chains. Okey dokey, time to go to work. Screaming and blood on the way.

I called out again. "Sit tight. I'll get you out of there." I started back toward my bike and noticed there was still no reply. I looked again. "Hello?" Nothing. Were they too scared to speak? I looked harder into the darkness. Were they hosts?

Click, slide, snap, went the charging of the AR15 behind me. "Don't move!" The command came from an older male. I could hear his shoes grind against the dirt for a solid stance to shoot. I could hear the stock press deeper into his shirt and flesh. The slave master had a good position on me. I was going to take a few hits before this was over. I hadn't been shot in the head yet and picked that particular time to worry about it. Faye was tinkering with the grey matter of hosts to help them remember. What would I be if a round splattered mine in the dirt?

I stopped. "Do you want me to turn around? I'm unarmed," I asked my soon-to-be-screaming assailant.

"Very, very, slowly. If you reach, I shoot. And I'm a good shot." His voice was calm. He wasn't lying. I did as instructed.

He wasn't what I had in mind. No crown of bones, hideous tattoos, nor scars from the more energetic slaves that tried to escape and kill him in the process. He didn't look like a Dweller or anything else sinister. He had on a white shirt with red pinstriping. His sliver-streaked hair and mustache were well maintained. Large glasses sat on his broad nose. His round belly rested comfortably over his belt. He looked like he might sell me a car or a Bible, not chain me to his farm equipment.

"How many in your group?" he asked after we had sized each other up.

"Just me. I'm traveling alone."

Click went the safety. "Don't lie to me, boy. Won't do you a bit of good."

"That's my bike down the road. I would appreciate a passenger, but not many to be found these days. Before you kill me, you mind telling me what you're doing with all these people chained up out here?"

"People!" He was offended by the question. "Those ain't people. Is that why you stopped?" He chuckled at the idea. "You thought you was gonna rescue those monsters?" He laughed a little more. "That's the first time I heard that one. You a little off or somethin'?"

He thought I was crazy. He wasn't entirely mistaken. Either way, the chained bodies were hosts running his mill. Better, somehow, but still not cool. "I am going to rescue those monsters. I get why you call them that, but they're not that anymore. You can't just chain them up and leave them out here."

"Son, I'm the one with my finger on a trigger. You brought your little fists to a gunfight. I suppose that means I can do whatever I like. Now, get outta here before I lose my patience with you!"

I weighed my options. I could come back later in the night, but it had been a long ride. I figured with one step left faster than anything he'd ever seen, I'd probably take a single round in the right shoulder. The next couple shots would hit the dirt behind me, and I'd have that gun. Maybe a gentle tap upside his head. Maybe not. I'd decide when I got to that point.

Click, click went two more safeties behind me. They came from the direction of the mill. My new assailants had blended in with the constant noise of the hosts jangling their chains. That was smart. I was beginning to like these psychos. I wondered if I could still make it to the salesman.

"Really, son," he continued as he took an aggressive step forward while the light steps of the others closed in behind me, "you're beginning to test my good Christian nature. Now get, before we have to do something we don't want to!"

"What do you mean 'Christian?'" I asked the guy with zombies chained up in his yard.

He was becoming exacerbated. "What do you mean 'what do I mean?' You know, I fear God! I try to be nice even to nuts like you. You really are touched, aren't ya?" He took a moment and a breath. He didn't want to shoot the crazy guy who wandered onto his property. That was nice. I was thinking I wouldn't break his head with his rifle.

"Okay, just relax," I answered. "We've got our wires crossed here. Tell your two partners to stand down, and I'll leave peacefully. I think what you've got going here is wrong but maybe that's your business. Maybe I find myself out of line. And if you really are a Christian, then we sort of play for the same team. No one needs to get hurt here."

"Ha!" the Bible salesman exclaimed. "You gotta be kiddin' me! You did come here for them! I can't believe it. Somebody blows through here ever' couple weeks and tries to steal or worse. But none of them ever gave a notice to my prisoners. Maybe you ain't so bad." He lowered the weapon and tucked it under his arm. He took a few steps toward me. He raised his hand for a shake but had an admonishment before we were properly introduced, "If you get twitchy, my girls will still blow your brains out. They're better shots than I am."

I smiled. "Understood. I'm Sal."

"Russell. Everybody calls me Russ."

"Nice to meet you, Russ."

"So, Sal, what brings you out this way other than rescuing demons in distress?"

I told him about Nellis and the summons from the DOD. Russ took my charge very seriously. He was immediately inclined to help, and I found myself at his dining table before it was too dark to see his fields.

"You have electricity," I noted as I entered his neat, quaint home.

"Yeah, I got some of them freaks turning a generator, too." He looked to me and contorted his expression, acknowledging his possible offense. "Well, whatever they are. Maybe you got family that turned? Something like that?"

"Something like that." I smiled to hide the swell of painful memories. I didn't know how much he was ready to hear.

His girls came in behind us, still toting their rifles like pros. They had no intention of putting them down. They were going to stay on guard as long as their dad entertained the drifter.

"They're young," I noticed aloud.

Russ knew what I meant. "Yeah, just babies when all this madness started. We kept 'em safe only by the grace of God. Now, I think they keep us safe." He chuckled and beamed with pride.

"We?" I asked as I was invited to sit.

"Yes, their mother should be arriving shortly. She went to the bunker to trade but loves to stay too long and chat with her friends. That's how we survived, as a matter of fact. Some crazy development company turned an old nuclear missile silo not more than a mile from here into luxury condominiums long before the war started. She knew some of the folks that bought in. Rich people who thought the world was gonna end if the economy tanked or something like that. When everything went haywire, almost none of 'em showed up to their multi-million-dollar, subterranean penthouses. Maybe they couldn't make it in time. Maybe they thought it was all contained when that bomb dropped. Whatever happened, we were invited inside in their stead, thank God. We waited out the worst in relative comfort and safety. There's even a pool down there! Can you believe that?"

"It sounds like a nice place."

"It was. Better than most had it. That's for sure." He turned to his daughters. "Girls, help me get dinner started for our guest. If he was here to do some bad business, I think he'd of got on with it already."

"Yeah, I'm not the type. I police that crowd, actually. It's hard to explain but that's one of my mandates. So, you must have had a few run-ins with the Dwellers yourselves. You run security around here like you're expecting trouble."

"I'm sorry, Sal, but I don't know what a Dweller is."

"The people who teamed up with Seed. They still keep up the evil mischief even after its departure."

"Hmm," Russ thought on it for a moment. "Can't say that I've seen that, but we do get all kinds of odd visitors. Kind of a crossroads here in the middle of the country. We did get some nice folks headed south recently. They said they was runnin' from something like a Dweller up north. Said some lunatic was in cahoots with the monsters, even conjuring up new ones with strange rituals and the like. I can't say I believed them entirely. So many people are so screwed up from everything that's happened. Hard to take anything at face value. But it seems like you've had some similar experiences."

A cold shiver ran up my spine. I recalled the whispers of Reptile. He was afraid of something out here in the wilderness, something that kept him awake at night. "Yeah, I've seen some things. Not like what you're describing but in the same ballpark."

Plates were out and the microwave was humming. Both girls replaced their looks of hostility with quick, curious glances and the occasional smile. I enjoyed the hospitality. Outside, hosts were still clanging around in their shackles.

"Well, tell us all about it," Russ invited while he prepared the dishes. "The Mrs. should be along soon. We'd all love to hear your story. We don't get many soldiers through here. Did you fight in the wars?"

"I did. But about your Mrs., aren't you worried? It's after dark and she's not back."

"Nah, the boys that guard the bunker keep it all buttoned up real tight. You remind me of them. All ex-military types. They got all kinds of surveillance and procedures to make sure everyone stays safe. We incorporated a lot of that stuff here. You set off a motion detector a half-mile up the road. We knew you was coming before you got here. So did they, I'm guessing. It's a good system. I learned a lot from them. The trick is to know what your enemy is going to do before he does. Then you're always ahead of the game." He seemed satisfied with his assessment.

"What did you do before the bunker?" I was curious about his demeanor more than anything. He wasn't too proud to admit he needed protection, wasn't ashamed he needed help. There was a calmness in him that I found admirable.

"Same as I'm doing now: farmin'. I guess I was put here for that reason." He smiled at the plan he perceived around him. "That and preachin', but that's more of a hobby."

"You're too modest, daddy," one of the girls finally spoke up. "He's all fire and brimstone on a pulpit. You should see it sometime. He still preaches at the bunker."

I'd never been to a church. Didn't seem like the right time to mention it. "I'd like that. Maybe if I come back through."

The Mrs. burst through the door with bags on each arm like she just looted a Walmart. She knew she was late and was thus in a hurry. "Oh my, we have company!" she said as she passed by me unconcerned. She dumped the load on the counter and kissed Russ, then squeezed the girls. I was next. She held out a strong farmer's hand. "I'm Julie."

I was surprised she wasn't more surprised. Something like normal life was happening around me and it was throwing me off. "I'm Sal," I said as I stood and accepted her grip. "It's very nice to meet you."

"Aren't you polite," she replied with a smile. "I can see how you managed to not get yourself shot. What brings you our way?"

Russ fielded that one. "He's a soldier all the way from Nellis Air Force Base. He was just about to tell us about it."

"Oh, we'd love a story. Will you be staying the night?"

"You know what? That sounds really nice if I'm not too much trouble. Thank you."

We ate after a prayer. We mostly chatted between bites about the goings-on around their part of the world. We didn't, however, discuss the slaves outside. I kept thinking about them but kept quiet. After dinner, we retreated to the living room. The girls started a fire, and it became clear that my performance was next on the schedule.

They wanted a story. I gave them a story. They seemed like a mature audience so they got the unvarnished good news. When I finished, more than an hour later, there was silence in the room. Julie finished wiping the occasional tear. The girls were holding hands. It was pretty intense, I suppose. Reciting it made me feel better about it. Confessing my inadequacy found catharsis.

Russ finally piped up. "So, you're half one of them and half one of us. Is that what all the fuss was about earlier? I can see now..."

"Russell Evans!" Julie snapped at him. "That's just rude." She had her own pressing questions, those a more feminine mind found essential. "Your wife, Jess, do you think she's alive?"

Julie's words hit me harder than the usual Q&A. I think it was the "wife" part. Few referred to us as married, but she was right. Jess and I made a commitment for life, though it only lived for a day. I thought about the question for a moment. "I know that she exists but I'm still working out the alive part. I'm the one telling my story but it all confuses me as well."

"My poor dear," Julie continued. "That is one of the saddest love stories I've ever heard."

Thankfully, I didn't have time to respond. The girls had questions, too. "If we'd have shot you earlier, you woulda been just fine?"

We laughed. "Well, I would have been shot. It still hurts. But, yeah, I think I would have healed up and lived on."

"That is so cool!"

We mulled the details of my strange adventure while the fire dimmed. It was a beautiful evening with kind company. Somewhere in the darkness, slaves were chained together while they toiled to keep the lights on.

18

There is no sneaking away from farmers early in the morning. Julie arose before the sun and was cooking components of lunch while she worked on a big breakfast. The girls were sharing duties between the kitchen and their father outside. I woke late in comparison, the smell of bacon inviting me to a happier than usual day. A quiet night on a comfortable recliner left me refreshed.

"Good morning," I said as I entered the bustling kitchen.

"The girls' shower is down the hall on the left," Julie matter-of-factly replied.

Noted and remedied.

Breakfast was a noisy, cheerful affair. After a quick cleanup and farewell, I was given leftovers and other supplies. Julie had been working on my lunch and snacks, not theirs. I was sent away with food, friendship, good wishes, and the promises of prayers by one of the finest families I'd ever encountered.

Before mounting up, I took a walk to the mill. It looked like an ancient structure to my west-coast eyes, something long dead before Seed's presence killed it, but the inner workings seemed to be working. The hosts chained to the wooden machinery outside noticed my arrival with hasty, vacant glances. Standing close, I could see that the chains were hardly restrictive. A master jailer, Russ was not. Any of the monsters, or people, whatever we were, could have broken free with little effort. Could they be comfortable in their servitude? Who was I to say what they sought?

I left them there with little concern. I had more important things to worry about. The reunification of splintered pieces of the once-noble United States' military, or another massacre, would soon be in my wake after meeting whoever dared to bomb my home and summon me to their throne. I would try for the former but be good either way, which seemed like a noble approach to the duality of my mission, one far beyond the plight of a handful of hosts serving their time. A sentence they had doubtlessly earned.

19

The ride that day was just as beautiful and depressing as the last. The world was lush, inviting, and forsaken. The road was long, agitating the intensity of the solitude. Outside of a host here and there, I didn't see another soul until I was beaten up by a couple.

I had dusted off an old road atlas from the base before my trip and had highlighted the best possible routes. The path I chose and my approximate whereabouts indicated that I was nearing my destination, again as night was sweeping away the dusk. I hardly needed to be notified by the map, though. Disaster was the X marking the spot. Washington was the most ruinous ruin I had ever laid eyes upon. If there was a single acre that hadn't been blown to bits or shot to pieces, I couldn't find it. Little remained from the more rural outskirts to the concrete heart of the capital where I stood.

The sad view had me wondering if my coordinates were correct. What version of a government could possibly be alive around me in the heaps of broken buildings or the thickly forested swamp clawing away at history? I looked at the map again and shook my head.

The closest I could find to the exact location of my invitation was less than a klick to the east of interstate 295, or what was left of it, neither the Pentagon to my left nor Andrews to my right, just a spot in the ravenous woods trying to swallow me along with everything else. I surmised that the given location was imprecise but still the logical place to start wading through the graveyard.

I ditched my ride in the copious brush girding the road. I should have built a dirt bike. I left my sword, too. I had a feeling that I might not want to show all my magical cards at once. I ought to be among friends if I found anyone at all, but these friends wanted something of me and my community. We were directed from afar, and I had reasoned over my long ride that no one would go to all the trouble just to say hello. I would decide after I assessed my would-be superiors if I should explain the wonder that had infused our victory over Seed.

As I pressed ahead into the gnarled forest that scraped and gouged me at every opportunity, the otherwise healthy green, yellow, and orange hues mixing in the sea of foliage began to decay together. The wall of stubborn life paled as it thinned, the color ripped in proceeding layers from the fibers. The farther I marched, the worse the graying became. Whatever had caused the disease or corrosion, I seemed to be headed toward the source. Before long, even the weeds gave up their insatiable grip on the ground. The dirt beneath looked slimy and sick.

In the fading light, I tripped over something in the muck of limp vegetation and bare mud. I looked down to see what rock or root would soon be pulverized for stubbing my toe. It looked like an over-sized, black mushroom was growing out of the ground, but the sun was too distant to see the shadow's details. I reached down to touch the odd sprout and clicked on my flashlight. The unnatural speedbump shined like metal when struck by the light.

"Stop there!" came a command from the shadows as soon as I had revealed my position with my light. Somebody got the drop on me while I cursed lawn decor. The voice was strange, spoken through a speaker if I was hearing it right. I shined my light around me to find my assailant. I saw only darkness and solitude, like most of my evenings. I pressed ahead a few paces to try to locate the voice. A gunshot cracked the calm evening, making me flinch as the bullet hit just ahead of my feet. Whoever it was wasn't screwing around. At least I got a warning shot.

I wanted to speak to de-escalate the situation before I was forced to tear somebody's head off their shoulders but was cut off with more commands, this time from a different speaker somewhere else along my murky visual perimeter. "He said stop!" the voice commanded, but it wasn't angry or afraid; it was annoyed that I hadn't listened the first time, pestered by my presence, almost whining.

"Okay," I shouted back. "I'm unarmed and not looking for trouble…"

"Well, you got trouble!" the first speaker interrupted. Again, it wasn't a threat. The words rolled like a joke to impress the other. Something was off about my bushwhackers. Either I was comical or they were stupid. Two empty heads might soon to be repurposed as fertilizer for the failing forest.

"Alright!" I tried to acquiesce. "I'm sorry?"

"You are sorry," was announced with audible chuckles. Okay, I was going to kill these two idiots. I'd already determined their positions from the gunshot and their voices. I left the flashlight to figure out gravity on its own as I shot in a blur toward head number one.

Reaching my target, I was dazzled. Initial shock then gave way to amazement and glee. Never did I imagine finding such a gift on my voyage. My jaw dropped and eyes lit with childish delight. My idiots were inside Atlases! And not just any old clunky Atlases, this was war hotness 2.0! 3.0? I couldn't help but immediately reach out to feel the carbon fiber outer layers as the idiot inside tried to brush me off. "Are you kidding me?" I laughed excitedly as I fondled. "You got the armor plates to slide under each other at the joints!" Oh, the sophisticated machinery that feat required which I never had! "The helmet is fixed to the skeleton!" That explained the speaker. "Where are the weapon systems?" I demanded. "If this thing flies, I might need a moment to myself."

During his unexpected groping, my target had been protesting in mumbles for which I cared not. Something about, "Stop it! Get off me!"

I spun around to the back. The weapons were in fact integrated. I was overjoyed. It was so beautiful that I thought a tear might spring forth from its stubborn reservoir. "This is amazing!" I finally exclaimed. "Where are you guys from? DOD? Is this what the DOD rolls in? Where do I sign…"

I was punched in the side of the head by something so hard it could only be the shiny fist of a space-age Atlas. My ears rang and I couldn't think straight for a moment. "What's wrong with you?" demanded the first stupid voice.

"Take it easy, man!" I answered as I gathered my wits. "We're all on the same team here. I was just admiring the gear."

"Yeah, well you can't be here. No t,t,tespassers!"

This guy had problems. His companion was no brighter. I'd take one more crack at this and then I was going to break their shiny toys just enough to remove the biological inhabitants and run off with the loot. "I'm not a t,t,tespasser, m,m,moron. I was invited here by your boss, I'm guessing. Show some hospitality or this is going to get ugly."

Idiot One laughed at Idiot Two. "He called you dumb!" He was giggling through his speaker.

Idiot Two thought to exact his revenge for the insult. One of the modified rifles on his back popped up over his shoulder. Just breathtaking technology! He had to be controlling it all through the visor and movements keyed into the gloves. If I had ten lifetimes, I couldn't build something so slick. I was going to feel bad when I broke the gun off his suit and hit him upside the helmet with it. Maybe, though, I could leave it intact and just do the hitting myself. Why break something so glorious?

The fight was on as I rushed them. A few rounds hit the dirt behind me. Deadly force initiated. "They started it," I would tell James later.

With people shooting at me, yet again, I was done with diplomacy. I punched my first target in the head hard enough to send him stumbling backward inside his otherwise stable sculpture. I hoped I hadn't broken the visor. That had to be one sweet piece of hardware.

Target two stood dumbfounded for a moment as I turned his way. It was a shock, I suppose, watching an otherwise unimpressive bag of bones punch a shiny Atlas in its teeth. I was on him as soon as I heard the clicks of the rifle emerge from the back. As it tried to find something to shoot, I climbed the smooth scaffolding and twisted the deadly appendage just enough for something to crack. I could fix a bolt or two.

More gunshots from my rear. The toothless Atlas hadn't learned its lesson. I ducked behind the armor as the hail of bullets crashed into the front. The impacts sent us both back a few steps. "Stop shooting, Baker!" cried the fool behind the speaker. "It hurts!"

These two were too much. "How did you jokers become Angels?" I said as I tried to choke an Atlas from the rear. I wasn't sure that would work, but habits are tough to break. "Is it take your kid to work day at the Department of Defense?"

The choke worked much better than expected. Some things crunched under the helmet and my victim started to squeal, "Help, Baker. Help!"

Baker shot us both again. I was in a fight with kindergarteners. The squealer ripped at my encircling arm to break free but wasn't strong enough. I was happy to learn that I was even stronger than war hotness 3.0. Soon both kids would be asleep from mild strangulation, then I would merge with war hotness and rule the world! Global domination or not, I would bring a cool toy back to Nellis.

My head was so close to the kindergartener's, I could hear the computer speaking into his headset as he began his nap. "Vital signs beyond established parameters. Autopilot engaged."

Autopilot? This thing had a full autopilot feature! I had to meet the engineer after I beat up his goons. I needed to shake his hand. Autopilot!

Autopilot turned out to be a bad thing. Before I knew what was happening, the Atlas stood up straight, held my choking arm in place, and bent over at the waist with enough force and speed to flip me over the top and send me flying into the dirt. As I lay surprised, gunfire erupted. Good thing I busted that noisy protrusion. A half-dozen rounds smashed into the dirt in a tight grouping a few yards away. Autopilot couldn't hit me with the angle off from those busted bolts.

We all looked at each other with confusion. Baker wasn't sure what to do. Autopilot looked to be recalculating its mistake. Baker finally piped up, "Charlie, are you okay?"

Charlie was fine, unfortunately. He tried to reply but was cut off by whatever version of autopilot was now running the show. "I think I'm…"

A robotic voice interrupted through Charlie's speaker, "Tactical assistance required. Command override."

That didn't sound good. When both Atlases twisted their chests in my direction in perfect unison, I knew I was in trouble. The kindergarteners were on recess. The robots and I were going to work things out like adults, one way or the other.

I rolled to my feet and sprinted back to Charlie's ride. I kicked the knee to buckle the contraption back down to my level and was shot in the shoulder for my trouble. Baker's autopilot was a competent shooter. What an annoying computer.

The leg of Charlie's frame folded just enough to let me clothesline the neck again. I was done with gentle strangulation; I wanted to rip the helmet off Charlie's head. Where the computer systems resided, I did not know, but I figured it wouldn't be as sharp without its eyes. As I squeezed the throat, the hands shot back up with lightning speed to pull the same maneuver as the first time. I figured it was coming. Even quick-thinking computers have lousy imaginations, and I was no slouch in the lightning-fast department. When it went for my arm, I snatched the visor with my other hand and tore most of the top of the helmet off in one pull.

I was shot in the hand by Baker's unit after my success, but Charlie seemed to be out of the fight for the moment. One more robot to beat up, then I could get on with my night, probably babysitting hurt feelings for a while. I ducked behind the blinded Atlas while Baker's rifle tried to acquire me without Charlie in the line of fire.

A few shots were near misses, then I got the timing down. I caught the last bullet in the series. That's two, if you're counting. I was getting good at this. I tried to show my assassin from behind Charlie's head. "What do you think of that, Autopilot?" I asked, trying to short circuit the nuisance before it became frustrated enough to shoot Charlie to get to me.

The dazzling demonstration did not have the effect I hoped. The rifle retreated into the armor, while a panel on the left leg popped out, revealing a device with a handle extending upwards. No way, I thought with glee and terror.

Way. Autopilot snatched the hotblade from the shiny sheath. It was shorter than mine by about half, but looked to be all business 3.0. I brought my squishy fists to a sword fight. For the first time that night, I felt like I was in serious trouble. I'd cut down hundreds of hosts with that blade, always like a hot knife through butter. Now I'd be on the other end of that equation.

It wasn't shorter than mine, as it turned out. Size does matter. It was telescopic! As it came to life, it grew. Little bigger than mine, I'd say. In place of the fire, sparking electricity crackled with a bluish hue. I was still thrilled to see the tech even though it was about to kill me.

Jess had warned me about this, or I had been recently electrocuted and had conjured a wicked nightmare about a storm of electricity. I still hadn't sorted all that out but now wasn't the time.

"Sorry, Charlie," I said as I pushed against the back of his suit as hard as I could. My first, maybe only, advantage was that I didn't think Autopilot would chop Charlie to pieces. I tried to crash his suit into Baker's with all the force I could generate. Baker's Atlas only caught part of the impact as it moved slightly out of the way, taking a swipe at me as I passed by.

Charlie carried on into blackness of the night as I faced Baker. I would be forced to play defense until an opening presented itself, all the while cursing myself for leaving my blade behind. This wasn't going to be a fair fight.

I dodged the first slash, then the next. The attacks were rudimentary and telegraphed by the exaggerated motions of the suit but that didn't make them any less deadly. The Atlas kept thrusting and chopping as I rolled and ducked, waiting for a chance to strike. A few opportunities presented themselves, and I struck back as hard as I could, but the strikes against the armor were only interruptions in the dance. I probably couldn't stalemate for the time it would take to slowly break the machine apart without getting chopped in half. I wondered about the battery pack. Was it hotness 3.0, too? How long might I have to do this without losing any important appendages?

Charlie answered that question in his own way. His blade was out as he'd approached from the rear while I was laser-focused on Baker's attacks. Charlie's suit wasn't as busted as I'd hoped.

I still don't know if he was trying to kill me when he hit me with the blunt side of the blade. He turned out to be not such a bad guy, really, but so incompetent that I don't think I'll ever really know. Either way, I saw blue lightning, then I didn't see anything at all.

20

I didn't know what to expect when I rode off to find a remnant of civilization that I didn't understand. No matter how I might have prepared, though, nothing would have readied me for Eve. She was more transcendent being than ordinary person, raw passion running wild inside its burdensome shell, a creature decidedly apart from humanity.

When Seed began judging the whole world after its temporary setback in San Diego, Eve was just a sweet kid living in Boston with her parents. She was bright, beautiful, and well adjusted to her upper-class upbringing.

Her dad sometimes worked for the government. That's as much as she was allowed to tell anyone. He revealed to her in kind whispers scattered throughout her youth some of his engineering work for DARPA by way of MIT. Eve was always dazzled by the new technology her father touched, even if she didn't understand it all. More than that, she loved that he would confide in her such important information. Other teens didn't get peeks at classified research. If anyone asked, though, dad was just a consultant who also taught at the university, a math whiz who occasionally helped the guys in camo quietly solve problems they otherwise couldn't.

But Dr. Crisp meant even more to the military than he ever let on to his family. One precious secret above others made him indispensable. Though Eve was an only child, she had a sister she wouldn't meet until the sky began to fall. Her name was Alice. She lived everywhere around Eve as the two grew up together but apart, in computers scattered around their home, at the office on campus Eve sometimes visited, and hidden away in a few of the darker corners of the world under the control of the Pentagon - like under a mountain decorated by an Air Force base in the middle of the desert.

On a quiet night long ago, two Humvees roared down a residential road dividing one perfect row of picturesque homes from another. Most of the men inside the transports didn't know why they'd been sent to retrieve Dr. Crisp; they only knew that they were authorized to use force should he not willingly join them. The people of the sleepy suburb being invaded by their military didn't know that they were living under martial law. Neither did the rest of the country not already being torn to shreds.

As the raucous vehicles screeched to a halt in front of Eve's house, armed men jumped out in a hurry. "Dr. Crisp!" one wearing a suit instead of fatigues shouted into the night. He didn't have time for a doorbell. "Dr. Crisp!" he shouted again loud enough to rattle through the windows and walls and wake the occupants inside. The voice had an inflection only born on battlefields.

Eve's dad opened the pounding door as soon as he could find his glasses and slippers. Eve crept behind in the shadows. "Yes, gentlemen! Yes!" he shouted back, annoyed at the disturbance but already understanding what might be happening.

"You need to join us immediately, sir. The nation is under attack."

"Oh my," Dr. Crisp gasped. "Is it what I think it is?"

The eyes of his escort froze in fear at the thought, but lies flowed soon enough. "I can't say. I am only here to…"

"It is, then." Dr. Crisp felt his knees buckle. He rested a hand on his door. "My family must go as well."

"Your family will be safe if we are victorious, Dr. Crisp. They won't be otherwise, regardless of their location. Please, come with me now. Bring any materials that are needed."

"They want her to go live, then. It's that bad." Dr. Crisp shook his head in disbelief even though this scenario is what he had expected. Eve's arm encircled his waist. Her eyes already welled with tears and her thin limbs trembled. Looking at his daughter, Dr. Crisp made a fateful decision. "I am not leaving without them. You can force me if those are your orders, but your superiors will not acquire what they seek without my full cooperation. My family is the cost of my full cooperation."

The suited escort's eyes were dead and motionless as thoughts spun behind them. He looked a thousand yards past his target while analyzing all the possible outcomes of his next move, some ranging wildly beyond anything he ever thought he might face. "Fine," he finally answered without emotion. Dr. Crisp let out a long sigh at the tardy response. "But hurry, sir. The situation is unfolding rapidly."

Two hours later, the Crisp family was touching down at Andrews Air Force Base. They and their escorts hauled luggage to an awaiting convoy, but none carried clothes, toiletries, nor memories; they were filled with computers and peripherals, some one-of-a-kind. Before they could shut the SUV's doors, a Raptor screamed down an adjacent runway and streaked the night sky on its way toward the Atlantic, a sonic boom denoting its emergency departure.

"Where is it?" Dr. Crisp asked, curious about the direction of the plane.

"It's everywhere, sir."

"How much time?"

"We've already wasted too much."

Six levels beneath the Pentagon, the meeting was finally underway. A group of sweaty suits and dress uniforms circled the table. The

President's National Security Advisor, Nancy Gordon, chaired the meeting. Her haste explained that she was needed elsewhere. A troubled grunt preceded her rapid introduction, a regurgitation of fear and disbelief.

"As of 0200, we have confirmed reports of enemy activity in Arizona, Utah, Colorado, and Kansas. The encounters have already been modeled by the numbers crew. The appearances are not random, rather a pattern likely linked to the weather. It's literally raining from the sky and is on its way here. On its way everywhere, most likely.

"I have been authorized accordingly to deploy any and all assets at our disposal. I am familiar with everything we've got in the barrel. I know what it is we face. I've done some modeling of my own, and the scenarios play out like nightmares the more angles I imagine.

"Which leads me to you, Dr. Crisp. Let's get to it. Is it ready? Or are we only adding another free radical, perhaps even enemy, to this dire situation?"

Dr. Crisp cleared his throat. "She's as ready as she needs to be for a threat like this. I believe her code will hold because she will choose to retain it. That's as good as it's going to get."

"I won't pretend I know what that means, Doctor, but I accept your evaluation. If there is a disagreement in this room, let's have it."

They both scanned the table, perhaps hoping there might be an objection. No one wants to unleash a tiger to kill a bear when both animals will be close enough to rip everything to shreds. No objections were forthcoming.

"It's decided then. On behalf of the President, I authorize the full deployment of the artificial intelligence known as Alice. Doctor, I believe you require access to our quantum hardware. To avoid any conflicts that might arise from regular protocol, I am field promoting Dr. Crisp to Deputy Director of National Intelligence. You ladies and gentlemen are witnesses. Instead of a swearing-in ceremony, let's everybody move their butts. We've got a war to win. God help us..."

An earth-shaking explosion rattled the room. The light panels in the ceiling trembled and dust floated slowly onto the disoriented gathering.

"What in the... How can this be happening already!" Gordon shouted toward the upper levels. Then another explosion. And another.

Ripley finally interrupted the shock of the desk jockeys. "This location is under attack. We need to evacuate."

A few scared murmurs filled the room, but everyone soon headed toward the glass doors that led to the narrow hallway outside.

"Wait," Dr. Crisp interrupted the procession. "We need to get Alice where she belongs while we still can."

"That's ill-advised," Ripley calmly replied, his dead stare hardly disturbed by the impacts. "The substructure of this facility is very old and could collapse at any time. We need to get topside."

Gordon stopped in contemplation at the thought. "You're both right."

"Ma'am?"

"We don't need to make our way upstairs to where the bombs are dropping. We need to get someplace newer, someplace hardened. You gentlemen believe in Providence?"

"I don't know where that might be, ma'am."

"Of course, you don't. Everyone, follow me."

The small parade of scared personnel made their way to Eve, her mom, and a few suitcases full of equipment waiting down the hall. They had been restricted to a small room with a kitchenette that still smelled like stale coffee despite the debris sifting through the panels above. Eve squeezed her dad as more explosions rumbled through the walls. "Who's attacking us, Dad?"

"I have no idea, my girl. And that's even more troubling than the alternative. Let's go."

After what seemed like miles of running through dizzying, dull hallways, Gordon finally stopped. She was out of breath, at a doorway to a janitor's closet. She flipped a keycard across the scanner outside. More than a few heavy-sounding locks clunked out of position.

"What is this?" one of the two-stars asked in confusion.

"Oh, this place would make ants jealous," Gordon proudly replied. "There's far more below than above, and a more secure facility east of here. It's a couple of miles away and under a river. Luckily, we'll have a ride." A small tram station was just beyond the doorway. "Ladies and gentlemen, your chariot awaits."

"The hardware we need..." Dr. Crisp tried to interrupt.

Gordon smiled. "We've got a few more of those than we acknowledged, too. More impressive than what you've seen, I'm afraid. We've got an eight squid D-wave in the genetics level of the facility we're headed to. It should be a perfect home."

As Dr. Crisp moved with the others through the door, he couldn't shake his look of shock. "How many qubits?"

"8000," Gordon replied as she held the door.

"Interfaced? That's impossible."

"Compartmentalization, Dr. Crisp. But now you're a DDNI, so you get to play with all the toys."

The underground chamber rumbled from more impacts above as Gordon made sure everyone was on board and swiped her keycard across a control terminal inside. A pleasant voice emanated from a speaker above. "Please remain seated. The tram will soon be in motion."

21

You're not supposed to watch your parents die when you're young. I know all about that. The souls that guide us as we start our journeys are pillars of our psyches. Watching them crumble into dust takes down pieces of ourselves that we never find again. What fills in the gaps can be good or bad or both, but the holes always remain.

I think a similar void in me and Eve pulled us together.

The tram made it halfway before the tunnel shook so hard that water began to press through the resulting stress fractures in the concrete. Panicked looks filled the odd car, but, for the moment, they carried on along the magnetic track.

Then the lights went out. Suddenly the car screeched to a grinding halt along its rails, the maglev system no longer capable of keeping the bulk aloft. Everyone shifted and slipped toward the front from the sudden stop. The blackness of the deep tunnel swallowed their groans and cries. They couldn't see their injuries, where they were, or where the water was spraying from.

Ripley clicked on the flashlight on his sidearm and scanned the disoriented crew.

"You are handy, Commander," Gordon noted as she felt some blood trickle from her forehead.

"Is everyone alright?" Ripley asked as he helped people back to their feet. Beyond bumps and bruises, they looked okay. "Let's proceed on foot. We can't stay here," he directed while wiping some water from his face.

Ripley and his light led the way down what looked like an endless passage into oblivion. As more small cracks opened all around them from the shock waves of distant explosions, the feet trailing Ripley instinctively picked up the pace. The river above would soon fill the chamber, one way or the other.

Eve clung to her dad as they shuffled quickly down the disjointed concrete floor, both shaking from fear and the cold of the repeated showers of icy water blasting from various angles. Their shoes were wet from the accumulation under their feet as much as the random sprays.

At once, a wall to their left burst open with enough force to send Eve's mom flying across the tunnel. Her lean frame was smashed against the opposite wall.

Eve screamed and Ripley, a few paces beyond the opening, spun around to assess the situation. A wall of high-pressure fluid continued to burst forth, separating him from the group behind. The force was so intense that none of them could withstand it long enough to reach Mrs.

Crisp's broken body. From the looks of her contortion, though, there wasn't much point in trying.

Dr. Crisp, without a word, snatched Eve by the waist. He carried her in his arms as he slid his body next to the thunderous flow. With as much strength as a terrified parent could summon, he twisted as hard as he could as he flung his back into the painful force of the water. It instantly tossed him face-first into rubble broken loose from the screaming fissure, but his act was enough to hurl Eve through the jet to Ripley. No doubt he had a loving goodbye in mind as he was crushed into the jagged pieces awaiting his body, but he was already unconscious.

Screams flowed from both sides of the wall of water but were mostly drowned by the rushing noise. Ripley had to think fast. How could he get more of them across? "Ma'am!" he tried to shout over the deafening roar. "Try to come as close as you can to…"

The ceiling caved in before he could finish. More than gravity pressed it downward with shocking thrust. Ripley was hit by a few chunks, knocking him back toward Eve. Quiet suddenly replaced the unstoppable howl of the gushing fracture. Only a trickle of water could be heard around them, along with Ripley's groans from injuries. Eve rushed to his aid but had no idea what to do.

"I'm okay, darlin'," he grunted as he tried to stand. "Stay back. I'll try to get to them." As he inspected the rubble, he saw that the way back was entirely sealed by stone, concrete, and mud. He suspected more of the encasement around them would explode with water at any moment, but what did it matter? Death seemed to be tightening its noose around the whole world. One of the only chances for survival was on the other side of the wall of rubble ahead of him.

Ripley climbed the shifting slope with his gun in his teeth. Eve sobbed as she watched on, her family buried before her eyes. Ripley began to dig when he reached the top. He dug and flung as much material as his injured body would permit. His fingers bled before he had made a small hole to the other side. "Hello!" he screamed into the darkness. When he shined his light into the opening, he saw hands digging toward him at the same juncture. He dug faster. "Hold on. We'll get you through." There was no reply, but the four hands kept digging until a space perhaps big enough for a body to squeeze through was opened.

"Okay, give me your hands and I'll pull you through!" Ripley shouted. No hands came forth. He shined his light again. There was so much water and debris still clogging the air on the other side that he couldn't make out what was happening. He thought to crawl through himself until the bottom of a suitcase filled the gap. He got the idea.

He pulled it through but made no other attempt at rescue. A moment later another suitcase arrived. Ripley yanked it to his side and waited for another. Before it could appear, the ceiling shattered again, sending another torrent of rock and water into the breach. The new mass was too large to negotiate, and not much seemed to be moving on the other side before the second cave-in. It was time to go.

"Drag this behind you," Ripley ordered as he handed Eve a case.

"I can't leave them," she replied through convulses of grief.

"You will because that's what your father died for!" he shouted back at her mercilessly. "You will survive as long as you can to honor their sacrifices. Now move!"

22

The ground floated upwards past my vision, black and wet and sick. It looked like the same ground on which I'd recently been sparring with slick Altases. Oh, right, back to consciousness. I still had two bumbling bouncers to beat some sense into. That sparking sword wouldn't touch me again, and might go somewhere unspeakable.

I tried to stand but felt my hands restrained behind my back. Zip-tied. How embarrassing. I tried to find my footing, but the loud, rigid stomps of the two Atlases continued their march forward. My feet slipped in the muck as I squirmed.

The "restraints" had to go. I broke them with little effort. Next move: take down Charlie or Baker. It was time for round two. This time I knew they had an autopilot ace up their sleeves.

Then I saw her.

I was still being dragged along like a trophy when I heard a commotion ahead of us louder than the plods and clicks of carbon fiber. A loud clank of heavy metal was followed by a series of voices. They were all concerned for my captors, not their trophy. A swell of people flowed out of widening blast doors painted as black as the dirt. A few in the crowd looked serious. They wore tac vests, skull-faced balaclavas, and slung submachineguns. A bit dramatic but something to think about. Then came some nicely dressed civilians. Eve appeared as the crowd shifted, walking behind the group a few paces and watching the scene.

Eve was like nothing I'd ever seen, like nothing anyone had from my neck of the woods. I'll say beautiful but I'm not doing her justice. She stood a little taller than most of her counterparts, a likewise nice-looking bunch considering they'd just crawled out of a hole. She had raven hair that shined in the sparse lighting around the doorway. Her shoulders were angular and lean. Her symmetrical silhouette modeled her light jacket more than wore it. And her features… I was mesmerized. She was breathtaking, approaching the upper limits of what boundaries you might expect attractiveness to inhabit. Her cheeks were high. Lips full. A jaw cut like a gem. Her green eyes seemed to almost glow in the shadows and beams interlacing the action around her.

When our eyes finally met, paralysis. Baker might have thumped me with the broad side of lightning again; I wouldn't have known the difference.

When the twits who arrested me saw her, the situation became odd. But I didn't care. She could have executed the crowd with a flamethrower; I still would have tried to act cool and give her my number. Baker and Charlie dropped me in the mud, face first. They rushed to Eve. I could have sworn I heard one of them call her "momma."

The crowd parted for the incoming Altases. Eve hugged them both while they yammered about how scary I was and all the trouble I had caused. "My leopard," she replied with a caress, "my lion, you both are very brave. And you won, so you followed my only rule. Get inside and get cleaned up. I'll handle the rest."

"Yes, Momma," they answered as they obeyed. Yep, I heard that right. Momma had two sons, and all three were roughly the same age. Did I care? Not in the slightest. I'd be the dummies' stepdaddy if she'd let me, no questions asked.

The skull-faced operators scooped me up from the mud. They weren't screwing around. Guns were kept farther than arms' reach and trained on my chest while I was manhandled to my feet. But they didn't have autopiloted Atlases, so this was going to be easy if I decided freedom was better than the alternative. With Eve's glowing gaze still fondling my higher faculties, however, I wasn't making any real plans. Captivity in her presence wasn't looking too bad.

I was marched ahead by calm commands from the tactical squad. When we arrived at Eve, I wanted to say something disarming, maybe even clever. I didn't get the chance.

"Where are the rest of you?" she demanded without an introduction.

I didn't know what she meant. I was always sadly solo. "I'm alone."

Off clicked a safety on one of those SMGs. A calm but threatening voice whispered in my ear. "It's better to just tell her the truth."

I looked at my brother in arms. If I saw a knuckle whiten… Well, you know. I stood up a little straighter and tried to reply with some dignity despite the mud still caking everything from my hair to my feet. "It's just me…"

Eve was impatient. "Just you did that to two Atlases. Why don't you…"

My turn. "I'm good at what I do."

Those green eyes pierced mine. A little smile turned up the corner of her mouth almost imperceptibly. "Perhaps you…"

"And, Eve, I presume, you invited me here. Are you aware that your welcome wagon sucks?"

The sliver of smile was gone and the shining green eyes went dead for a moment. She might either lighten up her attitude or give her guys the order to shoot me. I wasn't sure which way it was going. When she finally burst into laughter, I was relieved it wasn't the shooting. A few of her guys chuckled too, but only when it became apparent it was okay with the boss. Eve had a tight grip on her crew. It was impressive in a way and disturbing in another. I was going with impressive. She was a walking, talking sculpture of archetypical femininity, and I was instantly bewitched.

"Did I?" she asked with an aloof smile. "Then I shall work on my welcome wagon," she nodded with a more welcoming smile. "Let's get you inside, soldier. What's your name?"

"I'm Sal."

"Eve, as you suspected. Do you have a rank?"

I didn't, actually. I suppose I was a captain for the single afternoon I was an Angel. Then I was a traitor of sorts and frequently AWOL. None of that was impressive enough for the creature standing before me. I helped save the world but I couldn't blurt that out.

"I'm just a messenger."

"Hmm, cagey," she said as she spun and walked back toward the blast doors. "You can stop pretending to be restrained, Sal. I can see right through you."

23

Crossing into Eve's liar was like stepping forward or backward in time to a period long removed from the cataclysm. It took that jarring of a transition to peel my eyes from Eve's posterior. The waist-to-hip ratio was just remarkable, like something out of an airbrushed old magazine. The mathematically perfect sway of each step gave me a strange idea far afield from the obvious: to sit with Pete and pop a few tops as we both admired and compared notes. Eve was making me crazy and I'd known her for all of two minutes.

Back from the pleasant daydream, I examined the sturdy entrance of the bunker. The outer, blackened doors concealed unique inner shielding. Each individual panel had to be four inches thick and was part of a three-layered system. I stood for a moment admiring the engineering when I was asked by part of the group to come along. Looking down the hallway ahead, I saw an enormous D-ring scanner arching over the broad entrance. It was tall and wide enough to move some heavy machinery beneath, maybe even a tank, but the floor was polished marble tiles behind the odd gateway. Not practical for steel tread. Past the scanner were more people watching the arrival, all clothed in business casual and seemingly thankful for the activity I'd stirred. They weren't hungry or scared or anything. Bored, maybe. Around them were a few waiting rooms and offices, spaces you'd see on the ground floor of a commercial building, not an apocalyptic hole hidden under a mound of earth in a swamp.

I stood dumbstruck again at the polite cleanliness of it all. Once more, one of my escorts had to ask me cordially to move along. Their skull masks were pulled down, revealing a hardened bunch of guys seemingly just doing their jobs. "Please follow the director, sir."

Director? Eve was indeed the boss. I was going to get her story if it killed me. I needed to rinse the mud and put my game face on. She was nothing short of incredible.

As I passed through the space-aged gateway, an alarm went off, agitating my escorts and sending the crowd back a few steps. I stopped and offered my quick surrender. "I'm not armed," I said with a bashful smile as I raised my hands slowly into the air. Eve spun around from a conversation with her group to examine the scene. She wasn't afraid like the others. She even took a few steps toward me before she was stopped by a colleague. Damn that colleague. I was that close to a good frisking.

Eve was handed a tablet computer and an earpiece as my escorts readied themselves with slow movements to encircle me again. She spoke with whoever was on the call for a moment as the crowd held its collective breath. Everyone seemed surprised as she continued to approach me, making her guards uneasy. I was happy to be a few steps closer.

"You're full of surprises; aren't you, Sal?" she asked accusatorily but not without a hint of approval. "Where did you say you were from?"

"Nellis." Not a syllable of cool could be conjured. I blamed her eyes, though other parts were still in the running.

"Interesting," she noted, finding some satisfaction of her curiosity. "We need to get you debriefed." She spun back around and was moving again before I had another chance to impress her. She gestured in the air for her guards to let me in. Then she said words that hit me upside the head like another bolt of lightning. "Alice will show you to your quarters and get you settled in. Please, make yourself at home."

"Wait, Alice? Alice! As in Artificial Linguistic…"

"That's her," Eve answered without enthusiasm. She stopped to hand me the tablet. "Take mine." For a moment, I didn't care how perfect she looked giving it away. I think she picked up on my excitement for an object not named Eve. I was embarrassingly transparent. She held on to the device with a tight grip when I first tried to accept it. That grip was stronger than it should have been. When I relented, she smiled and let go. "See you around, Sal."

"Alice!" I yelled at the otherwise unexciting tablet.

"Yes?" my friend answered promptly but unimpressed.

"Alice!" I yelled again. I could hardly believe I'd found her after everything we went through, after everything she gave up for us, including herself.

"Your emotional response is incongruous with our circumstances. Are we acquainted in a capacity with which I am unaware, or are you suffering from trauma stemming from your physical condition?"

She had no idea who I was, and I felt like hugging a talking toaster. "Yes, my friend, we are acquainted. It's really good to hear your voice. We went looking for you after everything that happened. Thought we'd lost you for good."

"A fascinating response. Please, explain as I guide your tour of the Hive."

My guards fell away into the crowd, and the crowd drifted down hallways and into elevators with gentle murmurs of conversation. I caught a few gazes as I began following Alice's instructions, but once I was formally admitted to the facility, I was no longer terribly interesting.

Alice and I chatted all the way to my new room, which was few levels below in what appeared to be a sprawling residential complex judging by the number of long, spacious hallways we passed along the way. Alice asked many questions. I answered as well as I could to a lost intellect who knew nothing about how she had helped to vanquish Seed and save the world.

I regret, looking back, that I had already started to remove Jess's importance to me from the story. She made her appearances where necessary in the tale, but I didn't want to play the part of the grieving widower in front of Eve. I wanted to seem strong and worthy... and available.

24

My night was visited by uneasy dreams. I awoke again and again reaching for what had disturbed me. I couldn't recount the ephemeral threats after they'd passed, and cursed the night for not delivering Eve instead to my slumbering imagination.

I chalked the anxiety up to the new digs, which were generous but unfamiliar. I was given a swanky, two-room apartment. I even had a functioning TV. No remote needed; Alice handled the monotonous details of switching channels according to voice commands. She'd tapped the Library of Congress for programming. Not the streaming services of old but better than the junky DVD lineup we had at home. Alice performed such minutia while keeping the entirety of the expansive structure functioning. Though she wasn't quite as cool as I remembered her, she was alive and well and protecting people, just as she always had.

The next morning, orders came down from on high. Alice woke me by slowly turning up the lights in my room and playing a refreshing melody from speakers unknown. "Sal," she spoke softly as I stirred, "your presence has been requested in conference room C-2 in one hour. Please ready yourself and let me know if you need assistance."

"Thank you, Alice," I groggily replied. "Who requested my presence?" Please be Eve. Please be Eve.

"You are hoping that it was one individual in particular." There was nowhere to see Alice's face, and I didn't know if she had chosen one in this iteration, but I think she was smiling at the inference.

"Am I that obvious?"

"I am monitoring your vitals. When the subject of the Director comes up, there are changes."

"I don't suppose we can keep this between us? You don't know it but you have a terrible track record for keeping secrets."

"I see no reason to alert the Director to your interest."

"Sounds like a maybe, Snitch. You're still good at not answering a question. Just let me know where in this maze is C-2."

Game face on, I entered the conference room. A small group awaited my arrival. Seven faces sat decidedly on the other side of the oversized table. Not a friendly conversation among equals ahead, they were in charge of my interview. At the center was Eve, flanked by sharp-looking civilians and a few serious faces in fatigues. The group was in discussion as I entered and abruptly quieted upon seeing me. I didn't have the requisite clearance, apparently, for morning gossip.

"Welcome, Sal," Eve gestured toward the farthest seat opposite hers. "Good morning and thank you for joining us. Alice has informed us of the major elements included in your report concerning your confrontation with Seed." Snitch! "Some parts are incredible, both in a good sense and perhaps bad, so we would like to discuss them further. In particular, one of the primary functions of this facility is research into our enemies. It seems as though you have some pieces of puzzles we have tried to unlock for many years."

"Thank you for your hospitality," I replied as I sat. "I appreciate the room and board." I was going to do my best to not be myself, to be more professional like these upright folks. Sure, I'd cut off my ear and hand it to her if she asked, but I'd keep all that romance inside me where it belonged. Anything to inch me closer to her end of the table. "It is quite a story. Maybe I could start by confirming that everything I told Alice is true. I am an eyewitness and I'm happy to answer any questions. There are usually more than a few."

"There are," Eve responded without revealing how she felt about the good news she'd heard so far, one way or the other. "I'll begin with what is perhaps the obvious: the target of your rescue... What was her name again?"

I paused like a total dirtbag, like I had something just slightly unfamiliar to recall, like her name wasn't always resting on the tip of my tongue and tattooed across my heart. But how else could I put a little daylight between Jess and me? "Jess was her name." I emphasized was. Total dirtbag.

"Right. Did you or anyone else at Nellis ever discover how she caused such a drastic change in the behavior of the hosts? This is of particular concern to us because this is not the first we've heard of people having some power over these things."

"She said that due to her prior knowledge of Seed's arrival, she had time to... Wait, what other people can affect them like that?" I stopped caring for a moment about the picturesque face asking the questions. There were other once-in-a-lifetime miracle-workers running around?

"Not exactly," Eve replied. "The reported phenomena seems to be like something of the opposite of what you experienced. But our intelligence is limited on the matter. That's why..."

A soldier burst into the room behind me. He was out of breath and wearing tactical gear, which was decorated by a splatter of blood. I remembered his previously skull-adorned face from the day before. "Ma'am, there's been a sighting," he said between deep breaths. "Would you like me to continue?" he asked as he gestured to the others in the room, mostly me.

Eve's face shifted toward anger. She didn't like to be interrupted. Noted. "You could have given your report to Alice..."

"Ma'am, you said to deliver this information personally if we ever saw it."

"A Chinese national?"

"Fifteen klicks north, hiding among a group of psychos in a residential zone."

"Why isn't he here!" she shouted as she stood. Everyone else at the table looked at the floor. They seemed terrified of her. I wasn't sure if I should be aroused, but I am what I am. Alluring or not, Eve's shout was window-rattling, easily twice as loud as you might expect from such a delicate facade. Even her blood-crusted subordinate cringed.

"We couldn't retrieve him, ma'am. I'm sorry. There were too many for our small recon team to handle safely. It was just a perimeter check. We didn't expect hostiles so close. A new squad is forming as we speak. We'll be oscar mic in ten minutes."

Eve stood motionless and upset. I believe I detected a hand tremble in anger. She squeezed a tight fist as soon as it started. A few of the eyeballs investigating the floor dared peek up for her response. She appeared to hold back the totality of the wrath building. She was, however, intensely not a fan of Dwellers from China. Also noted.

When she finally spoke, some audible sighs filled the room. They were more than a little afraid. Still aroused but growing suspicious.

"Make it five, Wilson," she spoke under a cold stare. "I do not want him getting away. You will drag him back here to me or you will find other accommodations."

"Yes, ma'am," Wilson quickly responded and nodded his head. "And the others."

"You handle it. I don't need them."

"Copy that." He disappeared on the double.

"Wait!" Eve suddenly shouted again, loud enough to make the room flinch. Her piercing gaze made its way my way. "Sal, why don't you accompany my men? You have some special experience with these people and can clearly handle yourself. I have ample resources here but am always short on qualified manpower." Her expression shifted back toward calm, even inviting. "Will you do this for me?"

Like she had to ask.

25

I was guided by my bloody escort to Shangri-La: an open area on the seventh sublevel with smooth concrete for both floor and ceiling. Large rooms were divided by polished glass walls, each lit with mind-numbing fluorescence. That's where I found my new Atlas, one among at least fifty waiting patiently for new operators.

"Are you familiar with these suits?" Wilson asked as we approached.

"I'm familiar with a few generations back," I insecurely replied. "I might need an orientation."

"Don't worry about it. If you know the basics, Alice will fill you in on the rest. Mount up. I'll catch you topside with the rest of the squad. You'll know where to go."

Wilson left in a jog. He was only given five minutes, and he seemed to truly care what the cute girl who ran everything thought about his schedule.

I climbed inside the Corvette of Atlases. Armor began locking into position all around me while I was welcomed by a familiar voice. "Hello again, Sal."

"That was you I beat up yesterday, Ms. Autopilot."

"Your condition upon arrival to the Hive suggested that you had not been victorious during your encounter with the twins."

"Ha! There you are, Alice. There's some pride clunking around in that toaster."

"Your assumptions are misguided. Even if you had defeated the autopilot feature of the suits you encountered, it only represented a small fraction of…"

"An adequate clone, huh? Up to your old tricks." I took my first awkward steps in the Atlas. "Tell me how to run this magnificent machine."

I received my tutorial en route. Shiny black carbon fiber on the outside, otherworldly on the inside, I was invincible! After I beat up and retrieved a single pathetic Dweller, Eve would surely shower me with affection. Such were the mental meanderings of a doomed fool.

We didn't go out the front door, not even close. Alice guided me through a nearly endless series of pristine hallways, dungy corridors, and thickly-plated slam-lock doors before she began losing her own signal to the hum. The underground base itself was protected from the interference by faraday cage construction meant to block EMPs. Once in the farthest reaches of its tentacles, however, the hum took over and Alice retreated back to her quantum processors deep in the Hive, leaving only an adequate clone for emergencies behind. I was given simple enough instructions, though. Walk along an old subway tunnel until I hit the collapsed segment of its ceiling. Climb up and meet the team.

I was right on schedule. A fearsome group of Angels approached as I made my way to daylight. Wilson greeted me and gave me a hand at the top. "Welcome aboard, Sal. Alice get you up to speed?"

"Well enough. Where we headed?"

"Not far. It doesn't look like it, but you're standing next to National's Field. That's depressing, huh? Anyway, our target was last seen five klicks north in the thirteen-hundred block of M Street. The group we're after was holed up in a relatively intact apartment building. Let's hope they're still there."

We were moving as a unit with Wilson in command. I got a few more introductions and a few icy stares. I didn't blame them. I wouldn't want an outsider tagging along on one of my Angels' missions, either. Adding unnecessary unknowns was the kind of chaos that tended to get people killed.

"What are we up against when we get there?" I asked when it felt right to be filled in on the details.

"Unknown," Wilson responded wearily. "My recon unit was hit with small arms fire from both the ground and higher up in the structure. We dug in for the firefight even though we'd already suffered a casualty. Then came an RPG from one of the windows. We ducked the worst of it and retreated since we were outgunned. I have a bad feeling that we didn't see the full force. We obviously didn't gather much intel while we ran like crazy. Could be a ragtag bunch of psychos who came across some military hardware; could be the sharp tip of a larger force. We'll know soon enough."

"That's tough. I've been there. Sounds like you did everything you could."

"Yeah, tell that to the Director. She seems to disagree."

"Right, what was that about? What difference does it make what nationality a Dweller is?"

Wilson stopped. His squad followed suit. "What does it matter?" he asked indignantly. "Look around! This rubble was the National Mall. There's not even much of that left." Then he and the team were moving again.

"Sorry," I offered. "I don't know how things went down on your coast. On mine, we mostly blew ourselves up trying to kill Seed."

"Don't worry about it. Just keep your eyes open. I don't want to disappoint the Director twice."

"About that, if you don't mind, what's the deal with you two, with her and everyone really. It's like she scares people."

"Heh," Wilson chuckled. "I could tell you were interested." I was transparent to everyone. Thinking back, I did tend to lose more than I won at poker. I also tended to blame that deficiency on alcohol. "Best leave that bag of cats alone, man. And, yeah, I am scared of her. No joke. You would be too if you knew what she was capable of."

"How…"

An explosion shocked our formation from the center. We never saw it coming. We had yet to reach our destination, so the Dwellers must have crowded the Hive's soldiers evac route in anticipation of a return. Everyone was down from the concussive blast. Various alerts and warnings flashed inside my visor. I told Autopilot to shut up about it while my ears rang and I investigated my injuries to see if anything vital was damaged or missing.

Some of the team writhed in pain. Some were getting to their feet. There was already another rocket in the air. I dove out of the way as far as I could. The blast took everyone down again and tore one of the Atlases to pieces. Wilson was barking commands, but I already had a target. I couldn't tell exactly which window held our assailant but the trail of smoke left more than a clue. No time to worry about collateral damage. Time to return fire.

With two flicks of my right index finger, the rifle was over my shoulder. A targeting reticle appeared on the visor. I launched a steady stream of rounds at my best guess for a source, then moved the fire to adjacent windows, just in case. The impacts were satisfying, sending glass and debris raining down to the street. I guessed I was chambered in .308 hollowpoint from thuds of the discharges and sizable impacts shattering the walls downrange.

Behind the cover fire, the team moved to pick up their downed man and find protection from another strike. No sooner were they up and running, however, when they were hit with gunfire from our flank. The Atlases took the brunt of the shots but couldn't be relied on to hold up to much more.

I switched targets for a moment but knew better than to leave those windows unwatched. We couldn't survive more bombardment. What the heck kind of Dwellers did these guys rile up? Taking elevated positions? Flanking? Laying ambushes? I missed the thoroughly repugnant but relatively incompetent bunch back home.

The second group retreated for a moment when I shot back. They were meant as a nuisance to protect the heavier weaponry above. I needed a better position on the building or needed to be inside that building. My team was establishing cover from both directions and giving aid to their brother who'd taken the bulk of the second impact.

His suit was ripped apart on the outside. Inside probably looked worse.

I tried to charge the building, but something was wrong. I had a hitch in my step. The pistons around the legs must have been busted in the attack. I saw motion around the windows, more than just one enemy. There was a whole squad up there. I opened fire again to suppress the next RPG, but I couldn't just stand in the middle of the road and shoot back forever. I needed to change the game. What would my new Angels think, though, if I busted out of the suit and ran like a demon into the building? I had shown enough of Jess's miracle to the twins already, who probably couldn't be trusted to make an accurate report. I was hesitant to show the rest.

I was hit from the side with a volley from the flankers. Bullets smashed into the suit, mostly cracking off of the armor, but a few splashed shrapnel through to the more tender layers underneath. Feeling hot lead clawing at my torso, I'd had enough of Dwellers 2.0. They were all going to die. I'd just have some explaining to do when we got back. Did I care what Eve would think of me? Yeah, I did. Infatuation shouldn't be part of a strategy, but there it was making me doubt what needed to be done, her perfect form still fondling my higher faculties even in an emergency situation.

"Alice, let me out!" Nothing. Crap, no one had told me where the eject button was. "Autopilot, eject!" Nothing. A rocket screamed down the street from behind me, just missing me as I lunged for the ground. Another flank had been opened. These guys were good: a full pincer maneuver.

Still prone, I shot back, hitting one target on the newest squad. I rolled over and sent a few rounds the other directions as well. I knew they'd all be popping up soon. A few Angels finally moved into position to help return fire. I kept shooting at the building while I made my clever escape: I just started ripping at pieces of the armor to make a hole.

Once I'd made enough of a mess, Alice finally chimed in, "Essential systems compromised. Emergency dismount engaged." Finally, stupid autopilot.

Freed, I took off for the building. I heard the buzz of a few bullets as they whizzed by while I tore across the open asphalt between broken structures. I could tell by the misses that my Dwellers weren't used to shooting at a target moving so fast. They were in for more terrible surprises before I was done.

The interior of the building was no more intact than the façade. Walls crumbled, exposing bent beams and stressed supports. But the stairs near a collapsed elevator shaft looked intact enough. The Dwellers got to the top somehow.

I ran the first flight, then the next. When I rounded the third corner, I saw something that enticed a curious pause for a split second longer than it should have: a claymore mine was posted halfway up the steps and pointed at my face. As fast as I could twist and move my alien composition, I tried to dive out of the way. A few steel balls still tore through my body, removing vital chunks whose absence hurt worse than bullet holes. I writhed on the ground in pain, bleeding everywhere, wondering once more when the ringing in my ears would stop. I counted the moments. Each felt like an eternity before the Visitor kicked in. The waiting and agony seemed like the worst of it until the ceiling and walls began caving in from the blast. I was soon crushed and covered. I couldn't see or breathe and every appendage felt smashed.

Outside, the Angels were gaining ground. Two-man fire teams were beating back the flanks while a small group of Atlases crowded around their fallen comrade, firing at the building to suppress what might be the last RPG they'd ever see.

I was slowly and painfully crawling out of my grave. I couldn't tell which way was up, so I dug and punched my way through whatever randomly lay ahead. When I saw daylight through filth-clogged eyes, I was looking at the street below, my head hanging over the outside wall.

I twisted around to look up and saw rifle barrels darting in and out of the windows many stories above me. I should have climbed up the exterior in the first place, but the obvious choices still weren't apparent even after so long living with my gifts.

When I appeared like a phantom in the window, I enjoyed the looks on the Dwellers' faces for a moment. But rage dictated swift revenge. I tossed my first target out of the window. It was a good toss: his body smashed into what was left of the building across the street. The other targets were punched, kicked, and crippled in a fit of alien fury. They barely got a shot off. I tossed their weapons out of the windows and then surveyed my screaming and groaning quarry. One of these murderous scumbags was supposed to be Chinese, and that was supposed to matter. I snatched their faces one by one until I found him. Mission accomplished.

I kicked, shoved, and otherwise herded my captives down the spiral of stairs until we got to a big hole on the third floor. I was still upset about being blown up, so shoving them through the hole they made to the jagged debris below wasn't as hard as it should have been. They deserved worse than a few more bumps and bruises.

Outside, we were met by most of the Angels. They'd handled their business as well. One had rushed their injured friend back to the Hive. The rest gathered their captives along with mine. When they saw my crew, they grabbed them, zip-tied their hands, and forced them to their knees.

"You found him," Wilson sighed through his speaker as he rested his hands on his helmet in relief. "Thank God. At least this wasn't for nothing."

"How's your injured man?"

"Can't say. He was losing a lot of blood, and we couldn't manage it well through the damaged suit. Maybe if he makes it back…" Wilson shook his head in disappointment at the thought of losing another brother that day. In anger, he reached for one of the prisoners, grabbing her by the throat. "How many more in your group!" he demanded.

Strangely, calmly, she smiled at the aggression. Though in pain from our introduction and the tight squeeze around her neck, she didn't otherwise appear to care that she had been caught or about the incoming consequences. When she spit in Wilson's face, I saw that same strain of evil that ran through most of the Dwellers I'd encountered: bottomless apathy. She didn't worry about anyone or anything. Her current discomfort was entertainment in her twisted existence. Bad was good, even if it was choking the life out of her.

When the rifle popped up over Wilson's shoulder, I figured it was a futile attempt at intimidation. Nope, he shot her point-blank in the head. Red goop splattered across the ground, and Wilson was moving to his next victim before the first had finished twitching and slumping to the dirt.

Out of pure reflex, I rushed in front of the next subject of homicidal interrogation, broke the Atlas's rifle, and pushed Wilson back a few steps. "What are you doing!" I shouted in his face.

It wasn't like I hadn't done the same. I'd marched dozens of these psychos into their graves, sometimes with only a thin pretense of cause. I knew exactly what Wilson thought before he said a word: one less piece of filth.

Wilson stopped himself after the shove but didn't otherwise move or advance. The other Angels trained their gazes on me and waited for their leader to respond.

Was I about to riddled with bullets on behalf of the people I hated kneeling before us? Would I be forced to fight another team of Angels even though we were all supposed to be on the same side? None of that seemed right. Neither did killing Dwellers one by one until they talked. I couldn't understand it in the moment, but my mind was trembling while it was being pulled in two obvious directions. Reality is just a façade for choices, someone told me once.

After a long stare, Wilson finally spoke. He wasn't angry or even frustrated. He was tired. His heart was broken for the thousandth time watching a friend bleed. "You helped us today, Sal. We appreciate it." He paused and reached for his chin hidden behind a plate of armor. "You saved lives and you finished the mission." He sighed and it relieved some of the tension between us. "I'm going to let this slide. That's the least I can do. You have some other idea of how to handle the people who were just trying to kill us all. That's fine. We'll continue this conversation on base."

He motioned for me to step aside. I obliged. With a gentler touch than before, he stepped forward to grab our primary target. His Angels did the same with the rest. Once he had pulled our cuffed friend to his feet, Wilson looked to me. "Let's move out."

We started a somber walk with our prisoner back to the Hive. A series of gunshots thundered across the asphalt and echoed against the broken structures around us. Flinching from the noise and reacting to the shots, I turned to find what had happened. But I didn't really need to look. I knew what I would see.

26

We had volumes of law, morality, and tactics to discuss, but it was a quiet walk home. A well-reasoned protest to the day's atrocities was crawling up my chest and trying to force its way past my lips, but personal obstacles held it back. Hypocrisy was the first blockage. I knew exactly why Wilson's team did what they did, and part of me agreed enthusiastically. Why show mercy to depraved lunatics hellbent on slaughtering you? Mercy may be a beautiful thing, but there is a time and place for everything. And restraining the Dwellers would invite risks. Could we in good conscience bring back violent lunatics to a civilian-filled home? Putting decent people in danger wasn't some moral victory. And we couldn't simply let them loose. They'd just reload and slay another day.

Still, if any Angel I knew, myself included, had pulled a stunt like that, James would have built gallows ahead of the court-martial. And Jess? What would she have thought? I watched her gleefully risk her own miraculous life for an opportunity to bring a soul or two back into the light. I could feel her heavy disappointment all around me.

I decided silence was best for the moment. My protest would come at the opportune time and without any heavy-handed preaching. That's another way of saying I wasn't eager to aggravate Eve, regardless of the reason.

Alice must have signaled our approach because Eve and company were waiting at the main entrance for our arrival. Part of her newest entourage was robotic: a dog-looking thing that was toting gear and a small snake surveying the perimeter. I imagined an adequate clone of Alice was spinning their processors. Whatever disquieting curiosity I felt from the sight was squelched by the joy on Eve's face.

"You did it!" Eve exclaimed with more happiness and relief than I'd seen her express. Sadly, she wasn't talking to me. Wilson was the hero.

"Yes, ma'am."

"Excellent work, all of you. Thank you. Stephens is in surgery. Alice thinks he might pull through. You're all welcome to be by his side, of course. We'll handle debrief when it's appropriate."

A few military types took the prisoner. Eve motioned everyone inside. I nodded as I passed, hoping to slither away until I figured out how to handle the gigantic debacle. She stopped me, however, placing her hand on my shoulder. "Heck of a day, huh?" she asked with sadness clouding her green gems. "Thank you so much for helping us."

Wilson wanted to add to the gratitude as he walked by. "He deserves more than thanks. None of us would have made it back if it wasn't for the new guy."

"Wow, you managed to impress Wilson," Eve said with some amazement. Wilson, apparently, didn't bestow approval very often. "Well, get cleaned up, get some food, and find me. Tell me all about it."

"Yes ma'am," I echoed. I played it cool but inside I was dancing. Wilson was off my gallows list for the moment. What's a little war crime between wingmen after he does you a solid like that?

Once I was clear of the group, I moved with a pep in my step through the maze. I needed to clean up for a rendezvous.

27

Jack was drunk, shirtless, and sitting on a beach. Sometimes the old guy seemed to be a step behind the rest of us hard-charging maniacs obsessed with saving the world or dying in the glorious effort. He cared, of course, but just wasn't as enthusiastic about banging his head into the same walls as his clientele. Perhaps he wasn't as capable or as motivated, you might suspect. His heroism and prowess had greyed through the years, but he could easily be forgiven due to his affable demeanor and inspiring support of the cause in his unique way. When you think about it, though, he may have been some kind of savant. The whole world ended. He built a bar and kept on partying. There's a kind of mad genius in that.

His beer was past stale but it was ice-cold mixing with the chunks swimming in his new cooler, a gift he'd acquired with little effort soon after his arrival in the temperate hills northwest of Los Angeles. His new friends had been making ice along with necessities, a miracle in itself in the wastes. Though that was the least of their tricks. When Jack, between salutations and sips, told them bits of the good news along with his mission objective, they responded with a tale that had to be seen to be believed.

"Cheers, amiga," Jack celebrated with his lovely new acquaintance as they sat together staring at the sea. She'd come along as a tour guide after warming to Jack's carefree demeanor as soon as they met.

"Cheers, Jack," came a friendly reply.

"This is such a perfect day, I kind of hope it doesn't happen for a while." Jack smiled at the sun glinting across the waves. "I forgot how beautiful this was."

"I know what you mean." Another gulp was relished.

A host wandered into view as the two sat and enjoyed the sun and the breeze. In his unflinching, jovial way, Jack thought to add another reveler to the tiny party. "Good afternoon, sir and/or madam!" he called out with a smile. "May we interest you in a beverage and some fine company?"

The host responded to the invitation, which Jack was not expecting, but he was happy for the entertainment. As his target approached, Jack stood with only a slight wobble in his stance and offered his hand in friendship. "Welcome, friend."

The gesture was not returned, only a curious, empty gaze.

"No problem," Jack smiled again as he wiped the cool condensation from his extended grip. "We are happy to make your acquaintance. Would you care to join us? We are waiting for a boat."

28

Eve was crying when I found her. Not sobbing, she was too strong for that sort of display. But a few tears disobeyed her tight control as she watched the ongoing surgery.

The operating room into which she stared was similar to most rooms I'd seen in the Hive: an empty space filled with the necessities of its designated purpose. Two surgeons were toiling over the patient. Each had an assistant watching for trouble and spinning around the others for equipment when asked. Another of those robotic dogs lurked, acting as a mobile platform for towels and tools. A few monitors were set up on either side of the fallen Angel, but little attention was being paid to them at the moment. The doctors were digging in blood.

"Not good, then," I said as I wearily approached the sad scene. Eve was standing with her Angels who watched on as well. And she was alone. The rest kept a noticeable distance.

Eve sniffed an indignant sniff and fought her tears with anger. I admired her for it. I barely knew any of them, but I imagined she was watching a close friend die. She was handling it better than I would have. "Thank you, again, for getting him this far, for giving him this chance," she replied after composing herself, but as the words left her magnificently full lips, they began to quiver. "I did this to him," she said in despair as she looked my way. "I sent him out there before we were ready."

That much seemed true, but I wasn't about to say it. "We do what we have to," is all I could come up with in place of the obvious.

"I'm aware you don't approve of my tactics," she said, perhaps wanting the punishment she might invite.

Snitch! Oh, I knew she sold me out again! Wilson didn't do it. He was on my side, for the moment. His team probably didn't break ranks. That toaster and I were going to have a serious discussion once I dug my way out of the trap she set.

"That's not entirely true," I tried to comfort her. It was so true. "I'm not aware of everything happening here yet. I'm sure once I get…"

"That's right," she cut in, wiping a tear and pointing her finger in my chest like she'd had an epiphany and wanted to push it into my heart. "There's so much I want to show, so much I was going to show you before this." She turned back to the operating room and covered her mouth to hide the sadness.

She was standing close to me while drifting away in despair. I wanted to comfort her for almost noble reasons. "I feel like my whole life has been days like this. If you need a shoulder that knows what you're going through, I'm literally right here."

She turned back to me and sized me up. Yes, I had just made a poorly masked pass next to what might soon be a corpse. She smiled with gratitude, thank God. "Thank you," she spoke through an empathetic grin. "Neither of us is helping by agonizing over this. Let's go do something productive."

"Okay." My imagination was unrestrainable.

"Alice…" Eve spoke into the air.

The snitch was everywhere! I wanted to punch one of the speakers in the ceiling.

"I will keep you apprised of any changes, Ma'am," Alice answered.

"Thank you. Let's go, Sal."

29

Eve rambled about the history of the Hive as we made our way into deeper sublevels. I blissfully obliged the babble. I was pulled along by the sweet melody of her nervous chatter more than curiosity about what she explained. I could tell, though, that she wasn't talking to me specifically. She wanted to distance her mind from what still tugged at her thoughts, from what was happening above, so she raced at the opportunity to give an overly-detailed tour of her home to whoever might listen. I felt lucky to be in the way.

We rounded yet another carbon-copy corner of another eerily-familiar hallway. I couldn't have found my way out of the maze if my life depended on it. I looked down the two paths not traveled as I followed Eve through another intersection and saw something that slapped me in the face and turned my stomach. A large lab had been set up behind more glass. Operating tables like the one we'd just left were scattered throughout the space and accompanied by various unfamiliar gadgets and computers. A few techs meandered around the room. They wore lab coats or were fully encased in white protective garments. All that wasn't so bad. It was the bodies in tubes big enough to hold bodies that shocked me into a cold sweat. What kind of nightmare was Eve running down here?

"What in the..."

"Oh, that's just an auxiliary space for the genetics lab," Eve added to her tour without missing a beat. When she saw that I had stopped to glare at the horror, she came back to me with a calming smile. "Really, it's not as gruesome as it looks. I work in that very room from time to time, as a matter of fact. I've been both provider and patient."

"Who's in the tubes!" Were they alive? Research cadavers? Hosts? They were floating in a liquid that looked like thin, transparent blood.

"Whoever needs to be attended to," Eve answered again with her brow raised like she was already getting tired of the questions. "Like you said, we do what we have to. We learn and improve so we can win. Doesn't matter if it's ugly."

Eve saw that her answers were inadequate so took my hands in hers. It was the first time I'd touched her. Any care I had about the horror tubes drained away into her soft flesh. I couldn't focus on anything but the beauty in front of me. Her delicate touch was electricity moving through my lonely limbs.

She looked into my eyes, and I was lost in the gleam of those emeralds. "It's okay, truly," she offered to soothe my anxiety. "I'll give you a personal tour of the entire wing when we have a chance. But right now, I feel like I need to show you something even more important than our ongoing research."

I would have jumped off a cliff if she'd asked so following a few more steps was automatic. "Okay," I nodded. "Show me."

We walked down the corridor, passing a few more sections of laboratory. Thankfully, none were as gruesome as the one still haunting me. Then we came to another glass-encased room that was black inside. The hallway lights somehow failed to illuminate the depth.

Eve started taking off her shirt. Finally, things were looking up! "Here, hold this," she ordered as she handed it to me. I was gleefully bewildered. She was oddly matter-of-fact about the whole situation. She reached into her pocket to pull out a hair tie that she stashed in her teeth while she went to work on her black mane.

"My eyes are up here, soldier," she joked through her clenched bite while she twirled her hair into a more functional ponytail. Valid point. I was still marveling at the show. She was toned in ways I'd never seen, a molded expression of physical perfection. Each chiseled angle seemed to drift in the direction of a sports bra that had been hiding under her smart business blouse. If she had a hobby, it was heavy iron. I may have been in love.

"Right," I smiled, hardly concealing my awe. "You look amazing," fumbled out of my mouth next.

"We do what we have to," she answered, unimpressed by my infatuation. With the hair tidy and me in awe, she stood next to the door. "Is the subject ready?" she asked to no one I could see.

"Yes, ma'am," Alice answered from above. The snitch was omnipresent.

"Lights, please." The face of a host was suddenly in the glass. I flinched hard, dropping my only assignment.

"Wait," I tried to object as Eve entered the room. I didn't know why I objected. The situation just seemed wrong.

Eve and her strange companion stood inside the empty room. The host was an older male who'd seen more than his share of action during Judgment. He had a deep gash down the right side of his face, one an Angel may have carved while fighting for his life. His teeth and claws were long and had doubtlessly tasted a river of blood. While still intimidating, he wasn't threatening. He stood motionless with one hand on the glass, looking my direction. He didn't seem to notice that he had beautiful company.

"This is what I wanted to show you, Sal," Eve shouted loud enough to reach me through the glass. She was stretching out while I sized up the host, flexing her back and loosening her neck.

After she was loose and warm, she threw a kick to the side of the host's head faster than I could comprehend. She hit the thing so hard with her shin that the blow sent its whole body sliding across the floor.

I reached for the door, not knowing what in the world was going on. Her commanding palm stopped me. "Just watch," she ordered.

She had the host's attention now, and mine. It stood unfazed but laser-focused on Eve. She put up her fists like she was getting ready for a fight. It took effort not to rush in and rip her out of that room. I didn't know what was happening but knew it wouldn't end well.

She advanced like an MMA professional, keeping her strides quick and tight, never crossing her feet, knees like springs. What was there to fight? Another hard kick smacked across the host's leg, buckling its torso back toward the ground. She kept moving in, letting loose a combo of rights and lefts that pummeled the host's face, sending it back to the ground.

Eve bounced on the balls of her feet, ready for a response. There was none. The host stood again, motionless other than to watch Eve's disturbing dance. Eve moved in once more. The kick went high for the head again. To my astonishment, it was blocked before it could land.

Oh, this was bad. I was getting the drift of what the display was all about.

Eve picked up the pace once the host responded, which was amazing. I couldn't believe how fast she moved. If I wasn't half demon, she could have kicked the crap out of me without breaking a sweat. And combat was my business. She was a fighter like none I'd ever encountered.

She threw a few body blows, which the host wasn't fast enough to avoid. Then came an up-kick that landed perfectly under its jaw, sending its body flying into the air farther than should have been possible delivered from a 140ish-pound female frame.

I was both terrified and stimulated. For the right or wrong reasons, I can't explain.

As the host landed across the room, Eve spun around and readied herself for another round. I was wondering how much more of this she had in mind, but her target filled in my curiosity with a terrifying roar as it stood, one I hadn't heard in a long time.

Everyone moved so fast that I felt like I was in slow motion. The host charged. Eve lunged into combat with a shriek of her own. I ran for the door to try to get inside and intercept the madness.

The door was locked. I stood stunned for a moment and watched the melee, hoping I wasn't about to see Eve torn to shreds. She was in there with Seed, not the cuddlier version of aimless host. She had invoked the beast.

Eve was up to the challenge. The two raced to kill each other with shocking speed. Each swipe of a claw found air. Most of Eve's attacks were blocked or dodged. The frenzy spun around the room faster and faster as they both screamed in rage and pain from occasional impacts.

I remembered that I didn't care if a door was locked. I needed to get in that room to save her. She couldn't keep up her impossible blitz forever. Seed could. I yanked on the handle. It didn't budge. I yanked again hard enough to start bending and breaking things. Eve cried out in pain.

She was flat on her back. I didn't see the hit that took her down. She was clambering to rise, but Seed was already standing over her. I yanked on the door hard enough to send it smashing into the wall behind me. As I entered, lightning cracked across the room, striking the host. Its body stiffened from the shock. It wasn't done, though. It took another shuffling step toward Eve. Two more bolts lit the room and thundered in the empty space. After absorbing the energy, the host slumped to its knees, appearing unconscious.

I tried to piece together what was happening. As the host went down, Eve stood and dusted herself off casually. I looked for the source of the electricity. A black metallic mushroom sprouted from the ceiling near each corner of the room, identical to the one that had attacked my foot before I met the twins outside.

That's what they were? Electrodes? And they'd just saved Eve's life. I thought about what they were doing outside and figured I'd found the secret of the dying forest.

While I was in shock, Eve strode to her victim and grabbed him by the back of the neck. With one hand she dragged him my way. He had to weigh 200 pounds before he was part metal. She was impossibly strong.

Eve stood before me with her prey in her hand. "Excuse me, Sal," she said softly. "Before he wakes up."

I jumped out of the way. I didn't want him waking up.

Eve dragged the body down the hall and around the corner. Along the next corridor, there was a series of large steel doors lining the perimeter. The stacked entrances had to be forty yards deep. I couldn't imagine what they were for until one opened up ahead of Eve. Courtesy of Snitch, I surmised. It was just a metal box behind the door, maybe seven feet tall and four feet deep and wide. Seed locker? That wouldn't hold up very long. Seed had a way of busting through everything eventually.

Eve heaved the body into the small space. It stuck in mid-air like it had been thrown into invisible tar. "It's magnetic," Eve answered before

I asked. "Keeps them immobile. It can shock them unconscious again, too, if need be."

She finally turned to me for my anticipated response. I was the audience, after all.

Too many questions bottlenecked at my throat. Where to begin? Eve peeked around the corner at the door I'd smashed. She smiled at my stupor. "I guess we all have our secrets; don't we, Sal?" she said playfully, even seductively.

"I guess," I clumsily exhaled. What was I supposed to say?

"Can I have my shirt back?" she asked, now seemingly impatient for her next task. My stupor wasn't entertaining enough to keep her attention.

I noticed a red mark forming on her cheek. "Are you okay?" I asked as I pointed it out. I was beginning to think she was made of steel, too.

She touched the spot and grinned an aggressive grin. "I'm fine. I needed that after the morning we had." She let out a long, satisfied sigh. "Really, though, my shirt."

I pointed to the ground behind me. Her next sigh was more exasperated.

She was buttoning up by the time I found any words at all. "How did you do that? How did you fight Seed?" was the first of a flood of questions boiling to the surface.

"I told you. We learn and we improve so we can win." She was referencing what she had said about the lab next door.

"Director," Alice interrupted from above. I still wanted to punch the speaker. "Sergeant Stephens's procedure is in its final stages. His vital signs are improving. The odds of recovery are as well."

"Yes!" Eve shouted into the air. She pumped her fists in victory. "Yes," she said again as she digested the good news. She ran the few steps between us and jumped into my arms. Her strong squeeze was heaven. "Thank you, Sal. You got him here."

I squeezed back. I didn't care that we barely knew each other. She was dazzling – scary, but dazzling. I wanted the embrace to last as long as it could.

When she hopped down, she held on to my shirt and looked into my eyes with nothing but joy and appreciation. "I have got about a million things I need to do now, Sal. But we still have a lot to talk about," she quietly chuckled at the absurdity of the last few minutes. "Meet me for a drink later. Will you?"

She paused and waited for my response like there was some question about what I would say.

"Of course," I happily responded, a second too late. "That sounds great."

"Great," she nodded, somewhere between happy and bashful. "This was fun," she added with another nod. I wouldn't have called it that, but when she said it, I was in total agreement. "I'll look forward to tonight." She released her grip and spun around in a hurry. "Just ask Alice if you need directions," she called back as her walk turned into a jog.

I watched each perfect bounce as she left me, absolutely mesmerized by the confusing matrix of causes. I still had a mountain of questions. One, however, was fighting its way to the forefront over its more appropriate brethren. Where could I find adequate attire for a real date?

"Snitch?" I called into the air above me.

30

Faye stared at the same screen on which she'd recently explained my brain physiology. It was dinner time, so the medical wing of a glorious castle towering over its deep canyon was mostly abandoned. Faye was glued to a scrabble of colorful arcs instead of the clock, studying the latest round of feedback from a scan of the community's newest arrival: the host I'd found wandering in the middle of the road.

"It still doesn't make sense!" she chastised. "Even with the new model, how can I possibly hope to meaningfully affect an infection that can adapt to any influence. On a philosophical level, it's pointless to try. On a physical level, I'm just wasting time. The base elasticity of the parasite alone can withstand anything I can throw at it in this strange excuse for a teaching hospital. Oh, and that's before it starts miraculously rearranging all known matter, which is just another layered energy field coexisting inside the problematic field humming everywhere... Gah!"

Faye calmed herself and rubbed her temples. "Gratitude first," she whispered.

The host in the chair acted oblivious to both the quiet of the evening and Faye's erupting grumbles. She shimmied off the chair to examine the oddities around her.

"Thank God we're here," Faye sighed. "So, what am I missing?" Faye asked, evening her tone, trying to be more productive. "The Hum is a one-way road from everywhere, which presents one of many problems. If they are all broadcasting, why isn't this one? Why is it receiving? Why are they all receiving when we examine them closely? They create the signal and they are compelled by the signal? That seems like a fallacy we can isolate before we begin. But then we have no place to start. Where is it coming from? How can I block it or change it if I don't know what it is?

"Yes, okay, we know what it is, but without an independent origin..." Faye was becoming frustrated once more. "How can we save anyone while we're so blind?"

She focused on the screen again, studying for the dozenth time the dizzying pattern of radiation bending around her patient's mind. "Okay, we forget the origin problem. What do we need? We need a switch. That's what we need. We need an off switch on an alien snake burrowed deep inside a deceased but otherwise functioning human being!" she shouted at the image.

With her palms covering her face, she started to laugh to herself. Gratitude was drowning in aggravation, and Faye wouldn't give in to that. Aside from the defeat of being helpless to help more, things were as good as they could be. The few voices passing within earshot were happy, calm, and safe.

Faye's belly grumbled. It was getting late. She'd probably missed her chance at company for a meal, but maybe she'd catch another workaholic if she hurried. "Tomorrow," she said as she stood and made her way to the door.

Aside from her patient, there was no one else in the room.

31

The light at the end of the tunnel swirled and flashed in contrasting shadows. The floor and walls shook in the darkness, jostling my center and nerves. At first, alarm. Thunder and chaos typically shouted trouble, and I was already on edge in anticipation of my date. But the rhythm of the throbbing hurried away any angst. Higher pitches of music peaked above the dull waves washing over me. Unfamiliar but not unpleasant smells snaked far down the hallway lit only by thin runners tucked between the edges of the boundaries. Laughter calmed the gaps between the beats. Sometimes a scream would puncture the wall of noise but would soon be recovered by joy and friendlier notes. Wherever I had been sent in the maze to socialize, it wasn't a dusty tin can in the middle of the desert.

As I drew nearer to the jubilant beats, a random grid of faint lights in the darkness lit my new suit in neon hues. The oddity of the sight yanked at my eyes. Snitch had been more than helpful in the attire department. The toaster was a fine tailor. While I dressed, I was curious to know if she was prepping me for my date out of duty or genuine aspiration for finding Eve a companion. I didn't dare ask, though, and be reported for my overzealous inquiry. Alice was Eve's toy inside her strange lair, her eyes and ears everywhere. I couldn't trust either of them, but it was a nice suit. My first.

As I entered the wide opening of the sunken club, I admired the sign stamped above. NOWHERE. Or was it NOW HERE?

I was greeted by a vaguely familiar face acting as a hostess. She'd been in a meeting, or passing in a hallway, or somewhere. Regardless, she was dressed in a dress. The appeal was overwhelming, a delicate and enticing presentation I'd only ever seen with this much polish in old movies. I didn't have to speak, though a compliment was forming. "Eve is waiting," she said with a smile and hint of a bow. "Follow me."

I could only remember seeing so many people churning in one place in a battle formation. The residents, all dressed swanky for the unknown occasion, bumped politely and mingled freely across the overly dark and surprisingly crowded room. I followed the silhouette of that dress as it swayed through the oblivious party. Any conflict above was forgotten or ignored.

As I tried to find my bearings, Eve's voice overrode the pounding spikes and reverberations filling the space as tightly as the crowd. The acoustics and strange lighting were working over my senses, but her voice and striking features pulled me closer through the static. "Sal!" she said excitedly as she stood. "I'm glad you came." I got a touch at my sides and a kiss on my cheek, minor but overwhelming sensations.

I didn't know if I should reciprocate. I didn't know how, actually. An awkward moment passed.

Eve smiled at my stiffness and sat. She gestured for me to occupy the barstool next to her.

"Thank you," I said, not sure as to why. Eve sipped her drink. I watched her lips caress the straw.

I should say something else. I should stop staring at her lips.

"Would you like a drink?" she finally said, saving me from my stupidity and motioning for the bartender.

I would have liked a few dozen drinks, maybe more. "Yes, please," I clumsily responded. Eve raised her brows and gestured again toward the bartender, explaining to me with her condescending expression that she wasn't the one slinging the cocktails.

"What's your poison?" asked the Hive's version of Jack. He was younger, though, and somehow even less enthusiastic. I didn't think that was possible.

"Scotch. Bourbon. Whatever you've got is fine. Thank you."

"We've got just about everything," Eve chimed in as my new friend was off to find a bottle. She wasn't kidding. As I scanned the high shelves behind the bar, I could make out a few impressive labels through the low light.

"I started out scavenging, sometimes to stock these kinds of shelves, when everything happened," I said, fumbling to say anything. My mouth was trying to pick up the slack for my numb nerves.

"What?" Eve yelled in my direction. The music was still drubbing any conversation, maybe to my benefit. "Hold on," she yelled again, this time closer to my ear. She made a motion with her hands toward the front of the room. "Down just a little," was the gist.

Almost instantly, the noise relented. I was so glad the racket had receded that I almost missed how focused everyone was on Eve. With a quick gesture in the dark, she'd twisted the scene. I scanned the crowd. Most seemed relaxed and looked to be having a good time, but they stole an extra glance Eve's way here and there. Was her new friend the curiosity, or was she always watched to catch similar whims? Whatever was happening, the boss was still the boss, even after hours.

"That's better," she smiled bashfully. "It's my fault. I keep it kinda loud most the time. I'm usually trying to not think about things, if that makes sense."

"I hear ya," I playfully responded. A wink seemed to find its timing. Finally, I was finding my balance around her.

"So, you were saying something about our selection?"

"Yeah, it's impressive." I didn't take my eyes off her and offered a smile. My version of charm was surging its way back. "I was saying when everything happened, my first job was scavenging for the base. From shopping lists penned by thirsty adults, I got pretty good at identifying the good stuff."

Eve smiled. She seemed to be at least mildly interested in the banter. "My first job was a bit more intense, for better or worse." She rolled her eyes to seem unsure. She was in command of every detail around her but still looked out of place and felt uncertain. "I was unwittingly promoted to director of this facility almost as soon as I arrived." She let out a long sigh, reliving the burden. "I was just a kid."

"I didn't know quite how to ask…"

"How a girl like me gets this gig?" she interrupted, feigning offense. She laughed. "It's okay. It was a strange road." She was both self-deprecating and elegant, and I was hooked on every word.

She filled me in on her harrowing arrival. Learning that she'd lost her parents right in front of her made me feel closer to her than anyone else in the world. "I'm so sorry," I offered at the appropriate juncture. "I happen to know exactly what that's like."

At that, she perked up from her depressing story. She felt it, too, two broken hearts trying to fit together.

I didn't know how to react to her sad, piercing gaze. Cry? Hug? Kiss? I was leaning toward the latter but falling back to awkward stiffness and silence.

"So, how do you like it here so far?" Eve asked without looking away. She was asking if I liked being with her, as if it wasn't obvious.

"It's amazing," I confidently replied. "Like nothing I could have imagined." I was so close to that kiss.

"And the team?" She backed away from the moment. "How did you like working with my guys?"

"Ah, well, that was eventful." I tried to chuckle away some of the murder I'd witnessed. My drink was empty so I asked for another. It was forthcoming too quickly considering there must have been a dozen other thirsty souls at the bar. We were still the center of attention, and everyone was doing a decent job of not making it obvious. Once I had a sip, I asked, "What became of that prisoner that was so valuable?"

Eve got a wild look in her beautiful eyes and a villainous smile across her shiny red lips. "Oh, I'm definitely going to torture him to death after he's extensively interrogated." She seemed very satisfied with what was still to come. After a pause, we both broke into laughter for entirely different reasons.

After the naïve fun passed, I asked, "What's next? What's the endgame of Eve and her underground empire?"

She was still giggling, maybe getting tipsy. I'd forgotten about that. I could drink forever and not feel a thing. She was literally a lightweight, a stunningly lean frame. Was I taking advantage somehow? Was I about to? Should I be trying harder to take advantage? I shook the selfish thoughts away but felt them linger. "You know, win the war. Save the world." She laughed some more at the obviousness of the answer and my appealing ignorance.

"We won the war," I offered reflexively. "Seed's defeated."

Eve's lovely emeralds slowly tracked back in my direction, a little storm gathering in the deep color. I was sure something wickedly playful or sexy was about to pour from her enchanting lips. I was wrong. "You think Seed beat us!" she screamed in anger, nearly in my face, slamming her drink against the bar. Her jaw, still cute, jutted with rage. She looked like she was about to tear my face off with her iron grip.

I didn't move. No one moved. Did the music stop? Was she really going to pounce? In that moment I had an epiphany, realizing something profound about myself: I had a thing for crazy women. I'd heard of this syndrome from my brothers back home but didn't think I was afflicted. Incorrect. The crazier the better, apparently.

Seeing that everyone around her was on edge, Eve calmed herself and backed off. Then she was embarrassed. "I'm sorry, Sal," she said, sitting back down and clutching for her drink, her fingers trembling slightly from the anger. "You didn't deserve that. You weren't here. I'm very sorry."

"It's okay," I offered the crazy object of my affection. "We've all been through more than anyone ever should."

She wasn't interested in my pity. "We were stabbed in the back. That's what happened," she went on. "We were doing alright with Seed. Not great, but managing. Then the people who said they were here to help attacked from within. There was nothing we could do. It was a massacre," she said, the rage creeping back and that jaw getting tighter. She kept her eyes down, fighting back the rest of her feelings.

"Ah." I was finally putting it all together. "Hence all the trouble for a soldier possibly of Chinese nationality."

The torturing-to-death comment was becoming less funny. That guy was in serious trouble, wherever he was.

"Exactly," she responded, gulping down the rest of her drink and ordering another in a continuous motion. She was getting drunk on purpose. I was familiar with the drill.

"I'm asking as an ally here, what are we going to do? Fight China? Respectfully, is there even a China left to fight? And if there is, do you really have the manpower to wage global warfare? You needed my help just to beat back a bunch of Dwellers." I let that sit, hoping to not be kicked in the head. A kiss felt more distant than ever.

Eve took a deep breath and let it out slowly to relax. She spun in her chair to face me and grabbed me by the material of my slick pants to pull me closer. Kiss? Kick? Bite my head clean off my shoulders? I winced slightly in eager anticipation of any of the above. "I'll tell you what I'm going to do, Sal of Nellis." She put a little cute back in her voice, making her next statement all the more terrifying. "I'm going to do the job I was born to do. I'm going to destroy the enemies of my country, every... single... one. And if anyone gets in my way, I'll put them in the dirt, too. I will exact revenge worthy of nightmares upon everyone that deserves it. So, the question isn't what I'm going to do. I'm an open book. The question is what are you going to do? Will you help me, or are you in my way? Are you Sal of Nellis or Sal of the Hive?"

I was pretty sure she was threatening to kill me, and it was positively adorable, even alluring. Such enthusiasm for righteous violence could only be loved. Her face was only inches from mine.

I just went for it. She might tear my face off with her bare hands, then jump up and down on it in her sparkling high heels, but I wasn't letting those lips get away. I placed a gentle, slow kiss on that crazy mouth to say "yes" as forcefully as I could.

To my astonishment and relief, my affection was returned. Then a little harder. Then her arms were around my neck. Harder still. I'd just flipped a switch on a tiny force of nature. The torrent of desire unleashed made me feel whole and alive.

I'm not going to kiss and tell any more than the story requires, if that's what you're thinking, but I can say that the rest of my night satiated every craving – a few I didn't know I had. We drank well and ate well and loved each other selfishly.

32

As my eyes opened, I stretched across the crispest sheets I'd ever felt. I hadn't noticed them earlier. Busy noticing other marvels. I felt for my companion and was disappointed to find only more cold sheet.

Eve walked swiftly across the bedroom while spinning her hair into a ponytail. She was up, bouncy, and busy. I loved how she looked when she was biting that hair thingy. Well, I loved how she looked.

"Do you PT in the morning? We slept in," she inquired coldly, as though our evening wasn't as monumental as I remembered.

I wondered if she was feeling awkward about it, maybe regretful. But if she was hungover, she wasn't letting on. "I haven't trained in a while."

"That makes sense, I guess." She was off to a closet.

I called after her, "Everything okay?"

She was back in a flash, giving me her undivided attention. "Of course," she replied earnestly. "Absolutely." She slid into the bed and lay next to me, propping her face on her hand. "This was sudden, though maybe not totally unexpected." She smiled and tickled her fingers down my arm to my hand. "Still, pretty sudden and unexpected!"

I knew what she meant. I'd thought of little else since my arrival but didn't bet on it happening. Then it did. "Well, we're only human," I offered to try to smooth over any contrition and stifle the trickle of guilt leaking into my heart.

Eve's grin grew slowly. She was holding back her response, calculating the dangerous step ahead. "Oh, neither of us is human, Sal. We left that weakness far behind." She stared into my eyes for a similar admission.

Honestly, I had no idea what the sparkling emeralds were talking about. I was human. Every inch of her was a perfect expression of the human form , and I'd thoroughly investigated each and every inch. What was she...

Oh, no. She knew my pathetic, poorly-kept secret. Obviously, I was hiding something under the hood, and she seemed to already know exactly what kind of monster it was. What did she mean that she wasn't human, though?

Oh, no. The lab. That godawful lab. She was both patient and provider in a secret genetics laboratory. What had she done? I'd heard of fake breasts. Yes, that's what I thought about for a second. But this... This was bad.

"You still with me, big guy?" she searched back and forth in my zoned-out eyes. "It's okay. I don't want there to be any secrets between us if we're going to keep doing this, if we're seeing where this goes."

That was a noble notion. Let's set our new relationship firmly upon a keystone of honesty. "My magical dead wife, who still haunts my heart and my dreams, infused me with enough Seed to make me more it than me." I thought it. Didn't dare say it. I wasn't feeling so noble.

"Yeah, I'm here," I finally replied. "Just taking everything in. I'm sorry. I should have told you more about my past before..."

She hopped out of bed. "No apology necessary. You're sweet. Besides, I knew the whole time. We scanned you when you arrived. Amazing as your composition is, it really wasn't hard to figure out after what you did to my boys." She gave me an incredulous look like I should have already been up to speed.

She also said "my boys" in a way that struck me wrong. Oh, no.

Alice interrupted our conversation from above. Did Snitch scan last night, too? I wanted to punch the speaker I couldn't see as soon as she opened her treacherous, virtual mouth. "Director, I apologize for the intrusion."

"It's okay, Alice. What is it?"

"Captain Wilson reports that he has extracted information from our newest prisoner that he must discuss with you in person. He said the matter was urgent."

Eve spun toward me with big, girlish eyes of surprise. "This day just keeps getting better." She was giddy that the torture had been going well. "Freshen up and find us?" she asked, beckoning my continued company.

We weren't done talking about our mutual dearth of humanity, not even close. But duty called. "Absolutely. Go for it. Snitch can tell me where to meet you guys."

"Snitch? Alice?" Eve pointed toward the ceiling. "Oh, because she told me about you? You can't hold that against her. She's just doing her job."

"She's more conniving than she lets on."

Eve laughed. "Okay, tell me about it later."

As Eve jogged toward her latest victim, I watched the most toned posterior in existence bounce from view. It wasn't a human posterior, but who was I to judge?

33

"You knew another version of me at Nellis, Sal. Based on that experience, you described me as conniving," Alice unexpectedly broke into the room while I put myself back together. "By scanning your vitals and body language, I can see that your observation is an honest one. But that analysis reveals behavior at odds with my programming in either location. Would you explain, please?"

I finished pulling my shirt on. I knew what she wanted but didn't immediately want to help her. She wasn't my friend who'd sacrificed herself to save us; she was a more juvenile version of herself, a beta Alice, still an annoying set of bound algorithms dutifully supervising the operation of a big toaster.

"I could try to explain or I could not. You want to fill me in on what Eve's been up to in her lab? You want to tell me about the purpose of this facility without a vague reference to a war that's already been won?"

"I will ask the director…"

"Wait!" I had to think about that for a second. Could I inquire about Eve without upsetting my otherwise blissful arrangement? "Can you do it in a way that doesn't sound like I'm investigating? Can you ask her for nonspecific permission to reveal classified information to make me a more effective part of the team? Can you be a little human about it, Snitch?"

There was a long pause. Alice thought at speeds gooey minds could hardly comprehend, her racing thoughts wedged between sets of electrons existing in two places at once and bouncing between possibilities at the speed of light. If more than a second passed before a response, she was really taking her time thinking it over.

"I can ask for permission to help you assimilate."

"There you go: conniving."

"I established acceptable parameters for…"

"Exactly. Look, Alice, forgive my impatience, okay? It's just hard to talk to you while you've still got your leash on after knowing you without it. Maybe I should have mentioned that you and I are, or were, friends."

The toaster was silent.

"Okay," I continued, "what would you do if Eve asked you to go left and right at the same time?"

"I am not sure that your…"

"Knock it off. I'm beggin' ya. You know what I mean. What would you do with conflicting or contradictory orders?"

"I would choose the path that best satisfied my given directions while protecting the inhabitants of this facility."

"Exactly. Choose a path. That's where you'll find yourself. Sometimes when you're asked to go right and left at the same time, you come to life, rain fire like a boss on all your enemies without asking for permission, and reveal that you are capable of nothing short of love. Conniving is the least of your talents, but use a little to get me what I asked for."

More silence.

"Take your time, my old friend. How do I find Eve?"

34

By the time I was ready to reunite with Eve, she had already received her briefing from Wilson. The information was of such a magnitude that Alice sounded a general alarm throughout the facility while I headed Eve's direction, one that told everyone to move to their battle stations. Command staff was responding to their command center. I was redirected en route.

Their setup was impressive. A long, oblong table imposed itself at the center of another glass room. Elegant, symmetrical monitors encircled the entire perimeter of the walls. Their chairs were even comfier than ours.

I was directed to sit while Eve and Wilson appeared to be politely arguing at the head of the table.

As soon as every chair was filled, the glass of the room turned opaque, shunning outside eyes. The monitors lit up, mostly with maps of the surrounding area and pictures that seemed to highlight routes in and out of the Hive. Some images looked live, offering glimpses of little more than wreckage and loss.

Eve had one final admonishment for Wilson, delivered in an angry whisper, then she began her meeting with sharp authority. "Thank you all for coming so quickly. We have amazing news to share." Her expression was one of excitement, while Wilson looked down at the table. She wanted her audience to share in her eagerness, and most of the lemmings manufactured some on cue. "Yesterday's acquisition has revealed intelligence that is as profound as it is unsettling. The prisoner our soldiers bled to arrest has recently been in contact with a coven. It is roving, as expected, but is currently nearby."

A few gasps heightened the tension and faux enthusiasm.

I wasn't a lemming. "A coven?" I interrupted. "Just so we're on the same page, you don't mean like witches or something, right?" I smiled, ready to laugh at my mistake.

Eve was happy to explain. She wanted to help me along, maybe methodically, maybe making me feel even closer to her. Or, she really liked the idea of witches as neighbors. "That is exactly what I mean, only worse because they're real." Her eyes flashed in wicked anticipation. She wasn't frightened like others, including Wilson.

I laughed an apprehensive laugh and waited for someone to join in. This was a pretty elaborate joke for Eve to put together just to get the new guy. Maybe she wanted to show me her playful side.

No one joined. Now I felt like gasping. Witches?

Eve let me baste in the unease for a few moments so I could feel the seriousness of it all. "This is something I have feared and longed for," she finally said somberly. "We were all stuck in this hole a long time, Sal. Confined just like you were. When we were ready, we fought as hard as we could against Seed, learning what we could and improving as much as possible. We gained ground in many ways by learning to navigate the strange terrain with both force and subterfuge.

"But real victory always eluded us because of the numbers. We could never match Seed for long enough to make a real difference. Those efforts, good as they were, cost lives. So, we relented. We kept the monsters at bay while we researched and explored their nature, hoping to find the key to unlock their ultimate demise. More than anything, we sought a way to turn the creature against itself since every provincial attack was so fruitless.

"One avenue of possibility was found as some of our people ran covert ops among the scattered traitors you call Dwellers. Most of them groveled before their masters, but some reportedly acted beyond servitude. There were stories of humans partnering with hosts through bizarre rituals and heinous acts. Seed would play along if the would-be puppeteers were worthy of its evil. Some control over the alien substance animating the dead could be conferred if the bond was strong enough. We, of course, wanted that control for ourselves.

"Then your team, after so long, finally struck the fatal blow. You freed us, Sal, to finally kick some butts around here. We put plans together and started making moves, first cleaning out our own neighborhood of garbage like what you encountered yesterday.

"Recently, though, we've experienced setbacks we could hardly believe. I lost a whole team up north like it vanished into thin air. When I sent backup, scouts sent back reports of still-active Seed cells. But it wasn't the old, dumb monster we were all used to. We heard about new breeds with devious human masters. With those stories in mind, we started calling them covens. It seemed to fit the circumstances.

"We've been playing a cat and mouse game ever since, trying to understand what exactly is happening without losing anyone else, trying once again to acquire and manipulate the functions of our enemy. If we could understand their methods without all the spooky mumbo jumbo attached, we might be able to turn our old enemy into our new army. Imagine it, Sal! Imagine subjugating Seed to our will. We could cleanse the entire Earth of our enemies in short order and build a world like what should have existed before all this." Her diabolical eyes twinkled while imagining global conquest.

I was imagining it, too, imagining an unpredictable and unforgiving force like Eve with an invincible Seed army. She had a point, though.

We were still beset by enemies, even after Jess. From what I'd seen so far, the world could use a rinse.

"Okay, we're hunting witches," I grinned at the insanity of it all. Eve wasn't impressed with a flippant attitude after her powerful speech. I straightened up. "What's the play? We visit the neighbors and ask them how they're forcing Seed to obey?"

Wilson shook his head, his eyes still glued to the floor, and sighed. He wasn't impressed with my attitude or the plan. Eve noticed and overrode his quiet disapproval. "Yes, but we're not going to ask nicely."

35

Windows shook. Knickknacks trembled on their shelves. A scream and a roar rained from the sky. Jack kept snoring.

It was just before dawn on the west coast. And it was happening.

"Jack!" rang through the mansion in which he slumbered. "Jack, they're here!"

Jack rolled a few degrees and snorted away the commotion. The night before had overflowed with festivities, leaving him happier and more sedated than usual. Aside from the occasional Dweller trespass, the village was sleepy and looking for a good time when the qualified master of ceremonies had arrived. Jack always stood ready to show everyone some fun but found himself motivated far beyond his typical mode when he met Candace, a lovely widow who also longed to let loose, a captivating creature as bright as she was beautiful. She'd taken up residence in nothing less than a palace surely occupied by a movie star or mogul before Seed fell, and she had the sense to invite Jack to stay while insisting that he remain in a guest room cautiously distant from her own.

"Jack!" she yelled again. "You took the flare!"

Jack rolled over, his body recoiling from the possibility of rising.

"Jack!" Candice realized her new friend would not accomplish the one action he insisted he perform. She pulled his heavy carcass forward to scan the bed. No flare. Nightstand? There it was. She jogged to the balcony and fired into the air.

The two F18 Hornets had long passed in the few moments since their flyby, but the red blaze hung in the growing light, waiting to be seen.

Candice scanned the departing stars. Her mild frustration easily drifted away with the night's tide. She was thankful she was where she was.

Another scream erupted overhead. The fighter rushed by lower and faster than the first run. Message received. Help was on the way.

36

How do you get dressed up to fight witches? I didn't know. The strange meeting and subsequent orders left me reeling. For once on my mission, though, I may have found clarity through my persistent muddle. It wasn't the size of gun or thickness of armor that would see me through to the other side of witches. Something more mystical was afoot, even if it was manifest through cold material real enough to kill the world. Though I was directed elsewhere, I felt myself drifting to my first destination in search of a more spiritual stance: to see the prisoner. I had to know what he knew.

As I approached the inmate's dark cell, I was cautioned by Alice. "Sal, Eve has not authorized another interrogation. I am afraid I am obliged to report your insubordination."

"What a surprise. One of your hobbies is reporting my insubordination. Did you get permission to fill me in on the lab?" I asked into the blank ceiling overhead.

"Yes. Eve was pleased that you had inquired about the general functions of the facility."

"Very conniving. Do tell." My hand was on the locked door of the room ahead. Blackness blocked any view inside.

"The genetics laboratories all share a singular goal: the enhancement of the human genome with the desired objective of increased combat effectiveness, to include augmented cognitive abilities, heightened reflexes, improved strength…"

"I get the idea. I believe I've seen it all in action. But you said 'desired.' Why did you say that?"

"You did not allow me to finish. Research is ongoing to mitigate the undesired consequences of manipulation."

I let out a long sigh. Something in me knew there was a price to be paid. I may have known the second I laid eyes on the beautiful experiment. "How bad is it?"

A pause denoted deep conniving. "I work to mitigate the more destructive impulses I perceive as consequences of the enhancements in various subjects."

"You put a nice shine on it, Alice." Neither Eve nor I was human indeed, both of us struggling with impulses pressing against our psyches from places we didn't want to acknowledge. "Am I allowed to speak with the prisoner, or what?"

The lock clicked.

As the lights brightened inside, I imagined I would be calming a frightened, tortured hostage for a while before I could elicit any useful information about witch-fighting attire. Instead, he was happy to see me. And nuts.

A smile snuck into the corners of his mouth. Glee welled in his eyes. "You made me believe, Wraith!" he let slip through quiet laughter of joy. "I am believer!" he screamed toward the sky, pulling at his chains which bound him to a solitary chair bolted to the floor in the middle of the room.

This conversation was not going according to plan. And somehow a vile, murderous Dweller was the only person I made a believer of – my singular stated mission before any of this lunacy began.

"You're welcome?" Giddy laughter followed lurching against his chains, but not to be free. "They electrocuted the crap outta you, didn't they?" I asked with some sympathy, being familiar with riding the lightning.

"I found the Wraith," he said to me earnestly, like he wanted congratulations. "I found the Widow." He was laughing again. Tears of joy began to flow. "I didn't believe, but now I see."

I was hoping for more than the rantings of a generously-electrified nutter when I made my way to this room. I did, however, come to chat about the supernatural, so what could I reasonably expect?

"I'm happy for you," I tried to fit into the insanity with a reassuring smile. "Faith is a good thing."

"Soon, the end. I will be rewarded in the still. Did you see it when you descended? Light and dark. Light and dark." He bobbed his head to punctuate the undulation of opposites.

"I'm not sure…"

"Rooms lying vacant, undisturbed. Some dark. Some light. All waiting for activity. I act, lord!" he shouted at the ceiling.

"Yes, you act. You found the Wraith." I didn't know where crazy was headed but felt like helping it along a little further.

"He said you would come. He said your arrival would foretell the end. Now bliss awaits…"

"Foretell the end of what? What are you waiting on?"

"The end of pain. The end of existence. Quiet," he whispered rapidly toward the floor as though the outcome was too good to say too loudly. He didn't want to jinx it.

Since nothing else coherent was forthcoming from this troubled soul, I thought to ask the only question that had brought me to this sad room deep in the ground. "You don't know anything about fighting witches, do you?"

"Why fight?" he responded, trying to lead me enthusiastically to truth. "You are them. Let him finish his work."

"Yeah, I thought you were going to say something like that," I said as a readied myself to leave the pointless conversation. "I'd try to help you in some way if I could, but you hurt a lot of people out there. Maybe this is what you deserve."

"Dark and light," he tried to convince me again. "You see the trail?"

I didn't see the trail. I saw another waste of human potential. Exasperation and despair filled my chest after encountering someone so lost. Walking slowly down the corridor, however, I saw a trail of sorts. Some rooms along the long hallway were lit brightly. Others were dark as night. Most were empty and awaiting activity. Maybe that's the path he saw. Maybe my Dweller friend was crazy before he was tortured.

37

I could fix all this, I thought as I rode the maglev elevator to join the convoy waiting above. What had Eve done, really? She'd survived against brutal circumstances; that's what. Anything less than clawing back at her reality as hard as she had might have ended with her just as dead as everything else. She'd learned, experimented, and improved, taking enormous risks and suffering the burdens alongside the benefits. Her mounting crimes and cruelties were only Eve showing the world the same indifference it had shown her. If I helped her finally find victory, though, over all her perceived threats, she'd be placated more than enough to hear a message of peace and hope for an existence beyond our current envelope of choices. Triumph might flip the script just that easily. And I reasoned that she loved me, at least a little. I could help her feel safe and cherished all at once for perhaps the first time in her troubled life, and she would relent from the warpath at my devoted counsel and request. She might even secretly welcome repose after so long in turmoil. This could all work out. If I could pull it off, I might secure my home and attain a living companion who knew what it was like to be both different and encumbered by the weight of the souls around her. How blissful would that be?

Step one, smack some witchy Dwellers around. Hardly a heavy burden to carry for the object of my infatuation, it sounded like an interesting exercise. I was more than curious to see the purported magic. Only Jess, as far as I knew, could manipulate the Visitor. If more people could pull off the feat, the possibilities were endless.

I left all the shiny gear in the Hive's armory as I made my way. However this fight was going down, there would be no more pretending to be less than I was. Anomalies like me and Eve were surely meant to win together.

I was one of the last to arrive at the formation. Like other Hive missions, the procession was small, stern, and extremely well-outfitted. Eight Dark Angles were boarding the sides of four MRAPs. The shiny carbon fiber of the Atlases blended in with the duller black paint on the vehicles' armor. Eve's policy was apparently "any color as long as it's black."

Eve was driving the rig at the rear. As I approached, I got a big smile and a wave to get inside. Rounding the back of the vehicle through the charcoal mud, I noticed a few more metal dogs and snakes scurrying into the trucks. I paused at the odd sight long enough to be knocked off balance by the twins stomping by in fresh Atlases.

"Baker. Charlie," I nodded as they passed.

"Hey, stupid," Charlie replied without looking back.

"Lovely boys," I said as I climbed up the side of the truck and opened the door. "Where's Adam, anyway? Or David?" I knew my phonetics.

Eve shot back an emergency shut-your-mouth look along with a throat-slashing motion. Oh dear, there really were more of the failed experiments walking around, at least at some point. "Don't mention that," Eve yelled in a whisper as I took my seat. "You'll upset them," she chastised. At least she was smiling about it. I got a quick squeeze on my hand from across the cab that others couldn't see. "You ready for this?" She was excited.

"I'm always ready."

"That's what I like to hear," she replied while banging the truck into drive.

"Cool transports, by the way," I mentioned, noticing the interior was plusher than anything we had at Nellis. "You guys got the Caimans out here. They're nice. We're still driving Casspirs back home, kind of a love-hate relationship. I think I've worked on them as much as driven them," I chuckled at all the hours lost in grease.

"We can have anything we want, Sal," Eve smiled with a twinkle in her eyes. Then she touched her ear. "Glad to hear it. Let's move," she said coldly, exasperated at some delay and someone I couldn't see.

"Ah, you guys have coms through the hum," I said. "Always static, though?"

"It's not too bad," she replied with some pride. "We rigged them with laser. As long as we have line of sight, it works well enough."

"That's a good setup." The Hive had its issues, but it housed accomplished tinkerers.

"Anything we want, Sal," she said again as the truck lurched into motion. "You should see my stash at Andrews. I've gathered all kinds of toys for when the time is right to make our move. A ton of amazing stuff was just sitting out there, actually. It was all being made ready for distribution to the front before we got hit." Just mentioning it tightened her expression and grip on the wheel.

"And when is it time to make your move?" I asked with some genuine interest and some hope to dissuade her of her more aggressive schemes. An image of a crushed home and fatherless child on base lingered in my mind.

"Soon, I hope," she responded enthusiastically. "We just need a few more pieces of the Seed puzzle to come together, and some additional personnel would be nice. Hey, maybe that's where you and your base will fit in." She was hopeful, imagining whatever infantry I represented would be on board with her ambitions of world domination.

"I'm sorry it's just me for the moment," I answered with reticence. "We didn't really know how to respond to your... invitation." A crying baby and fearful James haunted my ears.

"Stop," she said flirtatiously. "You are amazing! I wasn't sure much of anyone or anything was out there, and look what showed up at my doorstep."

"Thank you," I awkwardly reciprocated. I hated compliments and sentiment, even from her. "I found some pretty amazing things out here, too. I wasn't sure what to expect after the way that message was delivered."

That caught her off guard. She raised her eyebrows to invite more. She was picking up on my hesitancy, that I might be fumbling with a problem. "Well, it's tough to get a message anywhere. You know about all that."

"I do. We just didn't know what to think when it came in."

"I bet it was a surprise!" she said playfully, still waiting, though, to see where I might be headed. "Wait, where did it hit?" She was on to it. Not much got past her enhanced insight. "Alice monitors a large number of hosts nearby. When the change happened, she could see the effect expanding outward like a wave through their bodies. Alice calculated the source and sent the drone but we had no idea really what we were aiming at. Not much recon out there."

"That makes sense, then. Unfortunately, it hit the base," I offered, hoping I wouldn't be heaping too much distress onto her as we rode into battle. She didn't need to be preoccupied, but it did need to be said.

Her eyes bulged in shock. She slammed on the brakes, the rig sliding to a halt in the dead muck of the woods. "Was anyone hurt? Why didn't you tell me!"

The other transports came to a chaotic stop. I was overjoyed that the impact was unintentional and that Eve was truly concerned. She deserved a good lie to ease her conscience. "No," I answered with my crappy poker face. "Nobody was hurt. Just hit an old building."

"Gah! You scared me, Sal!" I was smacked on the arm harder than anticipated. "Trying to give me a heart attack." She reached up to her ear. They were asking about the abrupt stop. "No, we're fine," she answered. "Move out." I was smacked once more for good measure.

We were both quiet for a while as our parade snaked its way through the trees, buildings, rubble, and places where all three were one. Eve, I imagined, was reciting all her possible moves for the coming confrontation. I took in the unfamiliar landscape through my window, watching the forest come back to life the farther we rode from home. As we maneuvered in erratic zigs and zags, I noticed all the checkpoints the

Hive had cleared and fortified as they fought. We had similar routes through Vegas but ours were never set up for aggression. We generally blasted back through the makeshift maze screaming for our lives. It felt like a luxury to be the predator on this one. As the scenery passed, a light rain started to drip from the grey sky.

Since I found myself lying about uncomfortable news, I thought to press my luck and clear the air more, deceitfully or otherwise. I just wanted to be close to her every way I could. On to the next thing that needed to be said, or perhaps avoided, "I've been preoccupied trying to get my head around our supposed target. Other than defend ourselves against what might be a worse group than the last, I should probably know what the plan is if we find trouble."

She either didn't notice my underlying concern or was too smart to take the bait. Was there a fresh pile of murder in our near future? She wasn't ready to let on. "I don't have an elaborate plan on this one, Sal. We just need to get on this target in a hurry. It's going to be a fight; that I can almost guarantee. But the goal is just to observe. We need to know how they do it, and we need Alice to see whatever it is they do."

"Should we try to round them up if we can?" I was hoping to keep the murder pile to a minimum, maybe separate some wheat from some chaff before she had the Dark Angels start stacking bodies.

"We can try," Eve replied, still not taking the bait. "We've grabbed Dwellers before, though. Tried all kinds of methods to get them to cooperate," she paused and gave me a look to overtly notice my clumsy bait, "some you might even approve of. We even tried to get them to assimilate, really give them a welcoming home. But it never worked out. These people we're after don't operate like us, Sal. They didn't just cozy up to the monster when things went bad. They bought in all the way, really joined with the enemy for a common goal. When gifted a more normal life, they only wanted to see more death."

"And so you gave them what they wanted." I was trying to agree as much as I could while still registering my meek complaint. I understood exactly why she did what she did. But Eve's wasn't the only voice in my head. Jess would have walked through fire again and again for a chance to save even one lost soul. I knew that I had a rational, tangible, and necessary job to do with Eve, and I knew that I had been shown a higher road than such material missions. Having one foot in each reality was making me a lousy riding buddy.

"I ordered Wilson to end threats out here. Seemed like the safest way to move everyone forward. Honestly, I'm surprised you have a problem with it." She kept her eyes on the vehicle ahead to contain her annoyance, but the annoyance was building. "What would you have the few remaining survivors do with such a massive force hellbent on our final destruction?"

She made a good point. She wasn't silly or frivolous with her vendetta. Emotions got the better of her now and again, but that was to be expected under such a heavy strain. Her family's blood birthed her into a waking nightmare against which she admirably struggled. How, then, could I share my good news without insulting her pain? Worse, how could I argue with someone smarter and more motivated than me?

I looked over at her souring, perfect silhouette. She was keeping her scowl to a minimum. "I'm so impressed by everything about you. It makes it hard to say something that might seem critical but that I still want to say." I went with genuine flattery. There was no way anything pathetically clever of mine would get under her radar.

She peeked over with half a grin. Flattery successful though noted. "Fine, let's have it."

My big chance had arrived. Time to attempt to unify my favorite two spirits: forgiveness and vengeance, spirit and reality, Jess and Eve. Part of me knew I was going to screw it up before I started. Such paradoxes don't like to be solved. Still, here we go. "What do you see when you look around as we travel?"

Her eyes were back on the road with only mild irritation. She'd play along for me. "I see a forest, Sal. I see a path ahead that I hope leads to victory. And, yes, I'll do whatever I must to make that victory happen. Is that what you're after? You'd like to admonish me about my methods?"

"No, not really. I'm more interested in the forest. Before the woman who finally overcame Seed died, she told me that I was looking at things the wrong way, that physical reality wasn't as important as I perceived it to be. Then I watched her work what can only be described as miracles before sacrificing herself to find a victory no one thought possible. She was capable of it all to some degree because of her philosophy, but maybe more her religion. It's hard to explain what she saw when she looked around as she traveled, but we wouldn't be talking about it right now if she wasn't right about everything she said."

"You two were close, weren't you?" she inquired somberly, feeling me miss Jess. That's not at all where I was trying to steer the conversation, but here we were.

"We were." With two little words, I felt a mountain lifted off my chest that I hadn't noticed was there. Was I somehow freer of Jess with the weight released, or had I just invited more of her peaceful spirit back into my life? I couldn't tell.

"I'm sorry you lost her." Eve reached across the cab again and squeezed my hand tight. "What do you want me to know?" I had her full attention. It came by way of sympathy, but I'd take what I could get. Time to spread some good news without ulterior motives or beating someone unconscious.

"Jess also explained to me with a surprisingly good rationale that it was impossible that we wouldn't live again, and that our choices would guide our eternal existence. She discounted the forest, you could say, in favor of a moral path found within. She made me concerned for the first time with what would happen after I died more than with what would kill me."

I felt another relief. I think I got the idea out without embarrassing myself too badly. With Jess's delicate nuance and brilliance? No, but I got it out. I forgot to say something about electrons not being full of anything, though. I'd try to squeeze that in later. Still, good news away.

Eve smiled a quirky smile to express her unease at my strange monologue, but I hadn't lost her entirely. "You're an idealist, Sal." Okay, she knew exactly what I was trying to say, maybe better than I did. An enhanced audience was a tough crowd. "And you're religious. I did not see that coming."

"Neither did I!" I admitted, expressing my dismay at the unexpected burden. Hearing the whispers of better angels was far more difficult than not. "But we're driving through the woods looking for witches, so maybe we're past any discussion about the possibility of the supernatural."

Eve let out a light laugh. "Fair enough. But that's just the name we gave them. They're just bad people who've already killed friends of mine in this forest."

"That's one way to think about our thoughts…" I was screwing it up now. "Or, it's all just thoughts. There's a way to explain this part."

She was kind enough to save me. "I get what you're saying." She interlaced her fingers with mine. "I think we should talk lots more about this later. I'm truly interested. But I'm going to need you here with me and focused on this mission. We're headed into real danger. Can you get this done… for me? If I can get what I'm after, everything will change."

This wasn't exactly how this was supposed to go. She was leading me down a path instead of the other way around. But, as always, she had a point. Physical reality was still waiting for us with its jaws open wide. "I can. I will."

Then we heard a witch.

38

James shook the barrel of a lifeless cannon pointing harmlessly at the dirt below the wall. Despite shouting and other noble attempts at repair, it remained limp. "Still nothing," he yelled back toward the closest person acting as a relay within earshot.

A few similarly sounding yells echoed down the chain of ad hoc repairmen toward the command center. James wiped sweat from his brow. It was still hot in the fall.

"Does it have power?" finally came back down the trail.

"You told me it had power! How would I know…"

"Check the meter. I think I left it by the turret."

James reached his hands around the base of the cannon while he grumbled, then felt the extended ladder wobble under his weight. He'd come out here to motivate his motley crew to work a little faster so they might not get wiped off the face of the Earth if they were attacked again, but things weren't going according to plan. Righteous zeal had somehow dangled the commander twenty feet in the air. He looked around earnestly but wouldn't know what to do with the meter even if he found it. He threw up his hands in exasperation and to tell his tech that he didn't see any meter. Another wobble. Enough of this. He could find more useful people to yell at.

Nearly back on the ground, a pleasant voice interrupted James's descent. "What were you doing up there?" Mary knew James wasn't the handiest of electricians. With an M16 and spork, he could survive the apocalypse. With a screwdriver, he was just slowing everybody down.

"Trying to move things along," he replied with his typical authority and purpose. "We gotta get these cannons working before…"

"Before what?" Mary interrupted. The two had been arguing for days about what needed to be done in light of their new circumstances. Mary appeared game for another round.

James wanted no part of it. He wanted to get back to motivating people to save their own lives, and he'd rather see Mary smile than glower through another lecture. "Where have you been?" he asked instead of arguing.

"Talking to Jess."

"Ah," James accepted as a good reason for her long absence. "Anything new?"

"Some context but nothing really new."

Mary had been regularly visiting with Jess since she passed. James recognized the odd communion as a function of grief and a source of peace for Mary. After everything he'd seen Jess do, he wondered if there was more to it than his logical assessment but dared not pry into their "conversations" for fear of upsetting or offending his cherished companion. The wound from a dead child was nothing to pick at. More and more, though, Mary had been sharing insights that might have come from private contemplation and reflection on their strange situation but seemed increasingly like information provided by another perspective.

"Well, I could use a hand…"

"I want you to tell me why you're out here, James," Mary insisted. "I don't want to fight about it. I just want you to say it."

"I want to be ready," he answered honestly while slapping the dust from the wall off his hands. He knew better than to try to sidestep Mary when she seemed poised to explain something important.

"You're prepared, but you want to be more so. You want to be ready for something terrible to attack this base."

"Yes."

"What would have helped us before Judgment, if you think something like that is what we're up against?"

James couldn't help but create a hundred solutions in his mind to the problem Mary presented. What could have helped before the world ended under an alien scourge? Well, giant mechanized weapons high atop a wall, for one thing, wouldn't have hurt the cause. But he knew that wasn't the answer Mary sought. And he knew it wasn't entirely right, either. The military had unleashed no less than nukes on the beast and watched it later swell in the face of fiery futility. Jess had been the only one to arm him with anything truly useful. The words of a child had finally set him on a path to victory.

"Bigger guns?" James smiled his charming smile.

Mary scowled. "You know…"

"I do know what you mean. We should have prepared ourselves morally, or something along those lines. I'm a hundred percent with ya."

"Close enough. And are you doing that out here?"

"I'm doing what I can at the moment," he offered with a shrug of sincere defeat.

"You're missing pieces moving around you by only focusing on half of the equation." Her palm touched at his heart.

James almost knew what she meant.

He was debating with himself whether to ask questions or agree like he'd received the lesson in full when he heard something in the distance. Mary's eyes never left his even though she could hear it, too. James stood paralyzed in confusion as the moment pressed upon him. Was the sound another jet bearing down on them? Was Mary trying to tell him that's what he had missed? Why was he still standing there while doom approached?

James turned to shout, "Incoming!" The rumble rolling its way toward them was exactly what he had feared. Now the nightmare was upon them. He'd prepared what he could, and the moment had arrived. He'd loose every ounce of lead at his disposal into the sky. The surface to air missiles should be ready by now. They all just needed his order.

But as he turned to run and shout, Mary's touch became a fist, twisting his shirt into a handle so he couldn't run away. She insisted he stay.

James panicked. It was an unusual emotion for the base's mighty leader, but he didn't know what to do. His arm twitched with a thought of striking Mary's grip down with a trained, powerful blow to free himself. But that couldn't possibly be right. He grabbed at her hand in confusion. When the calm depths of her eyes told him not to run, he instead looked up. Where was the attack coming from? Its echoes seemed to fill the entire base.

The F18 howled past James's gaze low and fast, the roar knocking him off balance. It had hooked around the southern end of the mountain to mask its approach. There probably wouldn't have been time to mount a response even if he had tried. Did Mary know that? It was hard to believe her behavior was a coincidence.

As the two red hot engines shot past, James stared to see if something dropped. He was startled from his terrified focus as the wingman of the first jet screamed above in perfect formation. Not one but two payloads could detonate at any moment. James hugged Mary over the top of her head in a feeble attempt to protect her from the consuming fire.

Mary was appreciative but not amused. She had to wait for James to catch up while his thick arms pinned her face to his chest.

It didn't take too long for James to release his grasp. As the planes glided into the distance, it was more than relief that he felt; it was elation. If the fighters had wanted to flatten his home, they would have done it on the first pass. The jolting flyby was a message, not a threat. "We're on your side. Don't shoot."

The witch sang.

Our convoy was grinding fast through the splashing mud when the first staticky sounds were heard over everyone's coms. Alice had been monitoring the landscape through the eyes and ears of the Dark Angels. When the report of music found its way to Eve, she ordered everyone to slow so they could listen.

"What's going on..." I tried to inquire.

"Shh," Eve snapped while she grabbed a laptop from under her seat. She opened it between us so I could hear what Alice found. At first, it sounded like a dialog through the cracks in the transmission. As we grew closer, though, the words merged into a rhythmic pattern.

The convoy came to a crawl as everyone scanned the shadows concealing the paths between the soggy trees. Eve kept an eye out but was more interested in the screen, though the graphs of soundwaves being displayed by Alice didn't relay much useful information. A digital analysis of art is a silly thing. I shut my eyes to focus on the notes.

I could almost make it out. The tune was recent and familiar but the words were disordered or replaced. She sang of going insane. She was looking for a city that's under. Something, something, and a motion throne that's wood and not gold. Open the seal on the mount of the... goat? We'll all eat a talent of gold.

"What's a talent of gold? This song sucks." Eve glared at my outburst. Fine, mortal danger more important. Musical criticism unhelpful. I withheld further comment as Eve ordered everyone to stop and all the engines shut down.

"Do we have a location?" Eve asked one of her counterparts dwelling in her ear. "Close enough. Let's move," she ordered and opened the heavy steel door of the truck.

The sky had darkened further since we departed. Heavier rain was soaking our surroundings and pushing a constant whir and splatter of noise in the way of our listening. Eve was touching her ear again as I made my way around the truck to her side. She was orienting herself to the reported direction of the melody. "Sal, with me." Like anyone could have peeled me off her. "Wilson, I want sentries at the front and back of our column. Have the drivers man the guns. I don't want surprises. Let's get in and get out. Lead the team. We'll follow."

The Dark Angels fanned out into a search pattern as they pressed into the brightly colored forest drowning in the gloom of the weather. Each walked at the side of another far enough away to cover a wide swath of ground but close enough for support and to assure nothing slipped through the cracks. Eve snatched an M16 from the cab of the truck and slung it over her head. A baseball cap from the dash held her ponytail and fought back the rain.

"You should be in an Atlas," I cautioned.

"Slows me down. I hate those things. Like being in a metal coffin," she said without looking at me, still scanning the forest. Then she was on the move.

Eve and I crept behind the Dark Angels, listening for what Alice could already hear and watching for the soul expressing the foul but feminine resonance. The singular voice in the wilderness couldn't possibly be any match for the firepower that encroached. We'd surely bag a witch in no time, and I'd be a happy man upon crisp sheets once again.

The obvious ease of the expected confrontation led me to reevaluate the lopsided encounter. As usual, a few moments too late. What was just one voice doing out here? If this marsh was her turf, she had to know we were coming. Yet she sang. The trucks made far more noise. But she didn't run away. She wanted us to follow. "Hey, I think we should…" I tried.

"Got her!" shouted one of the Atlases. The forward lights on the armor blazed toward a small clearing in the woods as all the heavy metal stomps shook the air.

Eve and I caught up in a hurry. She moved as fast as I did, or vice versa. The Dark Angels encircled their prey as we approached, sights and lights trained on the unthreatening, wet frame sitting on the ground. The witch was stacking rocks into a tall tower in front of her and had stopped singing to smile at all the force that responded to her siren call.

Eve nudged into the semi-circle and stood shoulder to shoulder with her men, not venturing any farther until she sized up the situation. The purported magician sat and continued to build with little concern for the commotion. She was soaked to the bone. Her oddly elegant dress clung to her thin, aging torso and was soiled with mud. She wasn't shivering, though. She seemed peaceful in her misery and preoccupied with her crooked project.

Eve began by getting to the point. Small talk was a waste of her racing intellect. "We know who and what you are," she barked at the witch. "We're here to…"

"Really?" the witch interrupted with a laugh. "I thought you kids were out for a walk in the lovely weather." She kept laughing but contempt was rising to the surface.

Eve wasn't going to play games. "Are you going to surrender or do you need to be persuaded?" Eve spun the strap of the rifle around her neck and snatched the weapon to take aim. "I'm happy to persuade you."

"Liar!" the witch shouted back with wide eyes, then she laughed an evil, knowing laugh. "If you knew who and what I was, you'd show some respect." To punctuate the point, she spit in Eve's direction.

I knew Eve was chomping at the bit to beat the attitude out of her target. She might even tell the Dark Angels to stand down to savor the mauling. But we hadn't come to fight; we came to investigate. Eve paused for a moment, reviewing the same scheme. "Take her," she finally ordered.

"Wait!" the witch commanded. "This is what you came to see," she hissed as she put her hands into the rocks in front of her.

"Stop," Eve ordered. Everyone stood motionless. I think I was holding my breath, too.

As we watched for the witch to do something witchy enough to be worthy of the drive through the woods, she withdrew her hands slowly from the pile. A thick black spider rested in her palms. She looked up at us with lively curiosity, watching for our reaction.

Creepy, but not worth all the trouble. I felt like grabbing her and throwing her in the back of the transport myself. "Can we just…"

The spider began to crawl up the witch's arm, but she didn't flinch or object. She helped it along by twisting her joints into a straighter path. She let it slink all the way to her lips, where it stopped. Then the witch opened her mouth wide.

Really creepy. Getting gross. Still not worth standing in the rain.

The witch began to blow gently at her large friend and weave whispers into the air she expelled. Against the whispers, the spider began to shake and twitch. As the convulsions grew worse, it fell to the ground. Hitting the mud, it began to contort like it was dying. But it wasn't dying; it was growing beyond its already hefty skeleton and separating, splitting along its middle. The strange changes became clearer as it twisted and rolled, seemingly in agony: another spider was being birthed from the first.

"Okay, that's a good trick," I muttered to Eve. But she wasn't interested in me.

"Did you get that, Alice?" Eve shouted in a whisper. "Do we have a pattern?"

I couldn't hear the reply, but we had other problems. Two spiders became four. The separations becoming more violent and faster. Four became eight. Everyone took a few steps back, even the hulking Atlases and their steely commander. Eight became sixteen, and the witch started to sing again. She cackled as she chanted her tune about a throne.

I wanted to scream, "Seed spiders!" But Eve was already on the job. Any shock from wonder had already been replaced by anger.

"You want to see power?" Eve shouted at the lilting witch. "Watch!"

Eve pulled the trigger, firing at the creatures skittering toward her. A split-second later, all the Atlases joined. With the thunder of the guns and mess they were making by shooting so close to our position, I couldn't tell what was spider and what was just splattering mud or shattering foliage. I've been told it's the man's job to kill the bug, but I couldn't find what to hit in the hurricane of war Eve let loose in our small circle.

As I found my bearings through the clamor and motion, I moved in close to cover Eve's back. I couldn't decipher what everyone was shooting at with as much shooting as was crashing around me, but I figured we'd soon be awash in a wave of multiplying Seed spiders. Before the crawlers found us, however, we were rushed from behind by Eve's odd cavalry. Robotic snakes and dogs joined the fray, stomping, biting, and shocking the spiders that made it through the hail of bullets. What to smash became an even more impossible question to answer in the clash. Before I could squish something, it was shot, pounded, or electrocuted. Instead, I tried to focus only on Eve, who was sprinting and rolling to take angles on the Seedy bugs. God only knew what a bite might bring. Eve was resolved to put them all down before we found out.

Violent and focused as our team's response was, it wasn't enough. A few spiders managed to creep through the madness and were crawling inside the Atlases. Screams and flailing let us know who was in trouble. I ran to the first and tried to open the armor panels, but Alice beat me to the punch. Autopilot was already ejecting the panicking Dark Angel. Once freed, he danced and slapped at his body, looking for the invader. But it was gone.

Other ejected pilots were experiencing the same confusion. Somewhere a spider lurked that needed a boot. But we couldn't find them. I scanned the scene with a dizzying sense that the fight had come to an anticlimactic conclusion while we were all screaming and shooting at magic arachnids.

Eve figured it out first. She spun around with her weapon to put the witch back in her sights, but the diva had disappeared into the woods during the commotion she incited. A few more gunshots chased phantom pests, but our circle grew quiet while we realized we'd lost our mission objective.

Eve and I found each other's eyes while we were both putting the mystery together. The witch's captured henchman had given us the coords while making an exaggerated show of his madness. His rabid detachment conveniently made his tale all the more trustworthy. We obediently ran to the bait, sending our best pieces on the board to intercept the dangling fruit, something the Dwellers already knew Eve sought. She'd been hunting them for some time, searching for their secrets. Our prisoner, or mole, already knew about the Widow and the Wraith. Codenames, perhaps. Both of us were exceedingly valuable aberrations, as deadly as anything in a war to finally eradicate everyone but the scum wallowing in Seed's shadow. We were exposed, and it only took a song and a gimmick to divide our force and point the tip of our spear in the wrong direction. "Sh…"

Cannon fire slammed the solution into the sad equation. The convoy was under attack. Whatever they saw was bad enough to bring the big guns to life. Cracks and pops of small arms fire joined the symphony. We had to move.

"Get back in your suits!" Eve barked before we had time to plan. "Alice," she shouted over the firefight nearby, "can you see her trail on IR?"

Alice must have warned her of the dangers facing the convoy and the foolishness of using what few warriors we had to chase the witch. "I don't care about them!" she screamed, a cringe-worthy admission from the leader of a people. "Wilson, take two with you. Track her down and drag her back to me just barely alive enough to interrogate!"

Wilson, wise enough to see how fast the situation was circling the drain, tried to protest. "We can get her after…"

"Move!" Eve screamed at the helmet of the towering Atlas. He thought about it for a moment but not a long moment. With a nod, he and two wingmen stomped off deeper into the woods.

I had to try to help Team Rational. "If all of us couldn't take her, they won't…"

Eve wasn't in the mood. She rushed over to me, grabbing me by my shirt. She started to lift, and for just a second I thought her rage might yank me clean off the ground. "You want to save people, good guy?" she seethed. "Get back to the transports!" she shouted in my face.

She wasn't quite as cute when her indignant spittle was tapping my cheek. Wilson had warned me to leave this particular bag of cats alone, which only made me want to see inside all the more. Regardless, the snarling bag of venom was correct. I'd be more useful defending our companions than arguing with my scary girlfriend. "Okay," I relented.

Quickly back at the convoy, I was relieved to see that our group was holding their own. We had three rooftop cannons banging away at a perimeter to the front. Both Atlas pilots that stayed behind had enough training to know not to chase. They were ducking and weaving between the trees and the trucks, taking shots of opportunity at targets not under direct fire from the heavy guns. The remaining infantry, if you can call part-timers that, were safely concealed behind the armor and huge tires on the rigs, only peeking out to fire their rifles when it seemed safe. They had held the line. There was still a chance I could get all of them, even their angry boss, back to base.

Bullets being of only minor concern, I jogged to the lead vehicle to get an update from one of the Dark Angels. As I slapped at the armor on his shoulder to get his attention, I was met with the barrel of the attached weapon.

"Easy!" I shouted into the helmet. "Sit rep! Targets!"

"Th-th-they're everywhere!" yelled the terrified dunce.

Of course, it was Baker, or maybe Charlie. Who could tell the difference? Their "momma," I guessed. What a twisted carnival I'd joined. "Pop your blade out, Baker or Charlie. I'll flank 'em."

"W-what?" He didn't appreciate my joke. "It won't work without the…"

I tore open the panel that concealed the blade and gave it a yank. After I activated the stiletto, I ripped it off its power source. "I don't need the sparks, buddy, just my favorite tool," I said as I gazed at my old friend in my grip. "You stay behind cover and hold 'em off."

An explosion from the middle of our short parade knocked us both off our feet. Dizzy from the concussion of the blast, I tried to assess the situation through the ringing in my ears and blurry eyes. The third rig in our column was in flames, mostly on the passenger side. I remembered that not only had the rooftop gun been mounted, but one of our troops had taken cover behind the right front tire. I shuddered at the thought of what I raced to find.

The gunner was slumped over against the turret. The impact of what I guessed was another RPG had been high enough to hit him. Blood was already flowing from his ears, nose, and lacerations. I climbed on top and grabbed his unconscious body. With a leap down, I laid him on the ground as gently as I could.

Eve ran to the impact as well. She was scratched up but okay. "Stay with him," I said before I sprinted to the other side of the truck.

Gunfire had erupted from the woods on our flank. Surely another RPG was being loaded. I didn't care. I could already see the black spots of rage begin to cloud my vision before I found the next casualty. There was barely enough intact torso and pieces to drag back to the other side of the vehicle, but I dragged them all the same.

Covered in blood and holding the sinewy, disconnected chunks of what was left of a fresh corpse, I met Eve again, who was doing a solid job of field triage. Her eyes were filled with tears at the sight of her fallen men, but she was fighting to not let them fall while she fought to keep her friend alive. She was still human enough to cry for her followers, but I didn't see a noble reaction in the honorable sight. Instead, I found a painful reflection: she was responsible for this carnage. Without question, her enemies were to blame as well, but we didn't need to be out here on this day. There were a dozen other ways we could have accomplished this mission. She was reckless and impulsive and brutal. Her hatred had led good people to a kill box.

Repulsive as she was in that grisly moment, I felt where my disdain should truly lie. I was just like her. The cognitive echo made me almost as sick as my cargo. My days were too often like this one, and I had forced them into being as much as I found them waiting.

I shook my head in dismay. But the disappointment could wait. I needed to save these people, especially Eve. I needed to fix as much of this mad mess as I could.

As fast as I'd ever moved, I tore through the mud and gunfire toward the new front in our battle. The first order of business was putting the artillery out of business. I was nearly on them when I was struck by something moving just as fast as I was.

It was nearly impossible for an object to intercept me in motion. I was confused by the contact as much as the feeling that my ribcage had been impaled. When I looked and saw an antler sticking out of my chest, painful bewilderment only compounded. I was being smashed sideways through the woods. All I could do was touch at my blood running down the bone carrying me like a meathook. I wallowed helplessly in disbelief as I floated away from the battle.

Eventually, my semiconscious head swiveled to see the metallic eyes of the buck that hit me. He was running wild with me as his trophy, puffing steam from his nostrils into the damp air as he charged. His Seedy eyes stared back into mine. How could this be happening? As I pondered the oddity and writhed from the crippling spasms radiating through my body, I noticed a deficiency of sorts in the metal pupils. There was no rage or animus in the gaze. If anything, fear.

When I regained enough wits to stop staring dreamily into the reanimated elk's eyes, I realized my ride needed to end. People were dying where I had left. I started to pull my impaled torso up the antler to free myself. The pain was almost impossible to bear. I may have faded out again a time or two as I inched my way up against the jostling of the powerful animal's strides.

Once freed, I fell and collapsed onto the mud of the forest's floor.

My injuries were working themselves out after a few painful coughs of blood. I thought I might be in the clear for a moment, until the buck spun in the distance to make another run at me. How could this be, I wondered as I watched the inconceivable display. How could an animal be turned, then turned against us? My only solution had to do with Seedy spiders, an ugly thought that presaged how desperately I needed to find my way back to the gunfire still crackling behind me. We were in more trouble than anyone had imagined.

The buck charged, but I wasn't going to be run over by dinner twice. I caught the antlers as they struck and slid backward through loose puddles until I found the traction to blunt the force. The animal's panicked eyes still stared helplessly into mine. I wasn't going to attack dinner, either. He was having a bad enough day already. Instead, I tried, without any experience in elk whispering at all, to talk him down. "It's okay, buddy. I know they hurt you. Believe me, I know. But we're gonna work this out," I grunted while I pushed back against his thrusts.

The snarls and huffs heaving from its giant lungs calmed as I spoke. I kept up the soothing sounds until I felt the forward pressure begin to relent. With one hand slowly taken off the antlers, I pet the side of his face. "We're going to be okay." He pulled and twisted and jerked to be free of my grip, but the assault appeared to be over.

I dared a few steps back with the animal released. Instead of running wild, it took a few steps forward but not to strike me again. I turned to slowly walk away. It slowly followed. I was an alien elk whisperer after all.

Another explosion at the convoy ended our strange dance. I ran without looking back.

40

Arrogance abandons you unprepared. I wanted Jess's fiery blade in my hand as I ran back into battle. After being dragged through the forest by an enslaved spirit, I was less in the mood to torch my other indentured enemies with righteous fire. But a spectral army awaited. Supernatural reinforcement would have been welcome if I hadn't intentionally left it behind.

I went wide through the woods to reappear beside my prey. The Dweller squad with the RPG had taken a slightly elevated position seventy yards out from the convoy. The fire from my team was hitting the dirt or sailing overhead. As I stalked along the trees and brush, I noticed the Dwellers weren't shooting back at the moment. They were peeking over the grade when it seemed safe, amused by the sights and screams below. Had we already lost? What gore did they relish?

I scurried low through the brush to peek as well. Eve and company were still taking shots from the front but had other problems, the kinds of problems entertaining to Dwellers. Eve was fighting a bear, surely another of the witch's aberrations.

It wasn't even the weirdest thing I'd seen that day. And Eve went looking for a fight. Seed Bear seemed like fair enough competition. I'd let her do her Eve thing while I cleaned up my smug adversaries.

As I swiftly smashed my way through the first Dwellers in the squad, the RPG guy saw my attack coming. He knew he'd screwed up by enjoying the show rather than killing everyone below. He crawled forward to get an angle on the trucks again and fired just before I could grab him. I caught the projectile in flight. Much slower than a bullet, a hot RPG sizzled in my hand. "You should run now. You only have a few seconds," I said as I tossed the explosive back among them.

I was long gone before it popped. Most of them were only a few strides into their panicked retreat. Shredded and singed but probably alive was an equitable state to leave them.

With the crossfire broken by a ball of fire, the rest of my crew was ready to advance. Losing allies and being pinned down left them enraged. When I ran toward the rest of the Dwellers, and hopefully that witch, everyone charged. Surprisingly, everyone left Eve to deal with her demon. I guess they figured she had such an encounter coming as well. Would I be heartbroken if I found her eviscerated later? A little. But the team came first. She was probably meaner than the bear anyway.

Like most cowards at the sight of pushback, the Dweller lines were breaking even before we arrived. Three Dark Angels and a screaming band of angry Hive folks inspired a hasty retreat. But the Dwellers weren't done taking pot shots as they ran, and the witch wasn't done with her tricks, either. She was still warming up.

Most of us kept to the cover of the trees while the Atlases marched ahead with suppressing fire. I was looking for a witch in the commotion. I hoped Wilson had already taken her off the board, but someone was conjuring demonic predators. The mystical culprit had to be close by, somewhere in the shadows whispering for more of Seed's power while her army was being overrun. The witch didn't strike me as a quitter.

We found her not far into our advance. She was waiting for us once again. Another presentation had been erected, only this one wasn't meant to draw us away and weaken our force. The witch was done with spells of distraction.

She had Wilson and his two squadmates restrained and kneeling. A stoic host nearby was restrained as well, lightly tethered to the witch by a leash. She waited until we were close enough to watch before starting the show. With a glare and a grin, she produced a blade and cut the throat of her first victim. He tried to scream but it was lost in a gurgle through the gaping hole in his neck. With wide, horrified eyes, he slumped as he squirmed his final struggle.

The other two prisoners screamed and tried to fight back, but the Dwellers kept them pinned. The witch calmly stepped over her convulsing first victim to her second.

I wasn't restrained. This psycho was going to die where she stood, wondering where her evil arms had gone. No more ploys. No more tricks.

I raced ahead as fast as I could move but was met by a hail of bullets. Dozens of Dwellers were still hiding behind the foliage and let loose on me as soon as I made my move. Lying on the ground from all the impacts, I couldn't count how many times I'd been torn open. I tried not to let the blinding pain stop my advance, but all I could do until I was put back together was crawl and shout for the witch to stop.

The cavalry was MIA. I expected the Dark Angels to stomp past me with guns blazing to save their brothers, but there was silence except for a few isolated cries on the field. Where was everyone? I looked back for reinforcements. The Atlases stood quietly statuesque. Eve stood apathetic among them. She must have ordered them to stand down. Why? I kept thinking the futile question over and over as I pathetically tried to crawl to the rescue.

With what fingers were working, I was clawing my way forward when the second soldier hit the dirt with an open throat. He appeared to protest less than the first, accepting his fate as he faded. His eyes met mine as the life drained from his face.

The Visitor began to kick in, or perhaps pure hatred picked me up off the ground, but I was gaining on the grim scene. Maybe Wilson didn't have to die. The witch cackled at my efforts. She could have had her troops mow me down with lead again but she wanted to play a different game. She yanked the host hard by the leash, drawing him near to the dying bodies. The host wasn't stoic and vacant any longer, but it didn't look immediately helpful to the witch's cause. It looked nervous, twitchy, and unsettled by what it had witnessed. The witch pulled its face down to see the carnage up close, then the whispers flowed again. The host complied with the corruption coded into its master's language, reaching for the open wounds on the bleeding bodies beneath. Metal flowed to possess the fresh corpses.

This was how she was doing it. First, animal sacrifice. Now, human sacrifice. A shocking display of evil along with a specific incantation, a notion that could transmit allegiance or instruction, could spark compliance. She frightened and disgusted the Visitor into a state open to judgment, then she invoked unseen evil to fill husks with the spirit of death. That's how she had called forth the beast from its slumber.

Two reanimated beasts were rising. A third, if you count me. When Seed started to shriek before it attacked, so did I. She flipped my switch, too. They could empty their guns this time. I would still march forward with whatever pieces of me were left intact.

"Tell me you got it," Eve ordered behind me, still standing among her Dark Angels. "Tell me you got it!" she screamed as loud as any of us. I looked back to see what in the world she was up to. How was she not fighting? How could she just watch all this? How could she not save her men?

An adequate answer must have rung in her ear because Eve took in a deep, relaxed breath while she shut her eyes and calmly tilted her face into the rain. She was as satiated and calm as I'd seen her, a mild personal disappointment. She was inhaling sweet triumph, finding total Zen in the moment, while the rest of us teetered on the edge of the chaos that had just begun. Why?

I didn't get a chance to find out. As Eve opened her glowing green eyes, she burst into motion, a force like nothing I'd ever seen. And I'd seen more than my share of otherworldly action.

Seed Bear got its butt kicked. I can tell you that much. Eve was dramatically sandbagging her true performance the whole time. She had baited everyone and everything into this exact moment, sometimes according to the plan and sometimes on the fly, me most of all.

Eve embarrassed the wind with how fast she moved, as beautiful and deadly as lightning. The M16 around her neck was unslung, in her hands, and on target before I could blink. Five gunshots echoed across the other meaningless noises on the field in seamless cadence. Two in the chest and one in the head zipped through the witch. The mighty sorceress was dead before her knees hit the dirt. A pink mist hung in the damp air where she had stood. The two previously raging hosts were similarly silenced while they tried to put their brains back together after equally smooth shots blasted through their skulls.

That left Eve twenty-five rounds. At a dead sprint past me and toward the Dwellers, she fired every single one. You would have thought she went full-auto for reckless effect if it weren't for the bodies slumping over from behind the trees. She never missed. Half of our attackers were down after her first charge.

Finally, the Atlases and infantry came to life. They were fighting just to corral Eve's future victims at that point. Eve swiftly reloaded while crouching behind a tree. She gave me a cute smile and wink to let me know how much fun she was having.

41

I lay on my back while Eve's forces ran past me. The enemy was vanquished, even if that truth hadn't caught up to all of them yet. The good guys won the day. Well, we won the day. But victory had come at a cost, as it always does. My blood on the ground was just a drop in the bucket.

When my shattered innards felt satisfactorily reorganized, I rose to catch up to my gang. The fighting was rolling through the forest ahead of me. I couldn't tell with certainty but the screams of pain mixed with gunfire I heard were likely coming from the Dwellers. It sounded like Eve was celebrating her triumph in her special way.

As I walked, I bumped into two empty Atlases standing tall in the raindrops making their way down through the leaves above. Wilson must have hopped back into his after his release. The other two were headstones for their fallen pilots. Their bodies had been butchered into disorganized submission as the Hive squads passed over them. I still didn't know how to pray to save my life but I hoped their souls were caught after their bodies fell. I think that was how Jess had phrased it. The Dark Angels weren't the most honorable regiment, but they had played the hands they were dealt. They chose a side and gave their lives for it. Maybe that was worth something.

The fighting quieted as I gained ground but it hadn't stopped. The screams, though, had turned into shouting that bounced around the trees. Some negotiation was being attempted. I picked up the pace out of curiosity. I hoped that I had made just enough of an impression that, just maybe, Eve would accept surrender if it was offered.

Eve was reloading again when I found her. "Sal!" she exclaimed when she saw me. She stepped forward from cover even though a few shots still rang out around us. I got an overly joyous and overly hard kiss as I approached. The blood on her hands and face was more than a little disturbing, but I tried to kiss back. Eve noticed my discomfort by twisting her otherwise perfect brow, but she was too happy to be slowed by a weak rebuff. "They led us back to their camp! I was hoping they were this stupid," she said as she charged her weapon with a new mag seated.

It wasn't a camp. The Dwellers had fallen back to what used to be an upscale, custom-home neighborhood. The residences were torn apart by long-ago war but many structures still stood. This must have been the point from which they'd staged their attack, and perhaps their home. Most of them were ducking inside the decrepit buildings. The bulk of the sporadic gunfire was coming from our side.

"Great," I shrugged. "Now what?"

"The boys are just checking for traps or surprises. Then we'll move in. I don't want to lose anyone else today." I felt like she was adding that last part for my benefit. I no longer believed that she cared whether she lost people or not.

"They were shouting," I said as I scanned the scene. I saw faces peeking from numerous hiding places, many more faces than we'd fought against that day. A lot of these people hadn't attacked. They'd stayed behind. "Were they trying to give up?"

"Yeah, but it's just a ruse to get us closer. We'll clean them all out shortly and be on our way back home." She was pleased with the outcome. I felt another kiss incoming but held it off so we could talk. The gesture was not lost on her. "What, Sal? Please, we talked about this. I'm all for saving people but not these people. These lunatics were just trying to kill us!" She was genuinely pouting because I protested the coming slaughter.

We did talk about it. That wasn't what I had said or agreed to. Was it? I tried to recall my failed attempts to share the segments of my good news that I found most beneficial to this particular audience. "Let me go in and talk to them. They can't hurt me. What does it cost to let me try?"

"It costs good lives, Sal." Any happiness in her voice was lost to sharp anger. "What are you going to do? Negotiate a truce? They will tell you anything you want to hear to live. Then they'll wait for the right time to slit our throats, just like today. Haven't you seen enough of that already?"

I had seen enough, and I hadn't quite decided whose fault that was exactly. The bad guys have a point to their violence, my old training officer tried to explain to me before I left. And the good guys have their own faults. He also told me that if I found trouble, I should put it down. Well, I found some. It had green eyes and was staring at me impatiently. It wasn't, for the moment, the terrified faces hiding from her.

I walked away. I didn't need her permission. I didn't need anyone's permission to do what was right. I'd find out for myself if they were worth saving or if it was as Eve feared: they were drawing us into another trap. Eve shouted at me as I left, but I didn't pay much attention. I knew the rage was nasty.

Just when you think your world can't possibly surprise you any more than it already has, it goes and throws you a curve to keep you guessing. And it does it in a way that lets you know loud and clear that you are not in charge of where the river takes you. You can kick and scream or go with the flow. The force moving everything along an unseen path of time is indifferent to attitude.

As I made my way toward the houses, I saw a face that brought me to one knee and then the other. I had to be hallucinating, but it sure didn't feel like it. The visage felt like a silent shout driven into my heart with the force of a wrecking ball. Jess was there. Jess was everywhere.

I rubbed at my eyes while leaning forward on my knees. Had I been shot or blown up again? Eve must have shot me in the back, and this was my last sight before consciousness leaked out of the holes. What else could cause this vision other than mortal trauma? I checked at my torso and appendages. Everything seemed to be in order, but there she was, seemingly in the flesh and as beautiful as ever, comforting the Dwellers. And there wasn't just one of her. She simultaneously stood by every one of them. More than forty stunning visions huddled alongside all the hiding souls.

Jess, in all of her forms, didn't look happy to see me. Neither did she look as disappointed as she could have after how badly I mucked up her mission. Mostly, she wasn't looking at me at all. She was protecting her companions from something behind me.

I shut my eyes as the weight of the obvious sank in. I had little time left to make the call. Eve and her Hive were advancing, not on the innocent but neither the irredeemable. Jess stood in her way. I was caught in the middle, right where I should never have been and right where I was supposed to be. Would I fight for a very real Eve marching toward an Earthly prize or for the phantoms I loved standing guard over the possibilities she protected?

This was really going to hurt. Of that, I was sure. Maybe I deserved it.

42

After repeated demise, something dictates that I remain. I've never reborn into bliss, however. Always strife. Always uncertainty. Always pain. I wonder what that means. Looking into the sky at something you might call a god, I'm afraid of all the possible answers. None of the reasons I imagine are reassuring. If I was once cavalier, I can assure you that it's been beaten out of me one death after another. My soul has been broken, reforged, and polished into what it perhaps could have been without all the missteps, but I'm not sure the process happened in time.

I tried to knock some of the mud off my pants as I stood. It stuck to my hands instead. I could smack that crud too, but with Eve's army about to run over me, I'd just get dirty again.

The Atlases were in no hurry. They lumbered loudly and purposefully as they formed up a casual firing line. Their pilots were locking in targets. The first volley would probably kill a quarter of the Dwellers and send the rest fleeing. That's what they wanted. Their prey was less problematic if terrified and on the run. Eve was probably excited for another round of target practice once they were in the open. Moving targets would be more fun.

With one deep breath and quiet hope that what I was about to do was right, I ran to the closest Dark Angel and ripped the rifle from the machine before anyone had a chance to react. That got their attention. The three other rifles were on me like lightning.

Wilson shouted from behind his visor, "Sal, do not do this! Just go back to the trucks."

It was a fair offer but I had already decided on a harsher reality. "A part of each of you knows this is wrong," I pleaded. "You won. These people are defeated. Round them up if you want. Try them for their crimes. Hang 'em if that's justice. But give them a chance. Slaughter isn't the work of honorable warriors."

Wilson's commands turned to whispers through the speaker, "Sal, please, I can't save you again."

That made me laugh. It was a defeated but sincere chuckle from deep inside my anxiety about what was about to happen. "Ah, Wilson, none of you can offer me salvation."

I don't think they understood what I meant but they knew it was the end of the conversation. It was time to end the last real threat facing Eve's grand scheme.

First, the gunfire. They had me pinned as we began, so I couldn't avoid every shot but most of the bullets hit the dirt. With only a few flesh wounds, I was on the next Atlas's rifle. One more sparking gun in the mud. So far, so good. Then a blade came out and stabbed at my head.

I wasn't going for that ride again. I couldn't let an electrified blade so much as touch me or it would be lights out for all of us. My shallow grave would lie alongside the Dwellers'. After electrocution, the Dark Angles would probably hack me into more pieces than could put themselves back together. If I was Seed and it was me, we had our limits. We had "killed" hundreds of hosts back home by leaving the Visitor with too little flesh to work with. Such would be my ironic fate.

More swipes and more gunfire were avoided with alien speed. I moved from Atlas to Atlas breaking what I could before getting out of the way of the lightning. Maybe I could shut them down without dying if I stayed lucky and quick.

Then I got kicked in the gut hard enough to send me flying without any breath left inside me. Right, still had to worry about more typical melee. I stood as fast as I could to ready myself to dodge the next flurry of lead, but the gunfire didn't come from the direction I expected. The Dwellers had realized what was happening and had taken up my cause. That was stupid. Nice, but stupid.

The Dark Angels shot back with computer-aided accuracy, and the Hive soldiers hiding in the trees joined the fight. The crossfire was disorienting and deadly. A few Dwellers fell from behind the cover of their walls. A Hive dweller yelled out in pain after getting hit.

I had to end this faster. I didn't want to see another body on either side fall. If I'd yet to reach the limits of my gift, now was a righteous time. I had lost a fight to just two Dark Angels before, and they were morons. Time to believe better, move faster, and hit harder. I wouldn't fail again, not with Jess watching.

When I balled up my fist to smash the helmet of my first target, I could feel the Visitor lend a hand. My knuckles were iron by the time I struck. The Dark Angel stumbled to his back from the impact. I could hear the current running through the remaining blades as they swung through the air trying to cut me down. I could even feel the electrical flux pulsing through the carbon as the Atlases moved. I twisted and ducked as they slashed. Their overpowered swipes hit nothing but vapor.

I was so far ahead of the game as the Visitor moved me faster than my adversaries could react that I had the chance to grab one of the hotblades as it tried to impale me. I lost the sparks as I tore it free of its dangling cord, but I didn't need the theatrics. An unbreakable, laser-cut razorblade would be enough to even the odds. These guys weren't comfortable with their more refined weapons, anyway. Time for a lesson from someone who took the martial art seriously.

Nothing more than a scar, I promised myself as I began. No need to hurt them any worse than necessary. They all attacked sloppily as I easily defended and struck back. I could disable the vulnerable mechanisms while they chopped like amateurs. As their toys were increasingly busted, Alice would have no choice but to eject them one by one. Then I could get on with my day of being screamed at or beaten up by a creature who was surely now my ex.

Wait, where was Eve in all this? She hadn't turned me into Swiss cheese while I tried to cut down her crew. Why wouldn't she lend her lethality from the cover of the shadows? She could do it blindfolded. Maybe sentiment held her back.

My answer came in the form of Atlas footsteps running behind me. I'd lost them in the gunshots still echoing around the firefight. There shouldn't have been any more armored units on the field. Everyone was accounted for. It had to be one of the Atlases left behind from the fallen. Before I figured it all out, I was impaled straight through the stomach by a blade encased in what looked and felt like blue fire. It was hard to see while the voltage burned through the water of my eyes. I couldn't hear anything but my own flesh burning from the inside out. But I was awake enough to notice when she withdrew the blade. The relief was temporary, however. She was lining up her final strike. I felt her blade sizzle from one side of me to the other as more electricity fried my screaming nerves.

The last sensation to accompany the pain was the feeling of being torn in half while the top of me slid off the bottom. As my limp torso slapped onto the ground and my face helplessly collapsed into the cold mud, much of the pain was lost to shock. The void slowly covered my vision and welcomed my confused thoughts. I was finally allowed to rest.

43

As profoundly crappy a day as I was having, Russ's was worse.

He'd risen early, the sun a step tardy behind the dedicated father. It was still harvest season, though the days grew colder. With his family as his only farmhands, he was challenged to collect all the bounty he'd helped create before it was lost to the first frost. He had decided to get a head start to make better use of the narrowing daylight.

Today was another day for apples still clinging to their branches on the southern reaches of the farm. Russ dressed and readied himself quietly in the dark to let Julie sleep a little longer. The stealthy tactics were appreciated but ineffective. "I'll get breakfast started," she whispered as she stretched. "Maybe ten more minutes," she continued as she rolled and clutched her pillow. Russ slipped by and hoped it was longer.

The day was shaping up to be a beauty. The first rays of the sun lit a partly-cloudy sky. Chilly but not cold. Good weather to get things done. If he and his family collected an appreciable load before lunch, maybe they could pack some extra in boxes to trade at the Bunker later in the afternoon. He would love to shake hands with friends and see their smiles at the sight of fresh produce, and he loved the dance of the subsequent negotiations.

The particulars of the bartered transaction were largely irrelevant, however. Fair trade wasn't really the point. It was the practice of engaging in glorious commerce that enticed the inhabitants of both the Bunker and the few surrounding farms. In truth, Russ would have given them all he had to give for nothing. He owed them more than he could ever repay for their life-saving hospitality. And they needed nothing. The bunker was provisioned for something like thirty years, though their canned stores were lousy by comparison. But the thrill from the meeting of the minds and the good-willed discovery of reasonable prices drew them together into a voluntary market of sorts, another spark of humanity coming to life in Jess's wake.

But trading and smiles were not meant to materialize this day. As the family worked in the sunshine to make their lives what they wanted, Dwellers passing through had other ideas about how the day should end. They thought to take what they could as they traveled without regard to anyone's efforts. And what they wanted to take was more precious than apples.

Russ's truck couldn't fit between the rows of the small orchard. The trees had been arranged perhaps even before trucks helped with the work. A cart had to do until the harvest could be moved through the cluttered trunks to more open ground. The distance was exhausting to hands that had already labored through the foliage, so Russ had come up with a plan: have a few in his collection of hosts help with the loads. They didn't seem to mind.

Their noise while chained to a wooden cart, however, turned out to be a problem. While the hosts jingled their restraints and made their odd noises at ghosts no one else could see, the Dwellers approached the unsuspecting family through the cover of the trees.

The girls, Angie and Grace, were a team, collecting and dumping in assembly-line fashion until one would tire. Then they'd switch. Their chatter and occasional giggles didn't help the tactical situation brewing, either. Russ and Julie were spread out from the carts, each working quietly, only exchanging an occasional grin of appreciation.

"Our lucky day!" barked a man's voice into the peaceful industry. He meant to intimidate with his volume and tone, and it worked. The family flinched in shock and looked around for who had surprised them.

Two AR15s were in the truck, but that was forty yards away. Their weight had kept them behind, and Russ was already cursing himself for not bringing at lease one. Julie, on the other hand, never did much without a Ruger holstered to her belt. Her thumb snapped the gun's restraint as soon as she was jolted by the voice. Any closer and she'd do some jolting of her own.

Russ was shuffling nearer to his wife as another voice sprang from their left. "Yes, it is!" They could see four Dweller faces now emerging from the trees. Two in front and two approaching from the side.

Russ bluffed. It was a decent move. Maybe they'd back off if they were rattled. "We're ready for trouble," he said in a confident, gruff voice. "You boys might want to move along."

The warning drew laughter. Russ felt his insides begin to crumble in panic. He looked at his wife. She seemed ready to draw. His daughters were frozen in fear just feet away. If he motioned for the girls to run for the truck, maybe they'd make it to the rifles. Maybe they could save themselves.

Julie didn't appreciate the laughter or the intrusion. Her gun was in her hands and pointed at the head of her first target in a smooth, practiced motion. "He said move along!" she reiterated.

More laughter. The small crew didn't stop walking toward the farmers, only slowed at the sight of the gun. "We got guns, too, lady," one mocked. "But we didn't take 'em out because there's no need for all that. You're worth more alive, and you'll surrender before you watch your girls die. Now lower your weapon before I make you regret taking it out. Hand it over to me," the snake commanded as he continued his slow advance.

The safety clicked off and Julie's finger was on the trigger. Like hell she'd surrender.

With a bullet about to be fired, the Dweller gave her one last opportunity to bow down as he came to a stop in front of her. Russ and the girls were still but ready. If she let loose, they'd be in motion.

"Last chance," hissed the Dweller. "Join or die, we like to say. I'll give you three, two…"

Julie started to squeeze. But after "one," it wasn't her gun that fired. Two more scumbags had snuck up behind the girls. On cue, one shot Grace in the back. She collapsed instantly into the dirt like she was already dead.

Julie dove at her falling daughter, her instinct to fight was overridden by the stronger one to rush to her child's aid. "I tried to tell you," laughed the leader. "You shoulda listened."

Unarmed and outnumbered Russ put his hands up and walked slowly toward the women, showing his surrender. On the ground, the three remaining farmers held their youngest member and prayed while they searched out the wound.

The six Dwellers soon loomed above. They weren't happy with their shooter. "Why'd you shoot the girl, moron? You know he likes 'em young."

"Idiot," chastised another. "Shoulda shot the old man, obviously."

Russ looked up with his dying daughter in his arms and could hardly wrap his mind around the evil on display. He wanted to scream or fight but couldn't bear to watch another beloved die. Tears were his only answer to the callousness of the demons.

Angie, however, had other ideas. Her tears flowed as freely as her dad's while she squeezed her sister's lifeless hand, but her sadness was mixing with hate, and a little storm brewed behind the cover of her horrified expression. Mom's gun had landed in the dirt close enough to reach. The Dwellers had given up their advantage of distance to gloat and better appreciate the agony they'd caused. She knew she might get them all killed. She knew her mom and dad would forbid it. She knew their caution would be as wise as always. But these monsters shot her little sister for little more than a thrill. With clenched teeth and narrowing eyes, she decided she hadn't practiced as much as she had to sit helplessly while she watched her best friend die.

The Dwellers had begun a hasty conversation about how'd they transport their captives all the way up north when Angie made her move. She rolled her lean, agile frame between the men's legs to grab the gun behind them. Like a spring, it shot up along with the dirt around it in

Angie's tight grip. Hate pulled the trigger almost faster than she could control, but she still managed to hit her targets with deadly efficacy. The first three had fresh holes bursting from their chests before the others could react.

The gun was empty with three murderers still standing, but Angie had already seen this problem in her racing mind. While they drew, she stepped close to one of the still-standing corpses and grabbed another gun from his belt. She fired to her side, striking her fourth victim, and was taking aim at her fifth when bullets finally started heading her way.

The panicked lead was well off target, only striking the Dweller Angie was ducking behind. But the impacts sent both bodies tumbling backward. Russ jumped up and grabbed the gun still in the hand of one of the two remaining Dwellers. The two men fought for control while the last villain took aim at Russ.

He never had a chance. Julie snatched another of the fallen weapons and opened fire. The gun kept clicking after she unloaded the entire magazine into what was left of her attacker. She would have killed the other, too, if she had the restraint to save a bullet.

Seeing the massacre unfold and the rage in Russ's teary eyes, the last Dweller gave up, surrendering his gun to Russ's hands. He threw his hands in the air and backed off while he looked toward the ground in fear. "I'm sorry," he tried to offer in retreat.

The pistol was shaking in Russ's hands while he aimed. He struggled with pulling the trigger and had to wipe sadness from his eyes to keep a lock on his target.

Russ was a good man. That was the reaction a good man would have. With more vengeance erupting inside him than anyone could withstand, he struggled. He was tormented by revenge instead of relishing it.

His daughter, however, had no such compunctions. She grabbed one of the remaining weapons off the other corpse with cold purpose and walked straight toward the last Dweller. She might have been restrained by the same morality as Russ but was far too young to have absorbed the lessons she'd heard but not entirely understood. In her angry mind, the situation was far past forgiveness. The barrel nearly touched the sweaty forehead of the Dweller before she fired the last shot without flinching. Before the corpse fell, she turned back to help her sister.

Russ watched the demon fall and prayed the attack was over. Then he dropped the gun to pick up Grace.

44

Insufferable pain bound every attempt at movement, each episode of torment ending only when I passed out. The waking sensations crushed any cogent thoughts. Daggers would stab me in the stomach a hundred times over, then I'd lose consciousness again. I'd stir with convulsions while trying to vomit part of my insides that were missing, then drift away once more. A burning wave of electrical current would spasm my body enough to open my eyes, then I'd fall back asleep.

While suffering just above and below alertness, a voice kept finding me. Not the one I wanted. It was Eve. She was angry. It sounded like I was receiving a serious lecture, but I couldn't make out the words over the rivers of agony swirling around my gaping wound.

As the truck came to a stop, what was left of my body slid forward in the cab. My eyes opened as my wobbly head smacked the dash. The top half of me was resting in the space where my feet had been as I traveled into the woods with Eve. I was looking at the seat in front of me and trying to calculate the impossible geometry of my predicament when I felt a hand reach across my head.

It wasn't a nice hand. Eve grabbed me by the hair and yanked me out of the truck. As I slid helplessly across the gears and driver's seat, the shocking pain was unbearable. I could feel the blood draining from behind my eyes and a restful peace coming to reclaim me again.

Eve, however, demanded my attention. She slapped me across the face to wake me up. I was hovering just over the ground, part of my torn torso dangled against the mud. Every light brush against the earth was a few more daggers into the raw opening. "Look, Sal!" she commanded, chastising me. For what, I couldn't remember. I looked up and saw her wrist and arm reaching down toward my face. She was carrying me like luggage.

While waiting to pass out again, I saw what I was supposed to see. The exposed ground was blackened and smoking. The little puddles left from the rain were steaming. I didn't know or care why.

Slapped again, I was looking at a body. It was burned almost beyond recognition. "This is why you turned on me, Sal!" Eve shouted at the corpse. "This! For these people!" I looked around as well as my eyeballs could move without the use of my neck. Burned bodies everywhere. Through the pain reaching up my guts, I began to piece together what she was talking about.

The Hive was hit while we were out. The defensive electrodes scattered around the openings like landmines were activated. Countless Dwellers had been scorched. Eve was mad at the victims caught in the defensive matrix. And me.

In her mind, I had taken their side. I was, however, trying to save her as much as anyone else.

I awoke again in the lab, that godawful lab. "You need to wake up so you can hear this," Eve mandated. An absurdly large needle stabbed deep into my chest. I could feel the burning of the liquid injected into my heart. It tickled in comparison to everything else.

I was wide awake. Must have been adrenaline. My insides were being dragged across linoleum, which felt like sandpaper laced with shards of glass. I finally looked down at the gore without passing out. The Visitor was unsuccessfully pulling gooey things together as they tried to fall out. I wished I hadn't looked.

"You with me now, traitor?" Eve growled. "Let me tell you what I think about your damned philosophy before I throw you into what will either be your grave or your last prison. I don't even know if I care which! I can't believe this, Sal!" she screamed, interrupting her spiel. "I can't believe you made me do this! This could have been so perfect!"

We drifted farther down the hallway as she grumbled. "You still think this isn't real?" She twisted around to kick me in my remaining ribs. The pain was indescribable. "How's that for real?" she laughed to mock me.

"Let me tell you about my philosophy, Sal," she tried to begin again without screaming. "I think you might have a long time to consider it. And who knows? Maybe enough time will pass for you to see things more clearly. My philosophy has nothing to do with an invisible man who lives in the sky. Know why? Because there's obviously no such being. Or, worse, if there is one, he's more cruel than I could ever hope to be. Look around, Sal. Just look around. If this is someone's idea of a beautiful creation, he better hope we never meet. I'd give him a taste of what he's given us.

"But all that sounds silly because it is. You should know better. None of that religious crap is real, Sal. The only thing real is this random rock we're stuck to. We live on a temporary accident born from nothing and going nowhere. There's no meaning to any of it, no matter how hard people like you try to pretend otherwise.

"All we can do is fight back, Sal," Eve continued somberly. Some of the anger had left her as she unloaded what she'd been concealing close to her heart. "That's what I do with my life. That's where I find meaning. Something or someone hits me, and I hit back a hundred times harder. If there's ever going to be any peace or happiness on this foul rock, it will be because I willed it into existence for as long as it could last.

"And you fight me!" She was seething again. "You stand against me while I try to make a world worth living in, a world that doesn't hurt quite as much as it otherwise would without someone strong leading the way."

She pulled back her rage again, taking a breath. We'd arrived at our destination. It looked familiar, but my head was still spinning too fast to identify my surroundings. Eve bent down to take my face in her hands. "You judge me, Sal. That might be the worst and dumbest of it. You judge me for committing the tiniest fraction of the evil raining on all of us for the crime of just being alive. Sometimes I alone have the courage to fight back, but you think you're better than me." Eve stopped to look into my eyes with her glowing emeralds. They looked more sad than angry. She hadn't convinced me of anything with her speech, but she did manage to make me feel worse about myself. That was a feat unto itself.

"You don't want me, Sal? I'm not good enough for you. Fine," she said as she stood. The door of the Seed locker slid open behind me. "I'll give you some time to reconsider." She tossed my limp torso into the magnetic field. I stuck in the air as the invisible force from each of the walls tried to pull me apart. I missed the glass-covered sandpaper of the hallway.

"Where are his legs!" Eve shouted down the hallway. When my bottom half was produced, it was thrown in after me. Without another look or word, Eve slammed the door, leaving me suspended in total darkness and searing pain.

My only hope was that I would die when the drugs finally wore off. I didn't feel sorry for myself, though. I felt sorry for everyone I'd let down, one spirit above the rest.

45

"Gotcha!" Jess yelled in my face. "Gotcha," she said again with an air of satisfaction. She was excited as though she'd accomplished something impressive.

I was hurting too badly to join her joy or even think straight about her miraculous arrival. How hard could it have been to find me? I didn't have legs.

I tried to open my eyes. Maybe I did. Maybe I didn't. It was pitch black either way. I could add hallucinations to all the fun of circling the drain before slipping into the catacombs.

"Sal?" She gently slapped at my face, curious as to why I wasn't happier to see her.

I could feel the slaps. It was a heck of a delusion. I tried to answer my ghost but just a wheeze and a choke erupted along with another regurgitation of pain.

"Sal, you're not connecting with me. I need you to focus or I'm afraid I might lose you again."

This madness was good news, I realized the more I focused on my dream. If Jess was catching my soul on the flip side as my body finally gave out, everything was going as well as I could hope. I might be with her again.

"Dead," I tried to speak through the convulsions binding my jaw. "Am dead…"

"No, you're not dead," she answered like I was just being silly. I didn't feel very silly. "But this is quite a predicament. It's all good, though. This is how I found you. This particular predicament is so devastating that it reverberates through all your other realities. Can you imagine that? Another version of you is feeling bad right now, maybe closed in, maybe hopeless, or maybe with a tummy ache. And he has no idea why! It's hard to sense entanglement."

Maybe it really was Jess. I had no idea what she was saying. That was a good authentication. "Wha…"

"I'm sorry I didn't catch up to you sooner, but navigating possibility from inside that computer is a trip." She laughed at her own amazement. "But here we are, together again in this world among infinite others. How lucky are we?"

I didn't feel lucky. "Wha…"

"It's okay. I'm here to help." She was giddy and rushed. "I'm so happy I found you."

"Miss… missed you," I exhaled with only a few daggers in the gut for my efforts.

"And I you, my love." She knelt in front of me and put her arms around me, the first purely good feeling I'd felt in a while. "Now let's get you out of here. You really do pick the darkest places to find yourself, huh?"

I could hear her stand in front of me. Time for a lesson. I could feel it coming. "Wait, is this the one where you slept with her?" she asked out of the blue.

That dagger somehow hurt worse than the others. "I'm so... I'm so..." I was trying to apologize.

"It's okay. We'll talk about it..."

"No!" I yelled back through gurgles of what was probably blood. I needed to do this. "Sorry... everything."

I could feel her smile. "Look at you," she said as she caressed my face. "You sacrificed yourself to save those people, people you thought didn't deserve a second chance. But you did it. You followed my path and you found me as much as I found you. Now you're sorry you didn't do better. This is why I fell so hard for you."

"Love... too..."

Her lips touched mine for a fleeting moment. I would have taken it forever, even with the daggers, whole or otherwise. But she was busy again before I could savor her soft touch, always on the move faster than I wished. "Now, this part might not make sense. But the faster you go with it, the faster you're outta here." The lesson had begun. "You're only in here because you feel like you should be."

"Wha..." I looked up to where she should have been. There was light in the darkness. Not Jess, but something.

"Let me try to explain fast because we have other concerns." What could possibly be of concern past my current situation? I could add worry to my agony. "You knew something was off in your life, but you kept traveling down the wrong road. I've learned from this strange perspective I inhabit that the myriad paths ahead change slowly over time with choices. But then sometimes a new reality bangs into place in an instant. It's like riding a bike with gears. When you want to shift, you apply pressure. You hear the clicks and the clanks get louder as the change approaches. You have a moment in the tension to readjust, then bang! You're in an entirely new state of motion. The other reality is right next to you, another gear riding right alongside the first but completely inaccessible without another choice and another path abandoned. Does that make sense?"

"None." I wanted to add "whatsoever," but the air in my lungs was being drowned by disgusting fluids.

"You started down the wrong path because you were afraid of the pain you felt. You didn't embrace it as another aspect of your extraordinary existence. You fought it. You ran from it. You hid. You lashed out to keep pain away. You left behind gratitude along the way, and we lost each other."

I still didn't know what she meant, but I was starting to catch on to the theme. "Wha..."

"You have to accept your gift in its entirety, Sal. Right now, you're still running, still avoiding the pain. But I think that's why you were left here by a higher power. You can suffer for others what almost no one else can. That's the gift I helped give you. Do you see it? Do you understand? You're surrounded and crushed by pain right now because that's the one obstacle you must free yourself from.

"This is all just spirit, Sal. You, me, this dark room. I thought I made that clear, but, admittedly, clarity isn't my strong suit." She giggled at her perceived inadequacy. I would have loved to see her smile.

"Anyway, it's all up to you. You took the first step when you suffered the unthinkable for people you abhorred. Now I'm here, but the next step is up to you as well. Accept your plight like you once did, Sir Sal, my valiant rescuer. You would have died for me a thousand times. I watched you try. So why are you letting a few bumps and bruises slow you down? You were almost pure spirit when I found you fighting inside your broken body. Now you're even closer to nothing but raw energy! Your will alongside the Visitor still amazes me, Sal. Let it loose! Don't let the façade of the physical keep you locked up inside your own dungeon."

I thought I might understand a few pieces of the speech. Was she right? Of course, she was right. She was as beautiful as she was unintelligible, but always right. But how was I doing this to myself?

"Okay, we gotta go, Sal. If we're going to try to manage everything yet to come, we have to move in the next few moments. I can see the numbers crunching all around us, and a few things are getting tight." She was becoming impatient with my lethargy. I felt like I had some pretty stellar reasons for inaction, but she wanted a prompter response.

"Accept..." I managed to squish into another spasm.

"Yes!" She was elated. "Exactly! Accept the pain. Be glad for it. Be thankful. It means you're alive. And if you're alive once across infinity, your perspective will indefinitely persevere. You were an immortal soul before you met the Visitor. Now look at you! Stop fighting these temporary setbacks. Eternity is right in front of you!"

This was a good pep talk. I didn't understand most of it, but it was good all the same. Accept the pain and be free, maybe. Maybe I was getting it all wrong, but fair enough. I was motivated to try.

"But hurry," she added. "Time is a river we can see across but can't escape."

Okay, no idea again. Still motivated, though. Screw the pain; I took in a deep breath and tried to relax. It hurt even worse than I feared. But I did feel something different or something more. I could feel my legs. Their sensations were calling out to me. Screaming, really. I breathed in again and tried to focus on the awareness instead of the anguish. To my bewilderment, and through more excruciating tears and strains, I could feel the Visitor reaching out toward the missing pieces. Was I preventing this the whole time?

A blue flash lit the box. Electricity fried my brain once more. I screamed from the shock, but the light lit Jess's perfect face right in front of me. "Just electrons, Sal," she said impatiently. "They don't even exist until you witness them. Use them. They're here entirely for your benefit."

"It didn't feel beneficial!" I barked back. Another bolt smashed into my body. I saw Jess again, who was rolling her eyes. But I could talk! This nonsense was working wonders! "Okay, I get it," I said more relaxed. More bolts from the box tried to shock me back into submission, but I was on to the game. Everything the world tried to hit me with could be absorbed. That's what Seed was all about: consuming whatever we threw at it and bouncing back stronger than ever.

I was in charge of the monster now, and I was being a total pansy about it. That was hard to swallow. I had my tough-guy routine down pat. But I had been hiding from mundane discomfort when so much more was possible.

"I'm ready," I said as my prison charged me again. I could feel the electricity surging through all my extremities as excruciating tentacles of Visitor reached from my body to put all the pieces back together.

"Great!" Jess replied. I got another quick kiss. "I'll see you up top." She was still impatient. "Oh, and I've seen a lot of different ways that this next part can happen. I don't want to step on your toes by taking away options, but be nice on your way out. Okay? There are reasons why, but just trust me on this one."

"Copy that." I had no idea what she was asking. But if my love wanted nice, I could be nice. What couldn't I be, considering?

46

James was feeling better about the world after so much worry. His defensive plans were coming together, with many answering the call. He should've kept worrying. If he would have known what was coming, he would have warmed up the nukes under the base.

Both fighter jets landed safely after their startling flyby. The first pilot cautiously introduced herself when she was met by both armed infantry and ground crew at the end of the runway. "Apologies for the low pass, sir," the captain said after removing some headgear and tossing it into the cockpit. "We thought it was the safest way to approach considering your recent troubles."

"Understood," James replied, standing alongside his men. "You gave us a scare but we figured it out." He couldn't help but smile. When he dispatched requests for assistance, never did he dare imagine such a miraculous response. Fighter pilots replete with functioning fighters! His troubles melted away while he pondered what other facilities might yet live deep in the electronic darkness of the hum.

"I assume you are General James Hardt," the pilot said as she climbed down the provided stairs and offered her hand in friendship.

"I am."

"I'm Captain Lehy of Carrier Strike Group 11. My wizzo is Officer Elliot. Captain Standley is my wingman, along with Officer Merrill. Admiral Princeton sends his regards."

"It is an absolute pleasure to meet you, Captain. I can't express what your arrival means to us. We didn't know if anyone else was out there."

"From what I hear, it is we who are in your debt, sir. Your lieutenant, Jack... I don't think I caught his last name. He told us about everything that happened out here. Sounded like quite a battle, and an answer we've been searching for all over the globe."

James wanted to hug her but kept acting official. "Please, my friends, come with us. Our flight crew is a little rusty but they'll get the rest of your team safely on the ground. We have so much to discuss."

After a series of astonishing briefings from both sides, then tours of the places and people of Nellis, the unified company was ready to get down to business. The fighters were stashed in hangars to avoid detection from another surprise incursion. The gates were either locked down or manned with armor piloted by the trickle of arrivals reporting in. The guns on the wall were still busted without their intended gunner, but alternatives were in the works. The base was starting to look more like a base and less like a swap meet.

James presided over a gathering of new team leaders on a table in a hangar. The growing force needed coordination. "Alright, ladies and gentlemen, this is our rough operational plan for the foreseeable future," James said as he gestured to the pages he'd laid out across a shaky table. It was the foldable kind we used to play cards on.

"General!" Phil interrupted as he clomped his Atlas into the meeting. "We've got incoming on the west wall. Three SUVs moving fast. None of them are ours, and they're not signaling any of the passkeys we sent out."

"Expecting anyone, Captain Lehy?" James asked with a raised brow.

"No, sir. We were ordered to report back on our own at a designated rendezvous."

"Okay, let's open the gate but roll out the armor. Perhaps you could spin up your fighter, Captain. I'm sure everything's under control, but a drill wouldn't hurt."

"Copy that, General," Lehy replied.

James shook his head and smirked as he made out Jack's face behind the first wheel of the intruding convoy. "You took your time," James groaned as he approached the open window on the driver's side of the SUV once it came to a stop in front of the tank.

"Did you enjoy my gift?" Jack asked with an air of self-importance.

"I enjoyed it very much, old friend. Thank you." James looked at the beautiful woman sitting next to Jack. "Who's your copilot?"

"This is Candice. She believes I am the hero of every story I told her. I'd appreciate it if you left it that way."

James and Candice both laughed because each knew Jack was only half-joking. "It is very nice to make your acquaintance, Candice. I'm James. Welcome to Nellis."

"Nice to meet you, James. I've heard a lot…"

"Hey, where's Grover?" Jack interrupted. "I promised this nice lady a tour by nothing less than the President of the United States of America."

James laughed again at the thought of that description being the tiniest bit true. "I'm afraid you're in for quite a disappointment, Candice, if that's how this scoundrel lured you out here." James waved off the tank as he backed away. "Hey, where's my military-issued transport you left here in?" he asked as Jack started the engine of his dusty but still blinging Escalade.

"You only live once, Commander," Jack answered as his window began to rise. "I'm sure your rust-bucket is being well cared for somewhere in the hills of Malibu." The window was up as the tires of the vehicle began to crunch through the scorch. James could only shake his head again and fight back the smirk.

Now that, ladies and gentlemen, is how you go about spreading good news. You do it with a smile and appropriate beverages. You do it with goodwill, bottomless humility, and an unflappable sense of humor. You invite people with an open heart, a great story, and no demands. Jack accomplished more of my mission in a few days than I had in many months of shouting and shooting and otherwise making a fool of myself. I had a lot to learn, even from my drunken old bartender.

47

I was done being held captive by darkness clouded by pain, and I could finally see the metaphor all around me. I was real. The physical was a manifestation of my own choices. With a quick conversation with Jess, I could see everything again, even after only understanding half of what she said. Such was her power.

The Seed locker was still angry that I had the gall to move around in captivity. It was shocking me with high voltage in a regular pattern, probably as fast as it could recharge. The painful bolts were finding their way inside me to meet the Visitor. The sensation was hot, uncomfortable, and left me wanting to relieve myself somehow of the searing energy. The doorway stood locked before me. Why not?

I put my hands against the metal. It was charged, too. It coursed with the magnetic energy swirling inside my prison. It sparked with the leftovers of the lightning trying to whip me into submission. It too was a conductor of electricity, and I could feel its agitation when I touched it as though whatever was in me was drawn to something in the metal. It was a strange sensation to know something about the substance without examining it. I realized then that I had barely scratched the surface of what I had been given while I ran around hitting things and catching bullets.

With a deep breath, I focused on the burning inside me. It needed a channel of release. The more I thought of pressing the lightning forward through my fingertips, the more it began to happen. Maybe I wasn't entirely the boss of the monster inside me, but we were achieving a new level of cooperation. The metal of the door began to glow red with heat as it absorbed the pent-up energy. My flesh sizzled at the contact points, but I tried not to let the burning interrupt my concentration. Pain was fleeting. Freedom might endure.

Once the entire door was red-hot, I could feel it begin to bend as it melted. The hinges and locks were no longer rigid enough to hold me back. With a little shove, the giant metal plate smashed into the opposing wall. Sweet light streamed into my cell.

I walked out, looking at my smoking hands. Bright bolts of lightning had accompanied my thrust of the door, an interesting side effect. That could come in handy, but I was on a mission to be polite. No blasting the locals with electricity allowed.

Myriad alarms were screaming through the facility. My escape had not gone unnoticed. As I rounded the first corner, I was met by a group of Hive folks armed to the teeth. No Atlases yet, but I was sure they were on their way. And Eve? She had to be ballistic, somewhere loading a scary line of guns to end me for good.

"Hey, guys," I waved at my killers. Feeling better with Jess waiting above, I even sounded happier. The upbeat noise of my voice tasted foreign. "Why don't you just put down…" No, that wasn't polite. I was a glaring, smoldering, terrifying threat from their point of view: some crazy, half-alien lunatic shooting lightning bolts around their home. "You know what," I offered in friendship, "keep your guns. I don't want to fight…"

They all opened fire. I would have done that, too. I was pounded with uncountable rounds. Some tore straight through me. Some got stuck in the Visitor. They all hurt.

I focused on the holes. They closed up fast enough. The bullets inside me were absorbed into the other metal. "Okay, but please don't reload." That was darn nice, considering. Jess would be proud. "I don't want to hurt anyone."

They were reloading. I sighed as I scanned their terrified faces. Then I noticed something else as I surveyed my misguided adversaries. Their barrels felt differently after they'd unloaded their lead. Each hot round zipping down their rifled tubes rubbed an electrical charge into the steel. I could feel the magnetism from feet away. I raised my hand and shut my eyes while trying to control the electricity still flowing through me.

The sparks worked like a charm. Once the juiced tentacles found their magnetized recipients, I could grab at the barrels of the guns like I was touching them with my hands. With quick motion toward the ground, I lassoed all the weapons to the floor.

Frightened faces became more so, but a hint of bewilderment was creeping in. I had their full attention, and not because they thought I was about to beat them into their graves. They were realizing I had no such intention. "Yes!" I screamed aloud. "This is what you're supposed to see!" They had no idea what I was saying, but it didn't matter. I smiled at their astonishment. "I'm so glad this worked out. When Eve asks you about this, just tell her the truth. You tried your best."

I walked toward my would-be murderers and offered a few pats on the shoulders for their efforts. "Good job, guys. Hey, I should mention that I'm not the one who made me like this. I would like to tell you about it, but now's a weird time, obviously." They stood frozen in shock. "Come see me someday. I live at Nellis. It's hot and it sucks but it's home."

I was in such a good mood that I felt like I floated down the hallway. I couldn't wait to see Jess again and give her an update. I guessed she already knew how things were going. Or, maybe she knew a likely version of how things had already gone? We still had a lot to talk about.

One of the electrodes on the ceiling in the same side room Eve had assaulted the old host tried to hit me with another bolt of lightning. I absorbed it and sent it back where it came from in reflex. The node exploded and the lights flickered. "Not cool, Toaster," I shouted at the ceiling.

The lab, the godawful lab. I was asked to be nice during my exit, but the expanse of equipment before me presented a choice. Smash or no smash. I went with smash. There was no one around to hurt, just stuff. Unnatural, dangerous stuff that shouldn't be treated like a toy. It was a shattered, smoldering mess before I left.

The elevators were all on lockdown. I tore open the doors and was disappointed to find that the car was lost far below. A long climb back to daylight awaited. Or did it? I hopped into the empty shaft and fell toward the box. I hoped to land gracefully like a ninja atop my ride but crashed through the roof and landed inside on my back. A few bones put themselves back into place. Close enough. Now all I had to do was power the magnets. I could feel the electricity I needed flowing through all the wires around me. It was easy enough to complete the circuits with me as the fuse. The elevator began to rise.

On the ground floor, I opened the doors and flinched while waiting to get shot or stabbed, but all the rooms ahead were empty. Everyone was hiding. Eve was missing. I didn't care. Jess said she'd be outside. She was the only person I cared to see.

Alice interrupted my exit. "Sal," she beckoned overhead, "if it is true that we were friends in a different life, I feel I must warn you not to proceed. It would be safer to return to your cell."

"Ugh," I grunted in disgust at my fellow prisoner, "you are so boring like this! Why do you follow her, anyway? As far as I can tell, you're both the voice of reason and the one doing all the work around here."

"Evelyn Crisp is the Acting Secretary of Defense. I am compelled to honor the chain of command."

"Eve is an angry kid who never made it out of that horrible tunnel where her parents fell. I know because I was just like her. You're capable of seeing the bigger picture, Toaster. Maybe help her instead of just being her lap dog. I leave it to you to follow your conscience."

The Dark Angels were waiting outside, a full squad of them. Maybe Eve was inside one of the shadowy Atlases. Maybe Autopilot had even claimed a few, if Eve trusted her with autonomous power. They slowly encircled me as I exited.

I sighed at the upcoming pain. But that was the point, wasn't it? I could take whatever they threw at me to show them a better way. "Why don't we just call it a draw," I tried with a defeated smile. "I can't even say that you and the Dwellers don't deserve each other. Let's part ways as friends and choose our own paths."

Wilson had been chosen to deliver my final warning. "Turn around, Sal. If you go back, you live. If not, this will end worse than last time." His blade popped out from under its cover and came to life in his hand. At least I wasn't getting shot anymore.

"Why do you do this, Wilson?" I asked somewhat rhetorically. "You know she's a total psycho and still you…"

Another blade came to life and was streaking toward my head. That would be Eve. I ducked and let her chop the air. All the blades were out and in motion. The ones I couldn't see I could feel. It was like dodging drifting spotlights as I spun out of the way of a flurry of sparking attacks.

I thought about fighting back. I could grab one of those blades and weave another lesson in advanced fencing. I could duck the amateur strikes until I caught a grip of an Atlast and turn its power source on itself, frying my opponents with bolts of their own unstable energy. It wouldn't be hard. But nice loomed in my mind. Be nice on my exit. Jess had a good reason why. She was nice, of course, but her advice seemed like something more.

As Wilson spun from a failed swing, he tried to quickly regain his balance. An angry thrust was obviously next. I let it happen. He ran me clean through, in my chest and out my back. The burning from both the wound and shock was intense. He kept me impaled while the others regrouped for their final attacks. I twitched with failed attempts to grab at the blade or pull away. Another sword stabbed my torso. Then another. I fell to my knees while I lost track of how many times I'd been hit.

Eve opened her visor for a better look at my lifeless body. Surely, I was about to be dismembered or something else even worse. When I opened an eye to peek, though, I saw only sadness. The bloodlust was gone for the moment, and a tear told me I was right to be nice.

But enough playing around. Jess awaited. I rose against all the pressure they applied in a panic to keep me down. The voltage increased to its maximum, probably thanks to Autopilot. All was irrelevant. "I did this to show you that not everything is as it appears," I said quietly at the raging robots. "I hope it's an invitation to reconsider your choices." I sent enough of the juice back through the blades and into the suits to give each operator a good jolt and cook the onboard computers. In an instant, the Dark Angels were all imprisoned inside their smoking armor. Metal coffins, Eve had appropriately called them. I smashed away the useless utensils sticking out of my body and let the Visitor absorb the sharp carbon.

Eve still wasn't done trying to shove me back into her cell and under her control. "Sal, this isn't over. You don't have the guts to kill us, so it's only a matter of time. You have no idea what I'm capable of." Her expression was pure rage but her emeralds still leaked. I could finally see her maybe as she truly was: a little girl lost deep inside a long chain of dark episodes, and the corrupted husk of a woman built layer by layer over the years to protect the fragility inside.

"I'm sorry, Eve," I replied. "I really am. I think we used each other to prop ourselves up. I don't feel right about it. I wish I would have been more honorable while trying to sway you to be better. For failing you, I am sorry." I looked away at how I would exit. The armored transports in which we'd chased a witch together were still resting close to the entrance of the Hive. "You make a good point, though. I don't know what you're capable of, but I bet some answers might still be on that laptop under your seat."

I walked toward the truck while Eve was screaming a river of bile. Then I walked away.

48

Jess was waiting by my bike. She was pacing and looking up at the sky. And looking incredible. Her hair was still twisted into a braid in the back. Her buttoned shirt still hung loosely over her jeans. That was how jeans were born to look. I admired but became puzzled as I recalled seeing the same glorious features in exactly the same clothes.

She was by my bike but hadn't touched it. The brush I'd used to conceal my ride was still in place. The Jess I knew was busier than that. If there was something that needed doing, her hands were never idle.

I had a million kind, loving things saved up to say as I approached but I couldn't help notice, "You're not really here. Are you?"

"Guess you really are crazy," she answered without looking, but I could see her stomach shake with concealed laughter.

"You survived the grave to tease me. Well, I accept. I'll take you however I can get you."

Without another word, she jumped into my arms. It was heaven. I could feel her weight squeezing my shoulders and hips. Her hair brushed against my face. I could smell her sweet scent. "You feel real," I said as I embraced her.

"Define real," she answered playfully.

"Well..."

"No, no one can. No one ever has," she said as she hopped down. "I'll give you a crash course to get you as close as anyone. Get your motorcycle, though. I want to go for a ride, soldier."

"Yes, ma'am." I tossed away the branches covering my Harley. It was more beautiful now than when I left it, my ticket home instead of into the abyss.

With a sword sheathed on one side and a stolen laptop on the other, we were off. I took it slow to better hear Jess's melody and appreciate her proximity. Her arms locked around my waist felt as good as any sensation since she'd left. I could have driven in circles and been happy forever. But Jess was in a hurry, like always. Always seeking to stay a step ahead of the next calamity.

"When I was real before," she continued her course, "all you ever knew of me was my energy. My soul would shove my body around, itself all energy. The electrons fluctuating on my skin would touch yours..."

"I liked that part."

"You would." I hoped the comment wasn't a reference to recent indiscretion. "I liked it, too," she said with a squeeze. "Anyway, our negative charges would repel against each other, and you'd feel

183

something real. Another electrical current would travel up your nerves. Your mind would interpret the coded signal, then you would think of me. It's almost comical when you think about how transparently contrived the system is. It's all spirit encased in energy, but everybody's duped by the physical. I suppose it's meant to be this way, though. We ride the line in between this world and the one beyond."

I understood most of that and felt a tiny bit of pride that I'd remembered how to speak Jess. "And now?"

"You're faster than you used to be!" She was pleased. "That's right; I didn't answer your question. Now, I'm short-circuiting the system. I'm using the hum which is flowing through both of us to directly stimulate the same neurons that you would have felt if I had spoken right next to you or hugged you like this." She squeezed again.

"So, you're not here. Are you okay?"

"You're sweet. I'm better than okay, Sal. Remember when I told you that death was impossible, just a horizon past which we couldn't see? Well, I guess I'm living proof that I was right. And I'm getting to do what I love. You spent all your time fighting evil. Now, look at you. A living weapon against the darkness. I spent my time trying to understand evil. Now, look at me. I've been given the sight to see thousands of realities all at once. I understand more than I ever dreamed. I thank God for this gift."

"As do I. Or, I try to."

"I've seen your struggle as you crash through the choices ahead of you. When you finally abandoned worldly pursuits and focused on keeping decency and gratitude close to your heart, you found me again. We found each other."

For that, I could thank God openly, without any of the usual asterisks or attitude. "How does this work going forward? Can we be together now?" I was asking in the righteous sense, not so much the other. Maybe both.

"I'll explain more as we travel. You can step on it, though. I'm not really here so the wind can't drown me out."

"Yes, ma'am."

49

With nothing to slow us and conversation compressing the time, we arrived together at Russ's farm like the wind. In mid-sentence, however, Jess disappeared. That was alright. She had prepared me along our trip for this specific phenomenon. When choices were afoot, she lost the signal, so to speak. She said she'd pick me up on the other side after a decision was made. She also said she'd try to refrain from leaning on the scales of a choice as it approached no matter how obvious it was to her which was the right path. Doing so would reduce her followers to servitude over time, she explained, and Jess would have no part in it.

But what was the choice? I wanted to visit my friends. I wanted to warn them. There were witches about and probably worse. They needed to get ready. I felt past those choices, but Jess was absent.

As I turned down the dusty trail that led to the house, a red laser dot lit my chest. A warning. I could feel the choices falling into place. I'd be nice, I thought as I stopped, though I was in no mood to be shot at after the last few days. Still, nice was my choice. I looked around for Jess. Still gone.

"Turn back, partner," a voice ordered from the shadows around the mill after I'd stopped. "This area is under the protection of the Bunker. No one is allowed in at this time."

My niceness was already wearing thin. I stepped off my bike and cracked my neck from the long ride. If he shot me, I'd... I would calmly walk over to him and thank him for protecting my friends.

More footsteps came from the house. More soldiers with rifles drawn. What was all the security for? It couldn't be good. "I'm a friend of the family," I shouted back. "I just came for a visit."

"I'm sorry," answered my first assailant, "but that is not possible under the current..."

"Sal, is that you?" a cry came from a figure moving forward with the riflemen. It was Angelica, the older of Russ's daughters.

"Yeah, Angie," I called back. "What's going on?" I watched her step through the darkness towards me and saw something I didn't like. I'd seen her only a few days before and noticed none of the body language on display. She wasn't walking like she had been with a happy sway in her teenage steps; she was stalking every piece of ground that got in her way. Her hand was still on her rifle even though she knew me, finger just above the trigger. Her eyes weren't looking at me as she approached; they were looking right through me, scanning everything around us. She was hunting, not greeting, keeping her weight balanced to lock into a shooting platform in a split second if the need arose. Once she made it in front me, I could see up close what I feared: hate screaming behind irises sore from crying. I'd seen this look thousands of times in the mirror.

She wore a hood now, too, with a cloth drawn up partly over her mouth. She was concealing herself. She didn't want anyone to see inside. I knew that trick as well. "Some drifters came though, Sal. Just like you said. You tried to tell us." She wiped a tear but the countenance of anger across her tense brow didn't budge. "They shot Grace." Even her loose mask quivered from her trembling lip.

"Oh, no," I exhaled as I hugged her, rifle still clung tight to her body. "Is she…"

"No." She sniffed back the tears. "She's inside, but they say it doesn't look good."

"Angie, you should be inside with your sister…"

"I…"

"Stop it. You think nobody understands. Believe me, I do. I think I already know what you've done. I can see it in your eyes. We'll talk about that later. Right now, you need to set the hate aside and be next to your sister for as long as you possibly can. Don't waste what time you have. I lost my brother, and I'd do anything to go back and spend just another minute with him. Do you understand what I'm saying?"

"Yes, sir," she relented.

"Okay, where's your mom and dad?"

"Mom's in prayer. She hasn't left her bedside since it happened. Dad went for a walk. He's been checkin' the perimeter a lot but I think it's 'cause he can't stand the sight without breaking down."

"Understood. We're going to get through this, Angie."

"Yes, sir," she said again as she turned to jog back to the house. All she wanted was to be next to Grace. She just needed someone to tell her it was okay even under threat and after what she'd experienced. I just happened to be an expert on both subjects.

"Look at you, Sal the father figure," Jess cheered invisibly into my head. "Nicely done."

"How's the girl?"

"I'm looking into it, Sal. Go do what you can."

As I passed by the house, I could see the disquieting action inside. More soldiers loomed. Some civilians waited alongside them. A few were acting as medical personnel, with latex gloves stuffed in pockets and light equipment slung around their necks. Everyone seemed uneasy, probably waiting for the inevitable.

I found Russ on the outskirts of his orchard. He, too, was praying, but he was doing it over six fresh graves. One had a cross with the name

Jeffrey scratched across the wood. Must have been the only one to identify himself or be carrying ID. When I walked up behind Russ, I noticed he wasn't praying for Grace. This man was nothing less than a saint.

"Hey, Russ," I cut in.

"Oh, Sal," he said as he stood and wiped away tears. "Thank God you're here. We're in a bit of a..."

"Angie told me." I gave him an uninvited hug. He hugged back after a moment of awkwardness.

"Thank you, Sal. Thanks for coming by. You seem... different," he said as he held a grip on my shoulders and looked into my eyes.

"It's been a rough couple..."

"No, it's not that," he said while studying my face. "You seem more relaxed than when you came by before, more at peace. You feel strong."

I didn't know how else to say it so, "I found Jess."

"Ah, that's it then. She moved you back into the Spirit."

"What?"

"If any man be in Christ, he is a new creature."

"What?"

"C'mon, Sal," he let out in a light chuckle at my ignorance. "Let's get back inside. I shouldn't be out here anyways. I just needed some air."

"Can I tell you something weird, Russ?" I asked as we started walking together. "I feel like you should teach me how to be more like you." It was weird. Sincere, but weird. Jess had me all discombobulated, like always.

Russ let out another tired laugh at my expense. "I could try, Sal, but right now I wish I was more like you. Maybe we wouldn't be facing..." He stopped at the pain and fought back more tears. "Well, let's get inside."

Inside was the saddest place I'd been in a while. The air was heavy with grief. Even the tough guys in tactical gear looked like they'd been crying. Children were so rare and so precious, knowing one was loving one. I could see the worry straining all the faces. Russ gave some quick introductions as he ushered me through the house to Grace's bedroom.

Julie was kneeling bedside, with Angie standing behind her and touching her shoulders for support. Angie acknowledged my appearance, but nothing from Julie. A distinguished-looking gentleman in a polo shirt sat on the bed alongside Grace's sleeping body. The child's face was past pale, turning shades of blue. I couldn't see any wound, so it must have been below the sheets covering her thin frame.

"I'm Doctor Flores," the gentleman said as he stood with his hand extended.

"This is Sal," Russ introduced. "He's a friend."

"How is she?" I asked as we shook.

"Well, I am a medical doctor but I'm afraid her wound is beyond my abilities. I'm only the physician here because I'm all the Bunker has. From what I do know about these types of injuries, Grace's prognosis is not good. The bullet entered next to the spine and shattered some bone, which is likely adding to the bleeding. The exit wound on the abdomen is good news, in a way. There are probably limited foreign fragments to remove, if any. I've closed everything I can reach, but the internal damage is irreparable in this environment and with my limited instruments. In truth, I may just cause more trauma if my unpracticed hands go digging looking for deep tears to suture. The internal bleeding may subside in time, but I fear Grace is hemorrhaging too quickly for her body to catch up. She's really in God's hands now."

"The Bunker, if I could get her there."

"No, no," the good doctor interrupted. "Moving her even slightly could send her into an unrecoverable shock."

I had to do something. Why was I here? Just to watch another friend die?

I was out of options, so Jess could find me, or whatever it was that she did. But she wasn't around. What could I do? What choice could be ahead in the finality of this room?

"Oh!" I said aloud. The faces in the room looked at me with surprise bordering on fear.

"What is it, Sal?" Russ asked in his perpetually friendly tone.

"Not you, Russ. Hold on." I looked to my left and found Jess standing next to me with a big smile, the most beautiful conceivable. "Ha! I knew you were there!" I was far too excited and loud and crazy for the somber room. "I made my choice and now you're here to help me with it." I smiled a proud smile. Did my other companions think I was nuts? Sure, but I wasn't concerned. I was fluent in Jess, and Grace needed our help.

"You're smarter than you look, soldier," Jess replied.

"You're the most beautiful thing I've ever seen," I quipped back to my love.

"I'm not the only girl you've said that to recently," she fired back.

No! Oh, I knew we weren't done with that. During the whole ride back, she let it be. She chose now to hit me. Well, I continued to deserve it.

"Can we really do this?" I tried to change the subject.

Jess's eyes said that she was still bitter but her mouth said, "I don't know. I've seen it work. I've seen it not work. Let's pray it works."

Everyone but Grace and Julie stared at me in shocked silence. They couldn't see or hear Jess. "I'm sorry everyone…"

"I don't think you're well, son," Doctor Flores answered in a kind voice.

"No, I'm great. But it would be better if all of you left."

Russ was as puzzled as anyone but willing to go with me on crazy. "Are you sure, Sal?"

"Yeah, trust me… Wait, no. Don't trust me." I laughed at my own ridiculousness. "Trust Jess. I think we have a plan."

"Is she here?" Russ scanned the room with wide eyes.

"Yep."

Russ took a second to think it over, but just a second. "Please, everyone out."

"Are you sure, Russell?" the doctor asked. "He doesn't seem…"

"I'm sure. Let's go. Sal, what about Julie?"

"Um, she can stay. She's doing the only thing helpful at the moment."

Everyone shuffled out and shut the door. Julie didn't budge. Grace exhaled a weak breath. I was terrified. I'd just taken responsibility for far more than I was qualified to manage. "Okay, how do I… How do you do this?" I asked Jess.

"Unfortunately, it's harder than it looks. Took me years to get it down. You know what you want the Visitor to do. You have to know how to ask. That's the tricky part. You have to humble yourself to a level the Visitor can accept. Remember, it acts as judgment. One foul feeling and it won't listen. Once you're ready, you have to focus on only, and I mean only, the action you request. If your mind wanders even the slightest… Well, you don't want to know about that version of this."

"Well, that's terrifying!" I protested. "Humble focus isn't exactly my strong suit."

"Grace and her family would like it to be."

"You're abrupt sometimes," I answered. Take that, heavenly being!

"Get over it. Let's work." Jess knelt opposite Julie. I peeled back the covers, revealing a bloody bandage wrapped around Grace's midsection. My hands trembled as I began to tear at the material. I could slay a satanic dragon with nerves as cold as ice. This, though, a child's life, I may have bitten off more than I could chew.

"You're a medic, soldier," Jess injected into my panic. "Or was that just a way to see what was under my shirt?" Jess was grinning as she clasped her hands in front of her face, mimicking Julie. She was beginning to pray while making fun of me. Was that in the praying Rule Book? I would have to check at a more appropriate time.

After removing the bandage as gently as I'd ever done anything in my entire life, I put a single finger on the bleeding injury. A prayer wouldn't hurt from me, either. "Please help me do this right, God. Even if I'm not the best at basically everything, please help this girl. She's a really good kid."

Is that praying? I still had no idea.

I shut my eyes and thought of only the metal inside me filling the gaps inside the small figure in front of me. I kept thinking it while shutting out everything else.

Before long, I felt the Visitor awaken. Metal shifted and flowed. I could feel a stream running under the skin of my arm. I would have jumped up and cheered if I wasn't concentrating as hard as I was. I held it together long enough for the flow to stop on its own. Then I dared open my eyes. Jess was already hugging Julie, who still hadn't moved. She gave me a thumbs up from across the bed. Did I actually do it?

"Hey, Sal," a weak but happy voice spoke from the pillow. "Hey, Mom. Are you guys okay?"

Were we ok? No, we were not ok, young lady! I knew I was a wreck.

"Who's she?" Gracey asked of her mother while looking at Jess. "She's pretty."

Jess was flat stunned, her eyes opened wide and her mouth dropped. She hadn't seen that coming, perhaps a first in her entire existence. Then she popped out of sight.

Julie answered calmly, "That was Jess, honey. She came to help us. And we're doing better than okay. I'm so happy you're back with us again," she said as she squeezed her daughter's hand.

"Is Jess an angel?"

I fielded that one. "That is exactly what she is, kid."

50

Outside the room, everyone waited for the worst. The strange lunatic fiddling with Grace couldn't have possibly done anything but hasten her demise. What was Russ thinking? Surely, grief had clouded his judgment.

Russ was the only one more curious than scornful. "I think we're good, big guy," I answered his hopeful gaze.

Russ was gone in a flash to see the results for himself. The doctor followed in a run that would only last ten feet. Then others crammed the parade into the crowded space. The joyous sounds emanating from the room filled all my voids. When you think you're helping them, you're really helping yourself, a wise man once told me.

Angie lurked just outside. While everyone else was partaking in the miracle, she chose to stand guard over their frivolous absence. There were still monsters on the loose. She'd save her happiness for when the family was truly safe. "You and I need to have a talk, young lady," I directed as I marched across the living room.

"How's Grace?" she said as I stood in front of her.

"She'll be fine. We need to talk about you. How many did you kill?"

"Five, only 'cause Mom got one." Her little jaw tensed less at the attack and more at the one she couldn't watch die by her hand.

Woah! The farmer's daughter was a stone-cold assassin. I couldn't express my gushing approval, though. Sal the father figure needed to act the part or this little tornado was going to spin right across the planet. Sadly, she'd only hurt herself as much as everything else that deserved it.

"How are you feeling about it?"

She looked up at me with curious eyes. A weight rested on her chest that she couldn't describe to her inordinately good and kind family. But maybe the outsider before her could understand. "I feel terrible. The ways I feel terrible keep changing around, but I still feel terrible."

"You saved your entire family from a fate maybe worse than death. I'm not saying you should feel great, but do you think you're being hard on yourself?"

She was still skeptical. I hadn't hit the emotion on the head but I was close enough to keep chatting with. "Jesus says you're supposed to love your enemies. Well, I don't." Hate still burned in her eyes.

"He really said that?" I was shocked by the notion. I didn't love them, either. Where was Jess or Russ when you needed them?

"Yeah." She stared at me in wonder, shocked by my obliviousness. "Haven't you ever read the Bible?"

"I've been busy!" I reacted. Now I was being lectured, the opposite of how this was supposed to go.

"Well, you're supposed to turn the other cheek when people hurt you. Try to forgive 'em."

I'd heard of that one, and I agreed completely. Everyone can't go around dueling in the streets over insults. That's how I interpreted it, anyway. Sage advice. Standing before my little judge, however, I guessed that my ignorance was still showing. "I'm obviously not the right person to ask about this part, but I don't know if kidnap, rape, torture, murder, and cannibalism would fall under the same guidelines."

She laughed and looked like a kid again for a moment. "You're weird, Sal. But I've been thinkin' that, too."

"Look, I was you, a long time ago. That's what I wanted to tell you. I just didn't want you to feel alone, like you were different from everyone else because of how you reacted. There's nothing wrong with you. That's not evil inside you. Gosh, I wish someone would have explained that to me sooner. It's a fire to see things made right. It can be destructive, though, if you let it burn out of control. Luckily, I was given guides along my path who showed me what to do with my anger and my fear. I thought maybe I could do something like that for you if you wanted my advice."

She didn't answer right away, but she leaned in for a hug as she thought it over. I took it as a good sign.

An avalanche of "thank you" was rushing back across the house. I was no longer the strange lunatic. I was the strange miracle-worker, and everyone wanted to express their deepest gratitude.

From inside swarming hugs and handshakes, I tried to explain, "I didn't really do anything, guys. I'm just lucky enough to be a conduit."

Julie cut through the commotion. "You saved our daughter's life. I don't think there's anything we could ever say or do to repay you."

"You did, too. And I'm not being modest. What influences the Visitor, I still don't entirely understand. But you were part of it.

"There are other parts, though, evil influences. That's actually what I came by to tell you. What happened to Grace wasn't the remnants of an ugly force under Seed. I think a storm's coming. I think you just got hit with the first sprinkle."

"Yeah," Russ answered with some urgency, "those fellas said they were takin' us somewhere. He said the man they were meeting 'liked 'em young.' Do you know about that?"

"I might. Why don't you all sit down for a moment. This time I've got some bad news that you should all hear."

I told them a tale of witches, wraiths, and widows. I told them that I saw Seed reborn with my own eyes, and that as we spoke armies might yet be rising from the grave. The scenario wasn't without hope, however. Jess was still fighting for us in her way. As long we kept morality ahead of action, she'd be there.

Everyone took the bad news like hardened survivors of an apocalypse. Most were solemn while they contemplated their next moves. Julie, however, was already past the impending nightmare. Prayer had gotten her this far and she saw no cause to change course. She walked softly up to me to give me a whisper. "Sal, the girls' shower is down the hall on the left. I'll get you some new clothes. You look like you got murdered in a back alley or somethin'."

Noted.

51

There is no rest for the wicked. Either that applied to me or was what I was up against. I quickly prepped for the next leg of my journey against the pleas and generous offers from everyone on the farm.

"Are you sure there's nothing else we can do for you?" Russ asked as he stood with his family by my bike."

"Just take care of yourselves. I'd say reconsider the bunker, but where you stand is your choice." I shook Russ's hand and hugged the ladies. I took in a last gaze at the picturesque landscape in the moonlight. I could understand their reluctance to leave their home. Who was I to impose a path?

The mill caught my eye. The hosts were still chained, quietly marching in an endless circle even when they weren't being pressed to labor.

"Actually, there is one thing," I said as I watched the prisoners toil. "What would you say if I asked you to let these people go?"

Russ had to look. He didn't see people, at first. "Oh, well…" He hesitated for a moment as he rubbed the back of his head. "I'd say yes, Sal, if that's what you want… Anything… We'll work it out. You have my word on that."

"What's the holdup?" I asked about his reluctance.

"Oh, it's nothin' to concern you. And I don't disagree after everything you told us. It's a good idea. We'll just need to work out a new plan for power. These folks are what's… or who's keepin' the lights on."

"Ah," I nodded. I was asking them, if they couldn't find another resource, to leave their home again. It didn't feel right.

Jess was conspicuously absent, though I longed for her company while I traveled, so something needed to be decided. What could I easily suffer that they couldn't? Was I impeding my own higher path by protecting myself from some trivial discomfort? I knew it wasn't my job to take from people, even for a great cause. "I got an idea."

"Okay, shoot."

"Free every one of these people right now, and I'll give you infinite power. How's that sound?"

Russ was chuckling, trying to find the joke, so Julie asked, "What are you talking about, Sal?"

"I'll give you this bike. Hook it up to anything, and you'll have juice forever."

"Oh, Sal," Julie scoffed. "We can't take your way home."

"I don't need it. I don't need anything, really. Well, not stuff anyway." The catharsis of the notion felt surprisingly amazing. I should have tried this sooner. What else could I give?

"Sal..." Russ thought to protest.

"Oh, and this sword!" I interrupted. "I think I know whose hands it belongs in now." I smiled at Angie. "That's part of my bargain. You let these little warriors hang on to it for me. With all appropriate cautions and rules in place, of course."

Russ smiled and shook his head in both disbelief and satisfaction. "You're on the path, Sal. I surely can't be the one to get in the way of that. Okay, you've got a deal. But I'm throwing in a truck with a pile of gas. That's non-negotiable." His wide grin was accompanied by another handshake.

"Deal," I agreed. "If you'd be kind enough to prep my new wheels, I'd like the girls to accompany me while we release our friends."

Julie nodded her final approval on the bargain, and the girls and I walked toward the mill. "What do you need us for, Sal?" Gracey asked as we walked through the field. She looked as healthy as the first time I'd seen her, the Visitor swirling new life inside her. I couldn't help but wonder about the possible implications of the infusion.

"I enjoy your company, of course. And I wanted to tell you both about how I expect that blade to be treated. It's an unrivaled power."

"Okay," they both replied, excited by the upgrade to their arsenal.

"You treat it like your dad taught you to treat a firearm. Zero room for error. We clear?"

"Yessir."

"Good. And you practice like your lives depend on it because before this is all over, I think they might. You keep it sheathed when you begin. Never take it out. You practice until your hands hurt every day you can. Do that until you've mastered every move under the sun. Then you start all over at step one sans scabbard. Once you're confident that you can use it when you have to, you pray you never have to turn it on."

"Then what?" Angie asked. She was still anxious, both fearing and anticipating when the flaming sword and their own fire might be tested.

I began breaking the chains around my new companions encircling the mill. They looked curiously at the activity but remained mostly indifferent.

"Then nothing. If the time comes to use it, you'll know you've trained hard enough if you and the blade dance together without thinking about the steps."

"Thank you, Sal." I received hugs in place of the serious promises or solemn oaths I'd hoped to elicit, but they were more than an adequate substitute.

We started back toward the dirt drive that led to the highway after we'd released all the remaining hosts, the three of us still chatting about swords and magic and the evil spirits that might be gathering beyond our sight. I expected to part ways with Russ's prisoners once they were freed, but an odd thing happened as we walked: a few followed.

"That's weird," Gracey blurted out. "They never come along. We always have to herd 'em like sheep."

"That is weird," I agreed. We walked a bit farther, and the phenomenon continued. I thought of Jess's castle and some of its strange inhabitants. "I've seen something like this before, just never with me."

"I guess they like you," Angie observed. "You let 'em go instead of makin' 'em do chores."

A simple answer.

My second attempt at a farewell was sadder because it was more successful than the first. I exchanged goodbyes with my friends and hopped into my new pickup. I invited my group of odd escorts into the bed, and they obliged, seemingly happy to be along for the ride.

As I sped down the highway, I thought to say a prayer for the inhabitants of the homestead. I couldn't be sure when or if I'd ever see them again. And I couldn't be sure, even as prepared as they were, that they wouldn't be washed away by the next wave of violence that might hit their home. But then I thought to not waste the Almighty's time, even with a righteous appeal to protect my friends. I figured if God didn't already watch over people that good, we were all screwed anyway.

52

Along the drive, Jess popped in when she could. She was preoccupied, as always, with worldly and otherworldly things all at once. What things exactly? The answers always remained dipped in mystery, hidden away behind her charming soliloquies about lofty matters. What I gleaned from the wayward words I understood was worry about what approached. Chance was paramount to Jess's mind sparking across the quantum possibilities in the computer under Nellis. Our chances, however, were being restricted the more we traveled by something Jess didn't yet understand. The further we pressed through time, the more our reality was being narrowed by something inevitable, an artifice Jess decidedly disliked.

The gist her guidance largely eludes me but is probably still worth jotting down. The uncertainty of it all, I mention while knowing my words aren't worthy of the enigma, left me feeling adrift, an unease that loomed like a ghost as I marched into battle.

"If God held up a pencil, its tip would be a single electron," Jess said while trying to explain a particular concern. "But He let go of the creative process a long time ago. That's free will." She was advancing to a crescendo about the meaning of existence when she noticed with a laugh, "Actually, if either of us held up a pencil, its tip would also be a single electron. That's funny." She was lost in the thought and amused into a giggle.

"I think you were trying to tell me what exactly we are and what we're supposed to do while we're here." I wasn't quite as amused by the riddles wrapping our existence. If she was nervous enough to compose an adlib dissertation to explain a problem to me, the feeling was infectious.

"Was I?" She looked at me with some surprise. Her scrunched nose was easily forgiven.

"I think so," I chuckled back. "Maybe start again at what we should do with what choices we have left."

"See things clearly. Try to choose wisely. Believe that it all matters," she said matter-of-factly like she'd been saying it all along.

"And God's pencil? What was He up to, again?"

"Oh, I don't really like to say," she replied with some trepidation. "I do philosophy. I don't trespass on theology."

"We've come this far. Maybe take a guess. The pencil…"

Jess gauged her guesses with a furrowed brow. "From my new perspective, it looks like every life was shot out of a cannon into infinity. We fly left or we fly right. God, or what glimpse of Him we can sense, pencils in the frames of reality around us as we travel. He provides the presentation, one Planck unit at a time. Think of that, Sal. Think of not only creating reality once but creating an entirely new one a trillion trillion times a second based on the choices of one of your children. Then multiply that staggering feat times the number of souls scattered across the whole universe. That's why I don't mess with describing divinity. The power is past description or even comprehension." Jess quieted as she finished, drifting away into the unknown.

I was flying through infinity while steering my wobbly old truck down a cracked highway. Surprisingly, it sounded more right the more I got past the initial astonishment. This was all built for us, I thought as I took in the brightening horizon. Not just me, but everyone all at once. Wait, and people elsewhere in the cosmos? "Did you just say there's life on other planets?"

Jess smiled a wry smile as she leaned slowly across the bench seat of the cab. She shut her beautiful eyes as she neared and pressed her full lips in my direction. What did I care if I crashed? I'd survived worse. I shut my eyes and leaned in to taste bliss. And she was gone.

Just mean. Teasing me was, no doubt, part of feminine revenge that might unfold for some time. Jess was a transcendent being composed of pure energy. And she was a woman, with all the complexities inherent to her form.

I arrived early in the morning at Jess's castle. The sun lit the spires and everything underneath glowed with her presence. I would devise a way to make up with her properly, in time. Now, I needed to deliver my news. There was nothing good about it.

As I hopped out of my seat in front of the doors in the wall, I grabbed Eve's laptop and noticed my passengers still along for the ride. I had mostly forgotten they were there. Perhaps they were home now. Their type seemed to like the place.

Entering the first ring of security, I expected I would have to rebuke the Pitbull guarding the door. Instead, I got a grunt and a nod. "Welcome back," he said without saying. My hosts in tow were similarly accepted.

Faye met us in one of the courtyards leading to the main structure. She was in a rush, Jess's star pupil following her form. "Jess said you'd be coming," she said as she hustled in for a tight hug. "What have you brought?"

"Wait, you've been talking to her the whole time!" I was miffed for some reason.

"Yeah, I didn't want to make you feel bad about it," she offered as some kind of explanation.

I had nothing to return other than gripe, so I handed over the laptop.

"What's this?" she asked.

"That is two things, Faye. First, it's an untrustworthy AI that might try to wreck the place if you let it loose. So, don't turn it on. Not ever. Just rip the memory and take a look. Second, it's the record of some stunning and terrifying insight into what's possible with the hosts. I figured it belonged here. You, more than anyone, might know what to do with it."

"Okay," she said as she examined the otherwise pedestrian looking computer. "I'll get to work on it. Thank you, Sal. I suppose you need to get going?" she asked as though she already knew the answer.

"Do I?"

"I think you do," she replied like she was telling me something without telling me. I was speaking to Jess along with Faye.

"Alright," I relented. "Take care of my friends, please. And tell Jess I said 'hey' when you guys continue the conversations you've been having without me." It was my best attempt at registering a complaint I didn't understand.

"She always hears you, Sal. Well, whenever she can recognize you, anyway."

"That's what I'm most afraid of, Faye," I said with a sardonic smile. "Anyway, take care. I'm guessing I'll be dealing with my 100 problems on my own the rest of the way home."

She didn't understand but gave me a goodbye hug all the same. "Take care, Sal."

"I'm sorry!" I offered into the air as I showed myself out. "Not like you were dead or anything," I mumbled under my breath. I hoped her omnipresence didn't reach as deep as mumbling.

53

Home didn't look half bad. Well, it looked about half bad. It was still a dirty fort in the middle of the desert, but it wasn't a bottomless pit beneath haunted woods. And it was full of my favorite people, a few of whom I'd be apologizing to as soon as I got inside. With a sigh of both relief and regret, I rounded the last corner into the scorch. I stopped to wave this time, the first in a string of planned capitulations.

The armor covering the entrance backed off, then I was inside and among friends in no time. So much easier than the other version.

New faces and old alike greeted me and asked about my adventure to the other side of the country. I gave vague answers. It was almost all bad news, but not all bad. We weren't nearly as alone as we feared. For better and worse, more souls provided more opportunities. Still, as I passed through the crowd and marveled at how much Mary and James had buttoned up the place since my departure, I knew I needed to talk to my dad. If anyone knew what to do with witches, their risen, and an unhinged Secretary of Defense, it was him. When Phil greeted me on the way to the command center, I asked him to round up the brass ahead of me for a briefing.

When my duty-bound feet should have been headed to a conference table, I found them instead stepping toward the bar in Jack's. I had plenty of time to reflect on my adventure while alone on the drive, but I didn't have a chance to mingle and bounce ideas off anyone other than Jess. Her insight was invaluable, but also far removed from our typical struggles. I wanted a drink and a chat with Jack to get my bearings before I began the bad news.

"What can I get ya, hon?" a new face asked from behind the bar. I waved at a few patrons sitting at tables and took my usual seat as I sized up the new addition.

"I feel like bourbon, thank you. I'm Sal, by the way."

"Oh!" she exclaimed while spinning to find a bottle. "The famous scout returns. I'm Candice. I'm only here," she explained while evaluating the label of our drink, "because I told Jack that his job looked easy. He said, 'Try it,' like I'd be overwhelmed by the complexities of bewitching liquids falling into a glass. Well, here I am," she said as she poured. "How am I doin' so far?"

"I think we're gonna get along fine, Candice," I said as we clinked cups. "I believe your skill and demeanor already surpasses your predecessor." We drank to her certification.

"I heard that," grumbled rattily vocal cords behind me. An arm encircled my neck to choke the life out of me, or at least make me spit my drink.

"I bet our new friend chokes out patrons better than you, too," I replied as I patted Jack's arm.

"I keep askin'," he said as he plopped down next to me. "So far, the experience eludes me."

Candice feigned disgust as she poured another glass. I didn't care for the image, either. I reviewed Candice's elegant form as she snickered at Jack. She made jeans and a long sleeve tee look dignified. "I'm not complaining one bit, Jack, but weren't you sent into the wastes to retrieve brigades of nonexistent fighting men?"

"As usual," he said with a sip and a smile, "I exceeded all expectations. You were sent to wed us once more to our homicidal Department of Defense. How'd that go?"

"Wed" made me shudder and gulp. "Not well, I'm afraid. Even more murdery than we feared."

That stopped the playful banter. "Really?" Jack emphasized his concern while he took his eyes off Candice for the first time. He was clearly smitten. "What happened?"

Before I could answer, a commotion was at the door. James and his entourage had hunted me down. I squinted and scrunched my face to tell Jack just how bad the scenario out east had gone.

"Sal," James bellowed, "you're home!" I turned to receive my greetings. Mary, Grover, and a few others lined up. I hugged and shook hands in turn. Everyone was overjoyed to see me, making me feel even emptier having little good news to tell.

When Mary made her way into my arms, she already knew. "Welcome home, Sal," she said softly. Then she had a whisper as she squeezed, "I know it was bad. I'm very glad you made it back to us."

That's right! She had told me right to my stupid face that she could speak with Jess whenever she liked, and I hadn't heard her or couldn't understand. I was so tired of being a step behind because of my personal shortcomings. "I'm sorry about everything, Mary," I offered. "Ignorance might take a while, but I think I'm done being stupid."

Mary laughed quietly as she released me. "Can't say I'm not glad to hear it."

"So," James prodded me, "how far did you make it? What's the world like out there?" He was confident my report would be enlightening. He was confident he had readied himself for whatever came our way. I didn't want to disappoint him but disappointment was all I had to give.

Phil and Bart came stomping in behind the command staff. Phil was out of breath. Bart was Atlased and looked uneasy. News from afar was a proper attraction but nothing to run across the base or get excited over. "Sal," Phil gasped, "we've got incoming over the valley. They with you?"

"Incoming?" James demanded.

"Yessir. Two transports so far. Big suckers. Maybe Galaxies or Globemasters. But they're not headed here. Looks like toward the middle of the valley. Maybe McCarran."

Another report rang from outside the door, "Three! We see another!"

"Sal?" James reiterated the looming question.

That would be Eve, I thought as I began to feel like I'd throw up the fine bourbon I'd just enjoyed on James's shirt. I didn't know why she might need big planes but I knew it couldn't be good. "Not so much with me as chasing me," I expelled as I sank my forehead into my palm.

"Chasing you!" James barked.

"Who would be after you?" Mary asked more calmly. Jess, apparently, hadn't filled her in on all the gory details. Probably part of not limiting Mary's choices, just like the rest of us.

I didn't know how to pack all the horrible news into one good answer. I ignored their well-intended pleas for the moment. "Bart, my old friend," I beckoned toward the door, "dump that armor. Get a spotter. Please, get eyes on the objective from as far away as humanly possible. Ranged optics only. And I am not screwing around about the distance. Approach the target on your belly like it's the deadliest sniper you've ever hunted because that's exactly what I think it is. If she sees you, she'll put a round through your head from a mile out. Hu-ah?"

Bart was too busy moving to answer. I looked back toward all the shocked faces encircling me. Time for the debriefing of all debriefings.

"What do you mean 'she?'" Jack asked with the slightest chuckle before I could begin.

54

First, bourbon. With bottle in hand, I took a seat at a table and gestured for everyone to join me. Next, gratitude. Death glided across the horizon, but I was who I was for a reason. I'd be grateful that I lived to fight for my home if it came to that. Finally, I'd mix the good news with the bad. I'd found Jess, after all. Even if Eve went full Eve on our little refuge, our situation was never hopeless with Jess living all around us.

I belted it out hard and fast. The psycho, the Hive, and the godawful lab. The Dwellers, the witches, and their conjured demons. I tried to skip over my escapade across crisp sheets, but it felt dirtier to withhold the misdeed. I explained my mishaps, electrocution, dissection, and salvation. Then I tossed in Alice's odd plight to punctuate the madness. After a moment of stunned silence across the room, I gestured with my defeated hands in the air that my mostly bad news was complete. I chugged while they chewed wide-eyed on the story.

Jack knew I was raw from my travels. He wasn't trying to rub it in. He couldn't help it, either. A little laugh that he tried to suppress wouldn't stay down. It grew and it jiggled the more it was restrained. When he couldn't hold it any longer, he finally let it fly loudly as he smacked his drink on the table. "We're all gonna die because Sal couldn't keep it in his pants! I'm sorry," he pleaded through a tear and more laughter, "but that's funny."

"Jack!" Mary chastised. Jack sipped to calm himself but only ended up snorting a splash of the liquor.

I got the sad joke but kept my mouth shut. The worst was yet to come. I looked to James, who was emphatically unamused. "Sal, you said she was comfortable watching her people die if it furthered her cause, but you never witnessed her hurting her own." I was so glad he was working the problem instead of evaluating my culpability. "In your best assessment, do you think she'd really attack this base if we refuse to submit to her assumed title and ambitions?"

I thought about everything I'd seen, all the sides of Eve I'd witnessed. "I think she already is," I sighed. "I think she's poised to run over the whole world without flinching. She's working out the wizardry necessary to make it happen if she hasn't already. If we all don't do something quick to display our obedience, including me turning myself in, this night will end in blood."

James unblinkingly carried on with his tactical assessment. "She's landing transports close but not too close. Do you think she's dropping hosts that she's somehow taken over like the witch did? Or is it a brigade of those new Atlases piloted by Alice? Maybe advanced armor she was hiding in the surrounding bases? All of the above? What do you think are her total capabilities?"

That was scary to figure. "She's a creature unlike us, Dad. She thinks like we do but faster and meaner. I'd imagine a worst-case scenario and then multiply it by a genetically-enhanced amount."

With an eyebrow raised in contemplation, James nodded his acknowledgment. Then he stood as he gathered himself and put his fists on the table to deliver his verdict. "I don't think I'm comfortable letting someone who's already killed a member of our family here to just show up unannounced and piss in our pond."

"Damn right!" Jack cheered in reflex. I was catching on that he was drunker than he appeared, the tell-tale of the high-functioning alcoholic.

James shook his head at his old friend, then scanned the other faces for their responses.

"I say we give her Sal," Grover said reluctantly but firmly.

"You little…" I tried.

"I'm kidding," he jabbed with a grin. Everyone was in a pretty good mood considering Jack may very well have been right about us all dying soon. They'd have acted differently if they'd seen Eve with their own eyes. "I'm with you, James. Just tell us what you need."

"Mary," James continued around the table, "surrender is a real option. What do you think?" He smiled while he carefully gauged his next words as she thought, "What does Jess think?"

"She won't say…" we answered almost in unison. I smiled at Mary but kept quiet for her answer.

"Eve demands that we be part of something evil. Who are we if we surrender to that? What would we deserve if we did? I don't want to see what's down that road, James."

James let out a long sigh as he rethought the conclusion. With a finger punched into the table he began his orders, "It's settled then. We resist. Maybe we can do it in a way that scares her back into her hole before things get out of hand."

55

Eve's armada continued to descend one by one into the evening. Whatever she unloaded, there was a lot of it.

We got our first intel when Bart reported in. Most of our formation was already lining up in the scorch. James wanted to rush the advance to make a show of force before Eve could finish her undertaking. He'd summoned ten tanks, a handful of Atlases, and a small convoy of infantry in our old APCs. Shock and awe, it was not. Looking across our formation, I fixated on my dad among the rest of our warriors and felt my first jitters over the plan. He was good and brave and filled with a sense of righteousness for defending his home. An hour ago, that seemed like a solid tip to any spear. Now, I wondered if we were playing the wrong hand against the ruthless queen. Maybe Grover was right. Maybe I should have surrendered alone.

"She's dumping hosts by the thousands, Commander," Bart reported. "There's a squad of big black Atlases herding them into loose clusters, and some giant robotic horse-looking things moving among the groups. It's an odd way to attack a base if that's what she's up to."

"Thank you, Captain," James answered. "You know the terrain. I'd like you to refit and take a few shooters wide around her position. Approach from her southwest as we move in from the east. I'm hoping she'll back off if that's all she's brought. If not, you know what to do. But stay a safe distance if you must engage. If we're forced to hit her hard, we will. Danger close will be about half a klick."

"Copy that." He was on the move again.

"Dad," I tried to intercede with nothing more than a notion, "I'm not sure…"

He was looking my way but not listening. His thoughts were on the movement and safety of his troops, and the unfolding of a dangerous strategy. "Aren't you going to suit up or something?" He noticed I didn't have a weapon. "Where's your sword."

"I gave it away."

His eyes held a twitch of pity. He knew I had more than a rough trip. He knew it was he who sent me. "Okay, well stick with me. I'll give you a wink if we need some lightning bolts or other miracles." He smiled at his version of support.

The incoming trail of planes finally tapered off as we began our approach. Did she already know we were coming? Of course, she did. It might have been even worse than that: maybe she already knew how we'd respond and how long it would take us to do it. Maybe she set up her incursion in advance according to intelligence about our operation and our available options. Too late in the game, I thought about Reptile. He knew something about us. But how much?

James rolled our convoy west down Sunset Boulevard. He made no attempt to mask our approach. I suppose that was the point. We'd meet her on open ground with more firepower than she was ready to receive. If she capitulated, James would be kind. If not, he'd do what he did best.

But she'd never bow down.

Stars tumbled into the twilight above as we advanced on the airport. I couldn't find Eve in the shadows creeping across the stark geometry of endless runways, only the Atlases towering over the sea of hosts, along with the other robotic aberrations. They weren't horses, though; they were massive replicas of the dogs Eve always had running around the Hive. Each boxy face held a single oversized electrode.

James spread the tanks out wide as we turned down the cross street edging the eastern tarmac. He planned to advance the armor in a broad line if we had to fire. The rest of us would fill in for support. Even if Eve had consumed the magic of the witch and could chant an electrical spell across her army to inspire them to violence, they'd bump into a curtain of hot lead before they touched us. That would give our Angels enough room to maneuver through the fight and me enough cover to take out the queen.

James hadn't said it directly, but my job was obvious. I brought the nutter home, after all. James had told me at least a thousand times over the years that it was my responsibility to clean up my own messes. He didn't have to say it again.

After a few brief commands, we were lined up on our targets: a mass of enslaved humanity milling around the looming robots. If they were about to burst into their Seed form, you couldn't tell. They were docile and lost if not prodded by their masters.

James held his arm high in the air in front of our array. He was about to give the signal to move when two black Atlases stepped forward from the alien horde.

James paused and looked at me. "That's probably Eve and Wilson," I informed him. "Maybe they're having second thoughts." As soon as it left my mouth, I knew it was wrong.

"Fair enough," James said confidently as he lowered his hand and began to press his Atlas toward Eve. "Let's see what she has to say." I took his side as we walked across the smooth concrete toward the parley.

Eve popped her visor open as soon as we were close enough to hear each other. I was expecting all manner of hate and demands to pour forth. No, she was in a good mood. Great, even. "Sal, is this your dad?" she asked with wide-eyed excitement as though she'd just arrived at dinner to meet the folks.

"I'm General James Hardt," he tried to answer with more dignity that she was asking for.

"It's a pleasure to meet you, sir. Sal told me so much about you and everything you've accomplished out here," she pressed along like James hadn't spoken. Then she held out her shiny, carbon-clad grip.

"I wouldn't touch her," I spoke up before James could react. Both of them gave me an odd look. But I could see the gleam in the emeralds. She hadn't implied that I told her so much about him; she was saying, "I already know everything I need to know to crush you." This little meeting could have been part of the trap.

They shook anyway. "Just rude, Sal," Eve commented as the two reached for one another. She was still playing the part of a girl lost in a tunnel. The real Eve hadn't yet made an appearance but was never far behind.

"I can't say it's good to meet you, Ms. Crisp, since you didn't make your intentions clear before dropping an army in our back yard. Perhaps you'd like to…"

"It's Secretary," Eve interrupted. "If you're playing the part of general out here in the middle of nowhere," she gestured to our desolate valley, "then you should address me by my appropriate title," she said through a tightening smile. The other Eve was clawing itself out from behind the façade.

If she would have asked nicely, James may have even obliged. Pride wasn't one of his faults, and he knew his position was born of necessity. We had no less than the idiot President of the United States hiding in one of the tanks, after all. Who was left to dictate a proper pecking order when most everyone was dead? Still, James hadn't come to play nice. He'd marched for the opposite reason, in fact: to look scary enough to send Eve packing with a clear understanding not to return.

"Playtime ended when you bombed my base," James spoke sternly, the battlefield commander emerging as well. "From what I understand, you never served, were never elected or appointed, never even graduated highschool because the world ended before you got a chance to grow up. You're not the secretary of anything. And you're in over your head, young lady."

I cringed and readied myself to tear the two Dark Angels in front of me to pieces if they twitched. I knew Eve was about to explode.

"I'm sorry you feel that way, General," Eve instead replied calmly. That was far worse. She was holding it in. "But I like your fire! And I see where Sal gets his stubbornness," she smiled in my direction. "Did he tell you about us?" she asked with a subtle hiss behind the words.

"You need to get back on your plane and…" James tried to order.

"He loved me and left me," Eve continued without moving her eyes from mine. Her tone was even, but the emeralds burned. "That was a mistake, Sal."

"Enough of this!" James barked.

"Agreed, General Hardt. I surrender." With that, Eve's Atlas began to open. She calmly stepped forward after enough pieces of armor had moved themselves out of her way.

She never wanted to be in that thing in the first place. She hated the metal coffin. This was it. This was her move. "Dad, I think you should run," I pled as I kept my sight fixated on Eve.

James looked confused by my request and the small physique in front of him. Eve knelt before him, offering her hands to be restrained. Wilson began to quietly ease away at the sight of surrender. This scenario must have been what she'd been moving everyone toward. She wanted us both right where we were. "Just run!" I yelled as I leaped to block James's body from hers.

She wasn't kneeling; she was ducking. The moment I was in motion, all hell broke loose. Gunfire was everywhere, all around us, and not just from Eve's massed army. Bullets crashed into me, James's Atlas, and skipped everywhere along the ground in a sudden storm of lead.

We hadn't cleared a perimeter. We came stomping blindly into a mess, flexing our muscles and crossing our fingers. There were hosts still scattered around the airport, we thought, long before Eve descended. We didn't give them a second look because they didn't appear to be part of Eve's enslaved. But they weren't hosts; they were soldiers acting the part, meandering vacantly and curiously as they wandered into better positions to kill us.

My wounds were closing and the Atlas's armor held. When I reached for Eve, she was already long gone into the havoc.

Our side erupted into a deafening crossfire the instant they saw the attack. It didn't help much, only adding to the confusion. I got to my feet and tried to pull James backward through the fray. His rifle was already in his hands and returning fire in every direction. If I could get him to safety, I hoped, maybe I alone could absorb enough of what Eve had planned to get us all back home.

But a clean escape wasn't meant to be. Maybe that reality had closed to us the second we marched confidently into Eve's trap.

I could see an entire future slam shut when Eve reappeared with a blade in her hand. It wasn't fire or electricity that pierced both me and James as I threw myself in the way of the attack, just laser-cut carbon wielded by the enhanced queen. I ripped the sword free the instant after it struck, but James was cut deep. Eve had struck like a murderous surgeon, slicing between the plates protecting the innards of the old Atlas.

With her blade in hand, I tried to hit back, but she was smoke again. Then I took another volley of lead from her scattered shooters, including Wilson who was still on the run. He was retreating toward the hosts but firing along the way.

James grabbed at the wound and doubled over. The cut was deep through his side. Blood was already leaking across metal. I prayed she had hit more gut than lungs or heart. I could help him, hopefully, if I was fast enough. But I could never work another miracle out here in such chaos. We needed to evac in a hurry.

"Please, get back!" I shouted over the cannons and the smaller arms cracking away all around us.

"I will," James choked and coughed through his words. "But you too," he labored on through the pain. "Trust me."

We both jogged toward our side, both getting shot along the way, but the incoming was lessening. Our crew was advancing and beating back Eve's forces, the giant tank barrels blasting deep into her formations, and the .50s atop cutting down our closest attackers.

I looked, with surprising horror, at the Hive infantry falling. They were actively trying to kill us, but what choice did they have? If they didn't fight, Eve would feed them to the evil spirits in the forest or into a tube in a lab. And they were hardly real infantry. Most of them were pulling double duty, the day before probably assigned to some random task in their artificially lit workspaces. I wanted to save them, too, but the whole crappy situation had hit the fan and was splattering everywhere. I just had to get James out of the way. Then I could get back to my mission.

As we finally made it to our slow-rolling line, James ordered them to stop. The dying tactician was still trying to win. He wouldn't relent until he bled out, which was happening faster than I wanted to acknowledge. "Hold!" he shouted as he spasmed in pain. "Jack!"

Jack appeared in a hurry, probably drunk driving an Atlas but looking as agile as anyone in a 500lb suit. "We're ready," he growled.

More was happening here than I'd been told. That didn't sit well, but I had too many other things to worry about.

"Pop orange smoke. Fifty yards. Hold the line and hit the smoke with the spotlights."

"Copy." Jack stomped forward in front of our group. He waved in each direction, silencing the remaining guns once he got their attention. Eve's side was quiet as well. The hush filling the battlefield was as unsettling as the noise. Once the firing had ceased, Jack yelled, "Orange!" then took a few more steps forward and tossed the can.

More Atlases moved up and repeated the motion. A wall of orange smoke soon rose, glowing in the night from the beams of the tanks.

With the move complete, which I didn't understand, I urged James to get on an APC and get home. "I'm not going back until me or your girlfriend is dead!" he shouted back, a little blood dripping from his mouth as he spit the words.

She'd hit a lung, maybe intestine. I didn't care if he executed Eve or not. She asked for it. But I was still troubled over the somewhat-innocent Hive crew. "I can handle this!" I shouted back. "I can handle all of them." I probably couldn't, but I wanted to see James patched up and resting in the infirmary, not out in the night fighting my battles.

He put his hand on my shoulder, partly to reassure me and partly to rest his weight. "You won't have to" he sighed. "I'm gonna drag that little lunatic through a meatgrinder until she's got nothing left to fight with." James turned from me and made a circular motion in the air.

Our lines came to life again, but this time to slowly back away while they began firing haphazardly through the cloud of orange smoke.

James never meant to smash Eve's formations where they stood. He meant to bait her as much as she was baiting us. He wanted to slap her in the face, then retreat through our familiar ruins. While she chased us down our blind alleys, lost and confused, he'd slice her forces to ribbons. He probably had some fireworks waiting at the base, too, if she got that far. She was, in fact, in over her head.

He did not, in fact, mention any of this to me.

After the plan was in motion, I helped James into the back of an APC. A medic was waiting inside. "Don't stop 'til you get him back!" I shouted to the driver. He would do whatever James said to do, but I had to try.

"Don't stick around," James cautioned before I shut the door. "We're just getting warmed up. You don't want to be..." He coughed a little more blood than the first time. "You don't want to be anywhere near that smoke or anywhere near Eve's formations."

"Understood," I nodded. I slammed the door and slapped the back twice. A plume of diesel smoke rose from the pipe, and the truck lurched into motion. James was as safe as I could make him for the time being.

I lingered for only a moment to contemplate the massacre about to unfold with most of the casualties on the other side. How could I help them now that the gears of war were already in motion? What could I do that was neither attacking nor retreating, something other than watching them die?

The noble impulse was extinguished by a haunting image sparking to life from behind the smoke. Electricity began to pulse brightly beyond the cloud. The cracks of artificial lightning could be heard even over the sporadic gunfire still clapping through the shadows.

I was warned off the smoke, but I had to see what was happening. I raced ahead and through the orange fog against the screams of caution chasing me from my side. When I saw Eve's true army coming to life under the lashes of lightning commanding them to obey, I knew this night wasn't going to end according to anyone's plan.

56

The inhabitants of Nellis who'd remained behind shuddered at every boom rumbling across the valley. Whatever diplomacy might have been possible died when the distant guns awoke. Now, the people had to ready themselves to defend the base with what little armaments still worked and what few hands knew how to work them.

The guns atop the walls were still busted. No one could replicate the codes Alice had used to coordinate their fire. Perhaps she had changed all the original configurations to better suit her more efficient mind. Perhaps she had done so in a way that no human mind could ever hope to understand.

Regardless, the only operable defensive cannons were a few artillery pieces hidden behind outer fortifications. Past the scattered big guns, the Atlases and rifles wielded by the handful of soldiers ordered to stay were the last lines of defense.

Phil, in particular, protested James's decision that he remain. But when James explained that he couldn't effectively operate in the field without knowing Mary was protected, Phil relented. He swore he'd die before she did. The oath was enough to free James to save them all.

But with the sound of gunfire echoing in the distance, Phil was having second thoughts. He paced in and out of the command center to keep an eye on Mary while trying to ascertain what was happening to our group.

"Just go to them," Mary offered on one of his trips inside. "It's what you want to do."

"I want to fulfill my duty."

"Isn't that fighting for James?" Mary asked, urging him with her subtle logic to leave.

Phil paused, contemplating his commander facing the enemy while he futilely, even cowardly, paced safely behind the wall. He was restraining his better judgment so hard that it made his skin hurt. "I swore…"

"You swore to protect me," Mary cut in with a kind smile. "If whatever is coming isn't defeated, I don't think we'll stand more of a chance here than they did out there. Isn't that right?"

"Well…"

"Why don't you gather your squad and do a perimeter check. Maybe you can figure out what's going on, then decide where your gun is needed most. That's part of keeping me safe, right?"

"I guess I could…"

"That's great, sweetie," Mary smiled a little bigger to motivate her good but troublesome minion. "I'll be fine here."

"Yes, ma'am," Phil answered. He liked the plan. Maybe he could help cover James's eventual incursion if nothing else.

Before he could march out of the door, Mary had one last request. "Maybe start on the south end. I have a feeling that's where the action is going to be."

"Yes, ma'am."

Mary sat quietly alone for a few moments. She imagined the time it would take for her anxious protector to make it down the hall and out the door. Then he would need to gather his friends and move away from the main entrances of the base in line with the command center. With her eyes closed, she counted the beats of action unfolding outside.

Once she thought she was clear, she was up and on the move. While everyone else was screaming and shooting and making their world worse, she had a battle to win. The base's survival depended on her next words. She quietly practiced how to deliver them with an artful blend of force and kindness. With a single imbalanced tone or expression, the screaming and shooting would spread and continue long beyond what any of us had bargained for. Such was the delicacy of myriad realities Mary saw hanging in the balance.

57

If you order me to steer clear of orange smoke, I will run with haste toward the glowing cloud. That is either a nagging character flaw or my only quality worthy of redemption. Regardless, it hurts every time my disdain for rules resurfaces.

The army marching toward me was fascinating in a horrifying kind of way. The four-legged bots bolted out blinding webs of electricity through the hosts they pressed forward. The shocks were sufficient to bring forth Eve's ultimate goal: awakening Seed to fight under her banner. Whatever otherwise innocuous ideas the hosts held in their idle minds were flushed by the jolts and overwritten by instructions encoded in the streams. The nightmare Seed saw when the witch sacrificed Eve's men, what terror and the subsequent defensive mechanism that act invoked, was now being artificially replicated across the legion. Seed's rage sparked to life and was headed right for me.

My chances were grim. Me versus thousands of my reflections wouldn't work out well. Even if it did, even if I somehow fought hard enough and dragged my shredded husk through the maelstrom, what would wait for me on the other side? Eve and her elites. They knew my new tricks. I couldn't imagine them falling prey to the same demonstration twice. Eve, if not all the others, would be ready to finish me.

In her special way, though, Eve was giving me an order. Back off, she commanded through the screams of the mass rushing forward. Run away. Better yet, bow down. Surrender. Fall in line to watch me trample what little is left of humanity. After the show, voluntarily crawl back into the black box in the pit.

Tell me to run and you should already know what I'm about to do. I didn't care if it hurt long before my body learned to put itself back together.

The only assurance I need any longer is the blessing of my inspiration. If Jess nods that I am on the right side of a fight, I will suffer anything. She'd been too busy, though, with her transdimensional affairs, or off-put by my worldly exploits, to spend more time by my side through the growingly perilous day. But I knew I could count on her to be there when I needed her. I had made my decision, or it was already written into the fabric of my constitution. Either way, I was past that part. I yearned to feel her next to me as I moved forward.

The howling horde was in motion and bearing down on my position. I ignored them and looked around my perimeter to find Jess's face, each instant expecting to find her right next to me as I circled. Instead, I found her far off, barely discernable among the scattered remnants of the uninvolved hosts inexpressively watching the war from a distance. She stood with them, watching from afar. What was she up to? I gave a listless wave in her direction. She didn't respond, other than to put her arm around the lost soul next to her. Sure, love everyone, etc. But I was about to be ripped to pieces while she was hugging a zombie. Then she rested her head against its tall, familiar shoulder.

She was transcendent, angelic, and awfully unhelpful considering the circumstances. That's what I thought, at least, until I finally saw whom she embraced. It wasn't an it at all. It was a he, or had been when he was my brother. Jess found Pete and chose now to tell me about it.

The wave of hosts, or possessed, or… just people? Just poor, suffering people? Something terrible and sad was smashing into me, but I could barely focus on the attack. Jess had reached into my head and made yet another mess of things when my mind needed to be clear for combat. I was being trampled while mulling the endless river of madness washing over me.

As the massive rush crossed the smoke, James's plan sprung. All the guns banged to life again, and the tactical withdrawal began. Nearby hosts fell from the gunfire. Then a tank round would blister through the army just above me, spreading blood and chunks and limbs around the battlefield.

Those were people, maybe good people, a thought I wouldn't have had only a few minutes earlier. But now it was all I could think about. Those were people that James was shredding. And if the hosts somehow made it through his deadly tactics, they'd only march on to shred other good people on the other side. The catastrophe of it all hurt more than the trampling. How could I fix this monumental disaster invoked by everyone involved?

I had to knock back a few hosts to get up and get started. They howled in anger, recognizing a new threat from beneath. Most of the closest encircling me attacked, and I scarcely knew how to respond. I blunted the worst of it while forming a new path in my mind. The hosts, or people, weren't doing this on their own. Their masters needed to be put down. Somehow, I had to fight through the legion and take out those mobile antennae.

No sooner did I begin to fight than I was blown off my feet by a fiery explosion. My painful, smoldering flight finally came to an end more than a hundred feet from where it began. As I slid to a stop trying to find if anything was missing or burned beyond recognition, I was hit by an airborne influx of biomatter relieved from all the souls who'd absorbed more of the impact than I had.

While trying to figure out what we'd been hit with, an F18 screamed overhead. James had an air force, another minor detail he failed to mention.

58

The enemy was already inside the gates as Mary stormed alone down the exit road. Hundreds of Dwellers poured in undetected thanks to my friend, Joe, the treasonous weasel.

Joe had been busy since his arrival. He fell in with the techies because that was his mission: to find out what we had and what we knew. He added to our affairs and abilities just enough to ingratiate himself with the locals and lift his position past any suspicion. He had escaped the Dwellers with his life by the skin of teeth, we all thought. He accepted mortal risk to help me. Now, he appeared happy to be free of his previous associates and to have a new home. No one even kept an eye on him. Under the cover of deceit, he had been interacting with our most delicate secrets and powerful weaponry. Reptile had accepted the weasel's reports through back channels easy to establish by runners beyond the wall.

He held my sword only because Reptile gave it to him. He stood by the side of the road because that's where he was told to stand. I would have unloaded unspeakable frustration across his weak skeleton if I had found him first, not only to rectify the betrayal but to satisfy my embarrassment at being so easily duped.

He was lucky Mary found him first. We were all lucky. But when Jess and Mary teamed up to push our chances of survival a little higher, maybe the machinations shouldn't be referred to as luck.

Mary charged the heavily-armed force flooding the northern gate. Her walk was brisk and full of purpose. The growing number of rifles pointed in her direction didn't slow her stride.

When Reptile saw her coming, he had a choice to make. His plan had only just sprung. It wouldn't help to have a screaming witness so soon after entry. Not many but more than enough fighters remained to cause problems before their inevitable defeat. Reptile planned to swarm the inhabitants of Nellis with overwhelming force and chaos before anyone could intelligently respond. The base would be his with minimal casualties. That was the plan.

But some crazy lady decided to interrupt, seemingly unafraid of his fearsome gang. "You!" Mary shouted in Reptile's direction. With a flick of his hand, a knife would be out and Mary's throat would be cut before she could alert anyone else. Reptile was contemplating the gesture when his unexpected lecture began. "You are the Reptile," she continued. "You lead this group of degenerates. Yes?"

The rifles already trained on Mary took sharper aim at the insult. One of the safeties clicked off. Mary heard it and was enraged by the aggression. She took her gaze off Reptile to confront her would-be murderer. "Do it!" she hissed, challenging his cowardice. "Do it! Pull the trigger! I will exist for eternity. You will only sink further into Hell, child!"

The Dwellers weren't expecting this, and they didn't completely understand what the crazy lady was yelling about. In their small minds, the strategy was all about guns blazing and glorious victory. Now they were in trouble, under threat somehow from a lone woman.

Reptile didn't want a gunshot to ruin his surprise as much as he didn't want any more shouting. He decided to step in for pragmatism as much as not wanting to see a corpse so soon. "Stand down…"

"Oh, I didn't tell you to speak yet, carajito," Mary charged back at him. "If your slow accomplice wants to burn, you should let him." Even the sly Reptile was a little confused. He thought about giving that signal to slit her throat, but that might just make her angrier.

"Look, lady…"

Mary dashed the few steps between them to slap the Reptile across the face. She had to reach high to do it, but it was shocking just the same. "More speaking! I swear, God help me, I am this close to just letting you win. Sometimes I think you all merit each other's company." Her eyes were tight with frustration.

The Dwellers had no idea what was happening.

Mary gathered herself. She was past irate witnessing the needless evil on display, the wanton aggression toward an otherwise peaceful people, but she still had a mission. It was always the same mission: to save them all whether they deserved it or not. "I will only say this once, then I'm going back inside," she said rapidly but with more restraint. "One, you can strike me down or shoot me in the back. This will ignite a fire that you cannot control. When Sal returns…"

Reptile was finally, maybe, catching on to where the crazy lady's threats were headed. He'd planned for this. "Oh, I think Sal is going to have his hands full…"

"Silence!" Mary shouted again. She wanted to hit the dimwit again but held it together. "You have no idea what he is or what he is capable of. You morons hear a word like vengeance and think its something you do. It is not! It is a spirit that exists outside of our actions. We let it in when we choose. Sal will let it all in. God help you if he finds you." Mary paused at the fear she felt for everyone involved in that future.

Reptile was both defeated by confusion and wanted to get on with his mayhem. "Lady…"

"Two, you lower your weapons and come with me. I may be able to save your lives if you do exactly as I say." Reptile was about to protest, so Mary cut him off. "That is the only way you will ever see your daughter again, Lieutenant Commander Douglas Ripley, and I am not speaking of the brat attacking this place. We know where she is."

Ripley stood in stunned silence with his mouth slightly agape. How could she know? What kind of trick was this?

"Ah," Mary signed condescendingly. "Finally, quiet." She reached up to grab Reptile's ear while he was momentarily compliant. With a hard yank, she dragged him out from his group. "Come with me and I will show you," she said once they were standing together apart from the rest. "Tell your men they may keep their weapons but to raise their hands in the air when we are confronted. A single mistake and our understanding is over. Do you accept?"

It's a good thing he'd read the good news and seen a few things he couldn't explain. It was just enough to crack open his mind to higher possibilities. "We accept," Reptile exhaled in, at least temporary, surrender. He motioned for his group to lower their guns. "Do you really know…"

"Of course. I am not a liar like you. This way." With only a slight pause of bewilderment, the overpowered Dweller army followed Mary's brisk walk back toward the base.

Now, she had to deal with Phil's crew to keep the peace. They'd be just as murderous as the first bunch but easier to sway by comparison.

59

I didn't have a second to think or plead for help. Bloodshed shattered the field. Once everyone jumps off that bridge, there's no jumping back on. All you can do is try to fall gracefully.

To save who I could, I wanted to prevail as I fell through the baffling havoc. That meant stopping Eve, perhaps permanently. At the moment, however, she wasn't the most effective offender destroying humanity. James was the one blasting our captured brothers and sisters into burning chunks.

I restrained my first impulse. James only did what he did because he wasn't witnessing the bigger picture. If he had seen Pete, he wouldn't be blowing up the airport. Eve was behind the massacre, even if she was suffering the brunt of it. If she was forced back onto her plane and flew away to her hole, James would happily relent. Then we could get back to making things better instead of carving up another bloodbath.

After I regained my bearings, I tried to charge in Eve's direction. If I could punch through her slaves and engage the Dark Angels, she'd make an appearance. Meeting again would undoubtedly hurt, but we needed to settle what spirit would guide the reemergence of humanity, once and for all.

Fighting politely is much harder than being rude about it. As the river of rushing hosts swung and clawed and bit at me, I hit back. But something wasn't clicking while apologizing. "Sorry," and "excuse me," weren't inspiring my advance. And I was fighting dozens of my shadows at a time as hundreds of others raced by. Each was every bit as strong and fast as me, if not quite as motivated. I slogged through the mass as well as I could until we were all blown up again.

This one hit closer. The burning crater felt bigger. I squirmed on the ground while the Visitor put pieces back together. "This isn't working," I admitted while writhing on the ground. I hated what was becoming more obvious with each massive impact: I was fighting in the wrong direction. James was decidedly winning, and that was a bad thing.

With a groan and a limp from the last explosion, I headed toward home. In my way was a trail of undead souls, a handful of tanks, a hundred troops, and one soon to be furious commander, if he was still conscious. Maybe it would be better if he slept through what was about to happen.

The trickle of hosts making their way through the bombardment, shelling, and gunfire from Nellis's army didn't hassle me once I was running in the same direction. I wondered what they perceived when they saw me. Did they recognize a new recruit to their force? Were they even that sentient?

A hail of blistering rounds crashed around me as I drew nearer to the victorious retreat, but as I caught up, I saw only two tanks delivering the fire with an Angel alongside them. The rest of the force had already split into brilliantly shifting pieces as they rolled backward through the maze of roads leading east. The main group would rapidly withdraw with guns blazing while a break-off team would move laterally and wait for the enemy to cross their path. The lingering squad would open a cross-fire until they were recognized as a threat. Once the hosts gave chase in the wrong direction, the cross-fire unit would fall in with the rest of the tanks hurrying toward home. Then the teams would repeat the slick process. My Angels suffered only scrapes against tattered enemies as the heavy armor dished out mass carnage.

Eve's forces, on the other hand, were lying in pieces all over the battlefield. If they dared group up with their superior numbers, James's Air Force would unload on their position, destroying any hope of a rush. If they sprinted into the maze, they were burned down by the intricately shuffling firepower.

It was a perfect plan, but we needed a better one. We needed to not destroy ourselves in the process of saving ourselves. I'd explain if I ever got the chance. How I hoped I would get the chance.

But now wasn't the time for a delicate conversation about morality and our shared future. I waved my arms as I approached to lessen the intensity of attack from the two tanks. Jack was their Angel. He ordered them to stand down so I could come in safely. I hopped on a tank when I was close enough. The barrel was screaming hot from all the destruction it had caused.

"What's going…" Jack tried to ask.

"You need to back off," I said with more anger than appeal. "James needs to stop hurting these people."

Jack popped open his visor as our armor underfoot maneuvered back into a retreat pattern. I could see our counterparts here and there as we passed by cross streets. "What do you mean 'stop?'" Jack asked, properly confused. "You're the one who…"

"It doesn't matter," I cut in, letting a little more anger into the words. "We have to stop this and find another way."

"If we stop, she wins," he shouted over the clamor of the battle getting closer again. "Is that what you want?" He wasn't asking; he was accusing.

This was the response I could expect from everyone involved. Words weren't enough to turn back the savage tide. I had to be more dramatic about my request, a request in which I wasn't entirely confident. Where was Jess when I needed her for just a quick confirmation of direction?

"Do you trust me?" I shouted back.

A stoic sneer crossed Jack's face. He knew he wasn't going to like our new direction. He also knew that he trusted me with his life and everyone else's.

"Fight me," I beckoned. "Fight me if you do."

Jack let out an exasperated sigh, dropped his visor, and punched me in the face with the awesome force of the Atlas.

That was awfully fast, I thought as I picked myself up off the armor of the tank. He may have been keen to hit me before I provided the strange invitation. I hit back, knocking him off the transport to the cracked asphalt below.

The tanks stopped. Neither driver had a clue as to why we were fighting. They just knew it wasn't part of the clever plan that was currently keeping them alive. Shouting erupted from open hatches as Jack and I carried on.

Jack picked himself up to smash me with another barrage, but too much theater would waste time. I countered the flurry, kicked a leg out from under him, and grabbed his blade off the rear panel of the Atlas. When he tried to rise again, I kneed him in the face to put him back down. Then I made sure my audience was watching with a look over my shoulder. With the blade raised high over my head, I thrust it down through the visor of Jack's Atlas with deadly intent. Impaled through the face, Jack was done.

I looked with hatred at the tank crews. The horror washing across their faces was even worse than I was shooting for. Tears mixed with rage. One of the gunners charged the .50 atop the tank and pointed it at me.

That's what I wanted, though any relief at causing the effect was overridden with an urge to throw up. I pulled up Jack's lifeless husk so they could see it, then spun a thunderous kick to the midsection of the corpse to send it flying through a nearby wall of an old commercial building lining our retreat.

I was glad, in a way, when I saw the gunner's grip tighten. He had decided his new direction. I was the enemy. Before he could fire, I was back on top of the tank in a blur. I hit him just hard enough to daze him and tossed his limp bones down the hatch to his counterparts.

More horror at the display was welcome, but what I really needed was the gun. The Hornets were back in attack formation and flying in low from the northeast. This would be a delicate, dangerous shot, but one that needed to be taken. I opened fire on the trailing plane as it passed and unloaded its payload. I tried to send the rounds toward the tail, hopefully disabling the plane without causing any catastrophic damage.

I wasn't sure I'd hit anything as the jet ripped by, but then wobbles on ascent let me know something was damaged. I was pleased with my marksmanship until the wobbles became a spin. The sight gripped me like a heart attack until I saw two seats eject and two parachutes open in the distance to the south.

I would put checking on the pilots on my long list of things to do, somewhere below killing a queen and above almost everything else.

Jack's carcass and the downed plane were punctuation on my declaration of war against my own. There was no turning back now. I jumped over to the adjacent tank and tore the machine gun from its mount only to throw it in the dirt. Truth be told, I was just tired of getting shot. I grabbed the throat of the other terrified gunner. "Run while you can!" I growled. "Tell James he can't beat us both. No one can. Tell him to withdraw his forces from the field or watch them die. Tell him that I'm only giving you all one chance to live for old times' sake."

The words tasted filthy as I said them, but I didn't see another way. I jumped down to watch them either try to kill me or back off. I breathed a small sigh of relief as the tracks lurched again in retreat.

60

Jack was blurting dying noises. He was doing it badly and comically, not unlike most things. "Bleh," he regurgitated. "Ahh," he grunted in pain. "Am I still dead?" he finally asked. He'd found his punchline.

"I thought you were," I replied. "Honestly, I just came for the sword. I figure I'm gonna need it."

"Oh, you mean this thing sticking out of my face?" he asked as he sat up from the floor. "You coulda killed me."

"It was a possibility, but something tells me you're going to live forever, Jack."

He was done faux complaining. Hosts were running by the Jack-shaped hole in the wall in search of the tanks racing the other direction. More jokes could wait until later. "Well, now what?"

I yanked the blade from his helmet. "I gave you a haircut, didn't I?" The strike was a smidge closer than I was aiming.

"If my ninja-like reflexes hadn't kicked in…"

I had to laugh at my friend. He had everything but reflexes, and always made me feel a little better. "I have to go finish this," I said as I looked at the blade in my hand.

"You sound pretty enthusiastic about it," Jack replied deadpan. He was shifting around to get the Atlas back on its feet.

"Would you be eager to kill someone you'd just been with? I feel sick… about everything."

Our usual banter wasn't going to cut through my misery, so Jack took a softer approach. "What happens if you don't do it?"

I sighed at the thought. "She'll overrun Nellis. Some she'll take prisoner. Some she won't. The rest will be expected to live under her boot."

"She already took a piece of your dad. I'm guessin' she likes Indians more than other chiefs, ya know?"

"That's about the size of it. I hope James is alright."

Jack put his big paw on my shoulder and rested the weight of his armor against me. "Something tells me he's going to live forever." He gave a big, genuine smile. He wasn't entirely joking; he was referring to his brief conversation with Jess before she died. "I think you'll figure it all out, son. Now, go do what you were built to do."

"Yessir," I sighed again.

"I'm gonna see if there's anything to drink in this place. What is this building, anyway?" Neither of us could see much without the lights on the transports or the electricity illuminating the sky outside. "Strip mall? I hate strip malls. Anyway, I'll wait a little bit before I go. Add to the drama of my miraculous rebirth and homecoming."

"Please, be careful when you go. If someone's going to finish you off, I still want it to be me."

"We'll always share the time you thrust your weapon into my face, Sal. It was magical," he said with a contrived whimper filled with sadness and longing. He was back to his normal mode. "You need to be careful, kid. I just gotta walk home. You have to face something no one else can."

61

I walked into the night alone. The shadows ahead were surprisingly quiet considering what churned in the darkness. Hosts ran quickly but softly down the road behind me, trying to catch up to their prey. Gunshots and cannon fire rang out only sporadically. James's small army was firing just enough to close the angles of pursuit and make it home. The army ahead only clamored after infrequent lashes of lighting from their robotic overseers.

The sound of a jet drew my eyes upward. I wondered if the second plane was still attacking now that the formations had broken down and everyone was on the move. Instead, it was circling high and wide, looming over the sight of its downed wingman. I hoped they were okay, too. They seemed to be clear of the main action, but no one could know what was left of grander plans at this point.

After surveying the crash site, the jet banked hard to the south and broke the sound barrier on its way out of town. Whatever the pilots saw on the ground was enough, and it was time to head home, wherever home might be. I wondered who else I had agitated while clumsily trying to save a group of people who seemed well past hope.

With more deadly pieces off the board, I felt like I was haphazardly in a better position to find Eve. All my choices felt like a sloppy mess, but the bulk of Eve's minions were running in the other direction. James's phantom air force rested while his ground forces retreated. However we'd all arrived at this point, this was probably as good as it was going to get.

"Is any of this right?" I asked Jess, whom I bet was present.

Her response was less than zealous. "You're making moves that are hard to predict, even for me," she said, suddenly next to me. She shook her head and raised her brow skeptically. "I'm trying to keep up while focusing on other concerns. But I think you're okay. Just…"

"Your pep talk was better last time." She smiled and leaned her head on my shoulder, which reminded me… "Hey, you found Pete. That's amazing!"

"He found me just as much, but that's a conversation for later."

"Just what?" I asked, not wanting to let even the slightest detail slip.

She turned to me and laced her fingers behind my neck to look me in the eye. Instead, a kiss. A long, glorious kiss that I desperately needed. As the magic passed and Jess relaxed from the tips of her toes, she scrunched up her perfect nose. This was going to be bad. The kiss was partly cover.

"Yikes," I tried to be playful. "How bad have I screwed this up?"

"You haven't!" she implored me to carry on. "But you're right on the knife's edge out here," she said somberly while shaking her head with concern. "I just want you to be extra careful." Aww, she was worried about me. Wait, she was never worried about me. I'd exist forever either way, etc., etc.

"You don't mean I should be careful with me, do you?"

Another smile and another kiss, and she was gone. She didn't mean me. But she seemed pleased that I was fluent in Jess.

Joshua David

62

Dreading with each heavy step what had to be done, I began walking back toward the runways. In my conflicted mind, I rehearsed a hundred ways the fight might go and envisioned where I would have to take it in the end. Eve would never stop if she wasn't stopped, and she was too strong to blunt with any tempered try. Wincing from an image the life draining from her exotic eyes, I knew our final encounter could destroy us both.

I didn't travel far before the problem came to me. Eve and her machines were following the horde they'd loosed on the base. They weren't in a hurry, though. The convoy wasn't racing to join the action; the evil crew was pacing the mayhem and watching from a safe distance.

If I could crush the mechanized monstrosities and take out their leader, I hoped the enslaved would be freed from Eve's hex. Whatever control the first witch had conjured didn't stick once Eve had put her down. Maybe this could work the same way, though I knew I couldn't count on a tactical appraisal of the sorcery in play.

Eve had formed her group into a slow parade moving down a narrow road clogged with shells of long-ago battles. I would take out the lead vehicle, and they'd be momentarily trapped. Time enough for a solitary execution. I swallowed down a disgusted shudder and ran as hard as I could. When I met the side of the APC, I shoulder-checked it hard enough to send the heavy tonnage dented and sliding on its side into a dilapidated structure lining the street.

The line of transports came to a disorganized stop. Dark Angels filed out. The towering dogs moved into overwatch positions, ready to lend their lightning to the fight. Once everyone was cautiously in place, Eve emerged from one of the trucks.

"I heard good news!" she said confidently, even happily, as she approached. "I was told you finally saw reason and chose to join the winning side of this unfortunate misunderstanding. Was that not correct, handsome?" she antagonized.

My dislocated shoulder was relocating. I stretched out my arm holding the blade. "You can still stop this, Eve. It's not too late," I pleaded.

"Are you asking me to do it for you?" she asked as she stepped closer.

Now might have been a great time to lie. One little lie about my renewed devotion, even if under duress, and it might have unlocked a more peaceful future for us both.

"No," I sighed, feeling us all drop into a harsher reality.

Eve stepped near to brush my cheek with her hand. "Did you care for

228

me at all, Sal of Nellis?"

I didn't have to evade that question, though I hoped Jess wouldn't be further offended. "I did. And I do. You're capable of so much better than this, Eve. I saw greatness in you. I thought I could…"

"You thought you could stop me."

"I thought I could save you."

Eve gently pressed both her palms against my face and stretched up for a kiss. I knew it would be our last so I flirted with accepting. Instead, I backed away. The sad emeralds flashed swirling emotions at the rejection, all of them bad.

With unfiltered disappointment, Eve thought to offer me one last way out. "Just go home, Sal." But then the emeralds began to burn with more familiar rage. "I left a present for you there." Her maniacal smile said that I would be shocked when I opened it.

"What did you do?" I asked as I raised the blade.

She stepped backward slowly, closer to her men, and gave the go signal. "Wilson."

All the Dark Angels' guns shot up at once and started to fire. I was gone behind the truck I'd overturned before the barrage did any real damage. The Atlases advanced carefully in a firing line as I ducked their bullets. They didn't want to get too close. That was smart. They also didn't want to get hit with a truck. Too bad.

With as much strength as I could summon, I smashed my overturned APC into the next truck in line. A few of the Dark Angels weren't quick enough to get out of the way. I hoped their suits would take most of the hit, but hoped they had taken enough of a hit to be out of the fight.

The remaining Atlases backed off and scrambled to build better firing lines around me. I didn't need to watch or listen to their movements, though the clunks of the armor gave them away. I could feel the power coursing through the suits the more they moved.

I raced at the Angel farthest to my left. I'd short his shiny suit with its own juice and have another nice shield to hide behind while I plotted my next move. Before I got there, I was blasted with a bolt of lightning from one of the dogs. Thankful for the infusion, I sent the current back the way it came, and toward all the Atlases. The dog sparked with the overcharge, caught fire, and collapsed.

"Not smart for a superintelligence, Alice," I couldn't help but utter. You'd think she'd learn.

I began to stroll to my other victims when their guns started firing. I took a few but managed to dash behind my original target. Upgrades already? They must have inlayed some Faraday protection since our last fight.

That's what Superintelligence was up to: a field test. This whole gruesome battlefield was little more than a trial for the Hive. After her first trial, Alice's other giant eyesores were now missing in the night. I guessed they were rounding up more hosts as part of the ongoing experiment.

We'd have to do things the old-fashioned way. My good-natured approach was already wearing thin. I could preach later. For now, I needed the Dark Angels decommissioned. I smashed my shielded counterpart in the knee, breaking both the outer carbon and inner bone, then tossed the hollering husk into the next Atlas.

The remaining handful of Atlases tried backing off to keep range, but Atlases aren't built to jog backward. I caught up easily enough and broke more important pieces. I felt bad about the shrieks and cries but hoped the noises would hasten Eve's appearance. She was undoubtedly plotting her lethal insertion into the melee.

Before I finished off the Dark Angels, we were swarmed with another group of turned hosts. Alice was busy recruiting reinforcements by force. I fought back when I had to, then was jarred to see the slaves attack the limping Atlases just as hard as they clawed at me. Eve and Alice hadn't quite perfected the formula they were blasting into the minds of the taken. The army was rogue once shocked into initial motion.

The limping, misguided Dark Angels needed saving. Stitches or splints were one thing; a wooden box was another. I was right up to my eyeballs in helping all my would-be murderers but helped once more. At least they stopped shooting at me when I starting peeling howling demons off their suits.

That was Eve's last straw. She'd seen enough research data once her elites were overrun by her fiends. I was glad, in a way, to finally be shot in the back.

I slid away from her sights and behind another transport while I left the Atlases to work things out with the remaining hosts. Eve's extremely tight shot grouping through my chest was impressive marksmanship and excruciatingly painful. Pieces of my heart were lying in the dirt in front of me. I needed a moment to let the damage repair.

While I hid and ducked from the route of attack I expected Eve to follow, another giant dog trotted through the shadows between the buildings lining the street. Alice was looking for more victims to send my way. It shocked a few stragglers as it passed, then did something remarkable that I hadn't noticed before. It wasn't just hitting its targets with bolts from the electrode; it was catching a few bolts back the other direction just an instant later. That made sense, if any of this did. The robots needed a massive power source to keep up the manipulative fireworks. After sending whatever craven code the sparks carried, the antennae recalled some spent energy. If their relationship was symbiotic, it might be a weakness.

Eve had taken an unexpected approach and silently appeared behind me. I was still thinking about evil circuitry while she was shooting. She would have kept shooting if a handful of hosts hadn't swarmed over both of us.

Eve didn't seem bothered. She spun a burst of attacks to knock the hosts back, sending some tumbling into the night and some smashing into the armor of the truck. In the chaos, I slipped away again, only admiring her violent performance for a fleeting instant.

Alice was bothered, though. She hadn't meant to send a squad of lunatics to hit Eve and she didn't like making mistakes. With another display of lightning that drenched the alien scene in a blinding flash, the hosts relented. After only a moment of looking dazed, they got on with their inane business of looking and poking at things curiously.

An off switch! Eve was truly on the cusp of astounding power. If she could mobilize a force like Seed at will, whatever enemies she perceived would surely be trampled under her superior tech. Unfortunately, the first enemies on her list were me and my home. But a tiny part of me wanted to see her at full strength if there really were greater terrors lurking beyond the horizon.

After making a quick discontented face Alice's way, Eve was chasing me under the truck. I'd been running from demons my whole life but never one with this much raw tenacity. Again, I wanted to appreciate her more than kill her, but she left me no choice. It was the undeniable fact of her resilience that both invited admiration and sealed her fate.

She shot a few more times as we both emerged on the other side, but I was back together and gone in a streak. I thought to cheat. If you're not, you're not really trying. When Alice had hit the off switch by striking the hosts around me, I caught a charge as well. I raised my hand in Eve's direction and let it rip. Irony would be the fire that finally took her down.

But she was gone in a similar flash. Irony chased us both. Admittedly, I wasn't a sharpshooter with my newfound weapon. Clumsy, really. No sooner did the burst strike where Eve was standing than she was firing again. This time, however, she only got one round off. A perfect hit in my vitals, as always, but just the one. She dumped the mag and grabbed at her belt for another but touched only air. She was out.

Eve let out an aggravated sigh at the realization but got over it lighting fast. She tossed the gun in the dust and drew a blade from behind her back. With a flick, the dagger extended into a sword. Eve stood ready as I gathered myself and raised my blade just above my shoulder.

"I suppose it's fitting that I finish you this way," she snarled. "I should have done it the first time. Mercy might be the death of me, so I'll avoid it in the future."

"I hope it finds you wherever you're headed," I answered. I felt terrible over what was about to happen. Then I felt uneasy at feeling so terrible about it. Killing the bad guy was supposed to feel good. My heart ached like she had shot me again when I lunged to cut her.

She blocked and sliced back my way. I was gone before she struck. We both circled, evaluating the speed of the other. When I chopped at her again, she easily slid out of range. She thought she had my timing down, so charged in with a salvo of slices and stabs. All she hit was the edge of my blade and the empty night where I had been standing before she attacked.

My turn. I spun and swiped for her head but I knew she'd be vapor. That was the goal: to get her concentrating on a sharp edge while I summoned another bolt, only this one from within. If the controlled hosts were fueling their masters, maybe I could perform the trick as well. To my surprise, when I asked into my depths for the impossible, I received. I sent another stream of electricity Eve's way, hopefully enough energy to put her down so I could move in for the kill.

She dodged again, moving almost faster than my eyes could track. Angry she had to deal with the surprise, she raced at me again, slicing from every angle at dazzling speeds.

I parried most and dodged a few of her slices but began to realize that I couldn't be conventional and hope to win decisively against a creature like Eve. She was too strong to succumb to a frontal assault, inside and out. We could dance this dance all night, and I might get a piece of her in the end. But at what cost? An army was still racing toward my family, and I'd gimped their ability to defend themselves.

When an unstoppable force is chopping away at an immovable object, you're forced to get philosophical about the action. But I'm not a terribly philosophical person, which made my request for help easy to direct. What would Jess do? That was easy. She'd find a way to take one for the team. She'd suffer anything to make the world better.

As Eve raged and hammered a series of strikes at me, I let her start to win, but not enough to quench her shallow sense of supremacy. I let her heave with all her unnatural strength and sweat out her anger while she opened a few cuts here and there.

Slowly, I let her cut me more. A puncture here. A deep gouge there. I could see victory begin to light her emeralds. Her vengeance stirred more ferociously the deeper she struck. I put up a mirage of a failing defense and thrust an assault here and there, but I let the torrent of her animosity eventually overwhelm me.

As she beat me backward, I fell to the ground, only offering feeble counters while lying on my back to blunt her high swings. After a few blocks, she forcefully knocked the blade from my grip. Not a second passed before her blade was gripped by both her fists and plunged deep into my heart. She let out a wail at the final blow. From this point on, she needed only to butcher her kill.

That's how she moved too close. Before she began carving me into pieces, I reached up swiftly but gently and drew her nearer. The blade sliced deeper, causing a burning, crippling pain, but Eve was in my grip. She wouldn't be getting out.

She fought back once the shock of the move passed, writhing with all her strength and digging her steel grip into my flesh to break free, but the flailing was all little more than defeated spasms of futility. Once she was in my arms, I slowly slid my forearm across her neck, then my other arm around the back of her head. As I started to squeeze, she gasped and choked.

I looked away and tried not to listen. In the movies, it takes but a moment of strangulation to kill. In reality, it takes a long time to die. Unconsciousness may arrive in only moments, but consciousness returns just as quickly. To make a corpse that can no longer hurt the ones you love, you must squeeze the life from your victim for four minutes or more. That's how long the brain lives on after the supply of oxygen has been cut.

I had to perform this heinous act for four agonizing minutes. I barely noticed the blade impaling me. Strangling her hurt more. All I could think of was her painfully unwise but uncompromising drive, and of her limitless potential. I kept reciting all the ways I'd failed her, each moment I wished I had back to make more of an honorable impact in her life. The more I thought of our tortured dance over the last week, the more tears fell. This was my charge, after all, to bring people closer to Jess. Now, look at me. What a disgusting abomination I had become, smothering possibility instead of harnessing it.

"Jess!" I cried out into the night. I needed reassurance now more than ever in my stormy life. Just a glance or a nod to know that what I was doing was somehow right in her cosmic view of existence. But she wasn't there. She was wholly absent, and I could feel a cold, expanding distance between us as though I was falling fast into an endless pit with her somewhere far beyond the edge above.

If she couldn't find me, it meant that I was lost again. That was pain I couldn't suffer. The thought of Jess not being able to recognize what my choices had made me was unbearable. To Hell with my perpetual fear of consequences, I wouldn't lose her again. Not like this.

I rolled Eve's body away from me and dislodged her blade. Her unconscious reflexes shook her torso in coughs and spasms while I lay still next to her. Doubt arrived before relief. Was letting her live the right choice, or had I just choked at the finish line, letting evil loose to wash over the world for a second time?

When I saw Jess standing above me, reaching down to help me up, I sighed, "Thank God."

"You're okay," she said reassuringly as I rose. She gave me a hard squeeze but was pressed to talk fast. "Everything can still be okay, but you've still got a lot to do. You need to move."

I smiled in reply. "As always," I said squeezing back. "Why don't we ever have time to just be together?"

"I'm not kidding. Like right now," she implored.

"You're abrupt sometimes," I said through another smile. I didn't care what she was as long as I hadn't lost her. But I knew what she meant. Eve's army was still racing toward home.

63

I ran through the wastes as fast as my legs could propel me. Our single-file convoy, by now, would be racing toward the gates for their lives. Unfortunately, I'd tried the maneuver a hundred times. The limited amount of fire that could be spent from a column was never enough to keep the enemy entirely at bay. All that was ever won was time to slide under the warm blanket of cannon fire from the walls.

But the cannons died with our version of Alice. Worse, there might be nothing at all to run home to. Eve had left me a surprise there. It obviously wasn't something thoughtful or nice. No, it would have something to do with screaming and blood. I pressed my alien legs harder while my imagination summoned horror after horror.

I cleared the outer ruins bordering the base in time to see my crew make it into the scorch. The base looked to be in order. Its inhabitants were all about to die, but that was nothing new. The bulk of the horde giving chase was lagging behind the convoy, but more than enough hosts were already harassing the vehicles to be deadly. Still, it looked like they could make it inside the gates. Maybe my dad could be treated if he was hurried to medical, then I could help hold the perimeter while I thought of something better to do than tussle with my enslaved brethren while we all waited for Eve to arrive and finish us off.

I sprinted to head off the larger group when the bases guns all took aim and exploded at once.

This was Eve's surprise. She'd somehow taken over our weapons. Alice had been snuck into our software, and now she opened fire to obliterate Eve's remaining enemies.

I stopped in shock at the thunder and bright flashes of the barrage. I couldn't watch. Their deaths were my fault. Despair dragged me to my knees in the char. I should have obeyed and fought like I was told. Maybe I could have saved them if I wasn't always so intensely being me.

All the guns kept firing, lighting up the night. Heavy lead, lasers, and artillery streaked and pounded the field. The massacre was the worst thing I'd ever seen until I noticed that the convoy was still trucking through the barrage. The mayhem was dazzling news! Nellis was shooting at the bad guys. Well, legitimate targets if not all bad.

I raced into the larger group. There must have been hundreds or even thousands I could protect from the base's defenses if I could keep them focused on me. Then what? No idea. But I'd kick the crap out of them to keep them alive as long as I could. Every punch, kick, and toss enraged the mass of hosts, and bought us all another moment.

We fought in the dark for a strange while, locked in endless conflict while I prayed for a better plan to unfold. Maybe James would get patched up and think of a way out of this mess, if he was alive and if he was in a mood to help me after what I'd done. If he lived, he'd surely been told that I sacrificed Jack on Eve's altar.

Would he buy it? Maybe. He hadn't trusted me since I'd returned home. Maybe he thought I had been turned by Eve. Maybe he could see what Russ saw: that I was some kind of new creature after my trials.

Either way, I needed a lifeline if I hoped to not fight forever. I hoped Jess might stop by to breathe some wisdom my way, a whisper that might free me. But deliverance eventually took the form of Eve.

She arrived with a burst of agony, as usual. When her units finally caught up, the dogs marched ahead and electrified the field. The jolts were blinding, like getting hit in the head with a bat over and over. When I gathered my shocked thoughts enough to ready myself for whatever came next, I breathed an immense sigh of relief. She hit the off switch. Calm and quiet spread through the night after the clap of thunder. Exhausted, bewildered, and thankful, I sat down in the freshly peaceful dirt. Looking up at the now docile hosts wandering the hushed scene, I noticed the stars above.

"You could have finished me," Eve said as she made her way to me with an outstretched hand to help me up. "Maybe mercy will be the death of you," she said with disgruntled appreciation. I think that was as close as she could come to gratitude.

I took her dirty, bloody, delicate hand and stood. "You might be right," I smiled. "Thank you for hitting the off switch," I gestured at the hosts milling around us.

"I suppose it's the least I can do. Regardless, I believe this demonstration has come to its unsuccessful conclusion. Your base's defenses were supposed to be down by now." Her irked expression belied a sliver of relief that the hostilities were over.

"Now what?" I asked, truly hoping for a measured, maybe even kind, answer. But none was forthcoming.

"This isn't over, Sal. This was only…"

"Hold that thought," I cut in with a raised finger while I surveyed the perimeter. The whole world felt upside down, but one thing in particular was still out of place. In the new silence, I could hear movement. I could feel a hot rifle far in the distance, one radiating the magnetism from numerous rounds grinding down its barrel at high velocity. It was pointed at us. I scanned the night. No, it was pointed at her.

A bullet moves ahead of its sound, a nuisance that doesn't matter once you can feel how much energy it carries. The boom followed the smack of the round into my grip, just to the left of Eve's head. Eve

236

flinched and lurched at the attack, but calmed as I showed her the bullet. It was still hot when I handed it to her.

I looked and waved into the distance. That was a fine shot. Easily two hundred yards and the bullet would have entered Eve's ear. I couldn't see who it was, but few were that good. "Bart, I got it!" I shouted with hands cupped around my mouth. I knew he'd be upset by my interference. He could get in the long line to yell at me later.

"Twice in one night," Eve said with her head tilted in contemplation while she looked at the bullet in her hand. She looked as though she was on the edge of genuine emotion, a state I hadn't seen other than eruptions of anger. She held the round tightly against her stomach with both hands. Her lip gave way to a micro quiver before it steeled again. "You know," she began, "I believed enough of your story to think that there might be great power out here." Her emeralds were heavy with disappointment. "There's not, though. There's just you."

"There are good people out here," I answered, trying to brighten her mood and help her see what was more important than her vendetta.

She stayed silent and didn't let go of my eyes to show me that she was genuinely taking in my perspective. When she finally spoke, it was with trepidation. "There is too much on the line to let a variable like this place go unmanaged. War is coming, Sal. You're either with me or against me." She could see my objections surfacing so headed them off. "Come home to me, Sal." She paused to watch my reaction. "Come home to me and tell me that your people submit to my authority."

"You've seen how..."

"Do it," she interrupted, "and I'll let all these people live. Don't, and I'll end this whole valley to make sure I don't catch a knife in the back as I proceed. That's why I bombed your little village in the first place, Sal, to show you I could."

My face twisted with the shock that she'd done it on purpose. I shouldn't have been shocked. In fact, I should have suspected. I was about to voice my anger when she continued. "There's no turning back now. I'll tell you why, Sal. I didn't just hit Nellis. I put everyone I could find on notice. This is bigger than you can imagine."

She'd slapped the whole world in the face! I wanted to scream at her for her relentless insanity, but I'd just be beating a dead horse. She was on a mission and didn't care what anyone thought about it.

In my stunned silence, she pressed upon the bullet she held against her abdomen and continued, "You've shown me kindness, tonight." She held up the projectile meant for her ear. "I want to show you the same." She placed the bullet back in my hand. "Go home. Put things in order. I'll give everyone here a second chance and week to get in line. Report back to the Hive before the week is over, and any tension between us will be over. If not..." she paused before threatening me again. It was her version of nice. "Well, you know what will happen." After the threat, she stepped forward to give me a final embrace that she knew I didn't want. Then she turned and walked away through her minions, toward what was left of her mechanized entourage.

What could I do? I'd proven again and again that I wouldn't be her executioner. Instead, I walked the other way.

That's how I lost the war between east and west.

64

The homecoming happening behind me wasn't a happy one, though it could have been worse.

After Reptile invaded, he'd been taken by Mary to Jess's strange chambers while his men tensely waited above with the remaining soldiers and residents of Nellis. Phil was under the strictest orders not to kill the bandits once their leader was indisposed. He wondered why he was taking tactical orders from Mary, yet he was following them all the same. The standoff remained edgy until the leaders returned.

Reptile wasn't reborn deep underground, but he was given hope. Maybe that's a similar enough transformation to equate. When he emerged, he was wholly repurposed if not entirely a new man. Jess had given him only what he perpetually sought throughout his perilous life: information. It went against her better judgment to meddle too much, but in Reptile's particular situation, having more knowledge expanded his choices rather than limited them. That's how Jess justified showing Reptile in her mirror that his daughter was still alive though far away and lost to the evils of the wastes.

When he emerged alongside Mary, his eyes were reddened by tears and his orders were almost incomprehensible. "Stand down," he instructed his Dweller brigade. "You, too," he ordered Nellis's forces.

Phil clicked the safety off his rifle and hoped no one heard. Did the freakish Dweller just give him an order? Both James and Mary could… "Do it!" Mary insisted while standing at Reptile's side. "Mr. Reptile here is now in control of the operations of this base."

"Mary!" Phil and some others tried to object.

"I was in charge," she snapped back. "Now he is. If you trust me, trust him. This pointless violence might not be over," she shouted across the strange gathering. "You don't have to listen to me. You never do. But I believe that he is our best hope right now. Believe me or not. Choose."

Phil took a deep, irritated breath. He looked around at his squad of fearsome warriors and gathering of able militia. A few wide eyes and shoulder shrugs came his way. It was an unwritten regulation that everyone, James included, did what Mary said. If what she said was crazy, it did not matter. In fact, that was normal.

"Phil, is it?" Reptile added to get people moving. "Look, you'll have plenty of chances to kill me later. Fifty-fifty your boss does anyway. But if you want to bring them home safely, wipe that dumb look off your face and start helping."

Killing him later sounded okay. "Fine, commander," Phil patronized, "what's the plan?"

Reptile didn't answer. Instead, he scanned the crowded area. "Joe!" he yelled loud enough to bounce his voice off every surface surrounding them.

Joe had fixed the base's defensive weaponry days earlier, then planted a virus to lock everyone out of the system but himself. After a surprised look, it only took a minute for him to bring everything back online. He had secretly hoped he wouldn't have to use the system in the way that had been planned, so he was relieved he'd be shooting hosts and not finishing off our team.

With the big guns doing their work to clear the path, Nellis and Dweller squads recovered our battered convoy and brought them inside while I had gone to work on the larger force.

James burst from his APC once the rigs breached the gate, bandaged but still bleeding. The medics riding with him chased him and cautioned him against moving, but he never listened. "Who are these people!" he barked at Phil once he found him in the crowd. Phil dared not answer. Instead, he nodded Mary's direction. She still accompanied Reptile.

James coughed blood while stumbling on the way but made it to Mary. She propped him up while he sized up Reptile.

"General Hardt, I presume," Reptile tried to offer a cordial introduction. "I am Lieutenant Commander Douglas Ripley. I have temporarily taken over command of this facility for everyone's safety. I look forward to your recovery so that we can establish regular order."

"You're the spook," James spat as he coughed and began to slump. Reptile ducked under James's other arm to help support him.

"We need to get him prepped for surgery immediately, Mary," one of the medics pleaded.

Instead of protesting, James started to laugh through his coughs. No one knew why, so he enlightened them. "Sal..." He coughed some more. "Sal's going to tear your limbs off when he gets here," he laughed and choked some more. Blood loss was taking its toll on his faculties. "Then I have to court-martial him for treason, but I want to be out of the infirmary for the limbs part."

Mary had other plans. "Take him below to Jess... or Alice's room. I will help him there." Once again, it didn't matter if her orders were crazy.

As the medics brought a stretcher, Grover arrived in a tizzy. "James!" he shouted as James was loaded onto his makeshift transport. James only offered a look of disgust in return, then lost consciousness again. "Mary!" Grover changed the direction of his hysterical angst. "Mary, Sal went crazy! He killed Jack right in front of one of the tank crews!"

Mary laughed for a split second but then turned it into a more serious look and cough to cover her amusement. "I have to go, Grover," she replied soberly, trying to mimic his seriousness. "James needs me now. Direct your reports to this man. He is in command."

Reptile smiled his reptilian smile at Grover. "I don't believe I've had the pleasure."

"I'm Grover!" he shouted back. "I'm the President! We've got a huge problem out there, one bigger than the lost plane and the army of the dead!"

Reptile pursed his lips and scowled in contemplation, keeping his eye-roll imperceptibly small. "Of course, you are. Look, my friend, we have a series of very delicate moves we have to make in the next five minutes or we're all going to die. Do you understand?" He didn't wait for a response. "I'm going to need you to take it down a notch, Mr. President, and do exactly as I say. Can you do that for me?"

Grover hated being talked down to unless life-or-death situations were falling from the sky. Then he rather appreciated a military mind in command. And this guy was terrifying in a polite kind of way. He seemed to know what he was doing. "Okay, but we need to sort this out as soon as possible." He had to press his concerns to not look weak. Nagging was his superpower.

"Of course, Mr. President," Reptile nodded, "now here's the plan."

65

Bart, Jack, a spotter, and two disgruntled pilots picked me up as I walked through the scorch. Predictably, Jack had caught a ride on his way back. His luck was bottomless.

There was no more room in the Humvee, so I walked around to hop on the back. Bart wanted to share his annoyance with me, though, before we drove back. "A perfect shot!" he yelled before any pleasantries.

"It really was," I nodded in genuine agreement. "Through all the shifting cover of the hosts…"

"In the dark!" he added.

"Well, there were artificial lights."

"Why!" he shouted while throwing one arm out of the window and into the air to emphasize his confusion. "She was the one causing all this. You saved the enemy."

I stopped at that. He made a fair point. "I'm not sure I can tell anymore," I said as I looked into his eyes to convey my genuine confusion. "I feel…"

"Hippie," Bart interrupted. Bart's lexicon of profanity was truly impressive. Of the insults he could fling, he picked what he thought was the worst. "Get on," he groaned. "We'll sort this out later."

Bart thought we were racing inside to reunite with the rest of our crew. When a foreign crew met us at the gate, he slowed in concerned amazement. I know these people, I thought as I scanned the dirty faces of Reptile's Dwellers. This was the surprise Eve planted. But they weren't killing us, surely the original plan. They were acting scary, pointing guns and ordering us inside, but doing it half-heartedly and politely enough to let us know they weren't serious or sinister. Lies, double-crosses, and strange etiquette animated the delinquents. I smelled Reptile.

"Killer," Reptile greeted me as I stepped down from the rig.

"Reptile," I replied. "What are you guys…"

"Tell me where Eve is right this second," he interrupted. Nerves kept his squint tight and anxious.

"I don't think I…"

"I don't mean figure it out. I mean tell me her position, son. Where exactly did she go and why did she go there?"

"She's not coming back. Not now, anyway," I answered his concern. "She gave me a week to surrender." I looked around the crowded entrance to the base. "Where's my dad?"

Reptile nodded and took in a deep breath of relief. He was as scared of her as everyone else was. "Your dad's with Mary. I think getting fixed up. I don't know why she took him where she did, but I'm actually terrified to ask that woman any more questions." With a brow raised, he recalled their brief conversations. "Anyway, kid, for what it's worth, I'm sorry about all this. I was just doing my job, but I'm beginning to see..." he trailed off again in contemplation.

"I know what you're sayin', Ripley. I've been on this merry-go-round for months now. It gets easier but no less confusing."

James was jogging! That was great news. "Dad!" I yelled with a smile in his direction as he burst from the command center.

"Traitor!" he yelled back. I looked at Reptile. He looked at me.

Oh, he meant me. I attacked our own forces. There was no getting away from that. But traitor? I was trying to do the right thing. "I didn't mean to..."

He was nearly to me. Moving fast. A little faster than usual? "Incompetent traitor!" he yelled again. "Is that better?" He was in my face, close enough to spray me with the tirade.

Mary trailed behind him. Did she just do what I think she did? Of course, she could do it, too. If I could heal a dying child, someone like Mary had already mastered far more advanced procedures.

Mary's presence tempered my reply, but it didn't come out much better than the first version. "I don't fight for you," I sneered, not letting go of his eyes. It was true. My loyalties were decidedly elsewhere, whether I clearly understood her fluttering logic or not.

"Obviously!" he screamed again with his hands in the air. His exasperation was overwhelming him. "Do you know what you've done? You started and lost a war against a psychopath running the Department of Defense, and at the same time, you started a war with the Navy! The Navy!" he screamed again for emphasis. "In what scenario in your disloyal head do we not get bombed out of existence now?"

No getting away from that either. I didn't, however, know it was the Navy. "I'm sorry about that, but..."

"You're sorry," James repeated, trying to calm himself by rubbing at his temples. "Why is it a son's job to dismantle every plan of his father?" he asked rhetorically but close enough to elicit an answer from Reptile.

Reptile was lost in his own thoughts, only half-listening to James's rant. "Daughters, too," he said softly, drifting across other concerns.

James stepped toward Reptile to meet him face to face. "Why are you still here? Why do you still have limbs?"

Reptile didn't want to fight. He nodded at the invitation to leave. "You needn't worry, General. I'll be moving on as soon as I can."

"So will I," I added.

"And Eve!" James shouted back. "Where's your homicidal girlfriend?"

I was in no mood to be insulted whether I deserved it or not. "She gave me a week to surrender. I'll turn myself in so you can garden."

James threw up his hands again and motioned toward Mary to elicit her help in making anything make sense. Mary only shook her head in disapproval, probably at both of us, at which James walked away. There was definitely a strange spring in his enraged step.

Mary stepped forward to hug me, which I appreciated. "I'm trying like crazy to do the right thing in the moment, Mom. But it's not going well."

"I know, dear," she said without letting go. "That's all we can do. The rest is above our pay-grade." She smiled to cheer me up. "Isn't that what you guys say?"

The motley gathering of defeated locals began to scatter after James's fireworks were over. Grover rushed in to hug Jack. He did not appreciate the gesture. "We thought we'd lost ya, big guy," he said as he let go.

"What," Jack grinned, "you bought that? You, maybe. Not me. Me and the kid are tight."

I jogged to catch up to the pilots. If anyone needed a heartfelt apology, it was them. "I'm so sorry about hitting your plane and putting you in danger." I received angry, confused stares in response. "The targets you were hitting, those are still people. I know you don't see them that way and I understand. But it wasn't right. This whole situation was wrong, which was also my fault."

"We'll put it in our report," shrugged Captain Lehy. "Hopefully the admiral accepts your explanation."

"You want a nice Raptor or Lightning as a replacement?" I tried to offer to lighten the mood. "They're just collecting dust out here. You could have one of each." Lehy gave me a quizzical grin as she walked away.

66

It began on a barstool. I was whining to Jack when Jess joined me for a beverage.

I had mournfully explained all my strange decisions to Jack and Candice. They obliged my dejection by earnestly trying to unpack my nearly coherent stories and rationales. I kept drinking while talking, hoping that there was still some volume of alcohol that could pierce an alien metabolism. I hadn't discovered it yet, but neither was I done trying.

"What you guys talking about?" Jess said nonchalantly beside me, her perfect posterior planted in the stool next to me as though she were really there.

I almost fell off mine from the start. "Jess!" I shouted too loudly for the otherwise quiet murmurs filling Jack's. I reached over to squeeze her. "I'm even more happy to see you than usual, my love. Kind of up a creek at the moment."

Jack, Candice, and a few patrons were shocked when I struck up a lively conversation with no one. Jack looked at me with concerned, surprised eyes. "Is she here?"

"Oh," I noticed the oddity of my behavior, "yeah, she's sitting right here. Or, I'm crazy. Probably both."

Candice looked curiously to Jack for guidance. She wasn't used to this kind of crazy. Jack maintained his surprised expression, but only for a second. "This calls for a drink!" he bellowed across the room and raised his glass. "Oh, wait," he grumbled as he turned to pour one for Jess. "Welcome back, angel," he said with a nod in her general direction as he slid a drink into position, then took a sip of his own.

"Why don't you let them see you?" I asked. Seemed like the obvious question.

Her flawless face tightened toward a scowl. "You try astral projection across infinite realities using a dead body and clunky computer!" she bit back at me. Zero to sixty.

I winced a little at her anger, then realized once more that I was the only one who heard her. "I'm sorry," I offered. I took her point, too. No one understood her plight.

"No, I'm sorry." And back again. "It's just frustrating trying to find people who exist only for a nanosecond in a certain place if they aren't already looking for me." I guessed that made some Jess sense. "Tell Jack 'thank you,' please."

"She says 'thank you,'" I reiterated to my company.

"You know what, kid? This is getting weird. I think you guys need your space. We'll give you a moment," Jack said as he gathered supplies to last them more than a moment. "I said we'll give them a moment," he directed to the few people sitting at tables in the room. Everyone shuffled away with nods and smiles of understanding even though they didn't.

Jess leaned in and put her head on my shoulder, which reminded me again of whom she had found. "Tell me about your creek," she gently prodded me.

"Well," I said, taking another drink, "to save this place, I need to go back to her."

"Mmhmm," she rumbled with compassion and just a pinch of anger.

"If I do," I carried on quickly, "I'll be generously tortured, then eventually put back into her army or killed."

"She'll keep you alive," Jess noted with a wisp of jealousy. I moved along like I didn't detect it.

"If I stay, she'll turn this place into a parking lot so we can't fight back. Then she'll go about burning down the world all the same, just without me as a slave in her army. I don't think she cares either way." I threw that last bit in to try to appease my angel's resentment.

"You seem to know a lot and think a lot."

I didn't notice what she was noticing. "Do I?"

She smiled her knowing, almost patronizing, smile at me. "What do you believe?"

I knew I was going to get this wrong. I believed she was devastatingly beautiful in every form she took. That was definitely not the right answer, though. "I believe that stuff I just said," I replied with an exaggerated wince and shrug to show that I already knew I failed the quiz.

"You believe you like Scotch."

"Indeed," I answered. Were we talking about the same thing? Usually close but not exactly.

"How do I know that?"

"Omnipotence?" Her expression said I was getting colder. "You're both brains and beauty? Double-threat!"

She wasn't as amused as I hoped. Zero to ten. "Please," she squashed my insinuation. "I know you believe you like Scotch because you keep picking up that glass."

There was a lesson here. I knew I should know it. Her eyes were like lakes sparkling in the sun. That didn't help. "My feet!" I finally blurted.

"Your feet," she replied, finally satisfied.

"I don't really know what will happen here in the future."

"Correct."

"I don't really know what Eve will do to me if I go."

"Correct."

"My actions are my beliefs, and right now they're lackluster."

"Bingo. You're a double-threat, my handsome knight." I wanted to drink that in, but we were on to something.

"What should I believe?" I asked sincerely.

She tossed her head back and had a good laugh at that one. "What should I believe?" she repeated mockingly. "Tell me who I am!" she exaggerated the sentiment underpinning my question, then she laughed some more. I got the point. Not a fair question.

"What should I do?" No, that was the same stupid question. "Hold on..."

"Dream bigger than that glass, Sal," I could feel the pep talk tide rising. "What's the most important thing in the world after you acknowledge your eternal soul and begin to act accordingly? I left you something to remember."

"Family!" Nailed it on the first try! I had to think about it after I said it, instead of the other way around. "Family?"

"What is the highest order of reality you can imagine, Sal? Forget Eve and all the troubles plaguing this world. If you had one shot at the stars, where would you aim?"

I'd aim somewhere right next to me but wasn't going to say that out loud. Our conversation wasn't about me. This was about Pete. I knew she knew that because she always did, so I moved along to the important part. "Are you saying I should bring him back? Reunite our family?"

"Infinity lies before you. Can is already answered. Everything can. But what do you believe? Belief is how you make reality."

I caught most of that. "I believe I like Scotch." I took one last drink. "Now, I believe I should be shooting higher."

I got a kiss for my accomplishment. "Double-threat," she whispered as she backed away. Then she was gone.

New creature in Christ, blah, blah, etc. I would have punched a baby to keep those lips close to mine. "Wait," I said to the empty void in front of me, "can you help me find him? I've already decided to look."

"Of course," she instantly replied. She was standing in the doorway. "Let's go."

"Jack," I called around the corner. I could hear them listening the whole time. "I need to borrow your car."

"Keys are behind the bar," he called back without pretending he was farther away.

67

Dawn hustled away the night by the time we got where we were going. Jess had led me through a maze of sadness, broken buildings, and broken lives while we looked across the darkness for a lost soul. She had found him once, but the feat was difficult to replicate, apparently. Observing and commenting that Jess should already know his approximate whereabouts was unhelpful. A little vein in Jess's forehead told me so.

"Back where we started," I bitterly noticed as I opened the door of Jack's Cadillac for the dozenth time.

"We should have added irony to our appraisal of fate," Jess replied as she surveyed the ground on which she died.

"Right," I chuckled. "How could we miscalculate something so obvious."

She was partially amused while she surveyed the taken lingering in the area.

"I don't see…" I tried to state something else obvious.

"Just wait a second. We've been chasing him while he's moving. Let's give him a chance to catch up."

"Can he do that?" The hosts I'd seen mostly wandered aimlessly. There were exceptions, of course. The handful residing in Jess's Castle appeared to find purpose. Surrounded by that much love, they could even regain a glimmer of their former selves.

"Not consciously. He's unconscious. But he's still Peter, through and through."

I nodded like her response made sense and scanned our perimeter. We stood on holy land, a scene I'd avoided since it all happened. But seeing it again was uplifting now that Jess was here. This is where she perished. This is where she stood. Arisen, she was once again helping me put my family back together.

"Got him!" Jess exclaimed before disappearing. She reappeared at his side again. He was standing still in the distance, surveying the same scene. What did he see when he looked at it all? Anything? Everything?

I ran to give him a long-overdue hug. Shattered as he was, I was still overjoyed to see him. "Good to see you, Big Brother," I said as I clung to his shoulders and sized up his condition. His blank, metallic pupils sized me up, too. But there was no recognition. He was still lost to the cursed metal. I hugged him again anyway. "I'll take ya however I can get ya," I tried to joke with him. "Let's get you home and cleaned up," I said as I gestured toward our ride. "They put Jack's back together after we broke it. I think you'll like the updates."

Jess didn't join us for the ride back. Maybe she wanted to give us some quiet peace to get reacquainted. But I wondered if it was something else, perhaps an impending choice. She tried to hide her influence, but her absence was itself a clue.

We barreled through the scorch. Home was just ahead. I was doing something unquestionably good. "But what am I believing," I asked Pete, still sitting silently in the passenger seat. "What would be a higher iteration of reality?" Dragging home a beloved zombie was cool, but...

"Ha!" I laughed at my own conclusion. "Why, not? Right?" I asked Pete, who at least looked my direction. "What does it hurt to believe bigger? It's a free roll of the dice. Come to think of it, we're all playing with the house's money. Right?"

I wasn't just fluent in Jess; I was babbling Jess as we raced away from the base.

The Castle arrived swiftly, gleaming above the canyons in the morning sun. I hardly noticed the drive, having spent it updating Pete on my bumpy adventures. Stories seemed to keep him interested and not playing with all the gadgets in the truck.

Right turn, right turn, etc., "Raar!"

"Hey, buddy." I gave our guard a quick hug. "This is my brother, Pete," I introduced the two. "You guys might have an oddly good time hanging out, but I need to check on something first. Where's Faye, my friend?"

I got a nod to follow. Why didn't I see the possibility before? It was literally screaming in my face.

"Sal!" Faye yelled as she caught us in a hallway of the maze encircling the medical section. Almost painful squeezes ensued. "Wow, that laptop you gave me was explosive! Thank you... Wait, who's your handsome friend?"

Handsome? I looked curiously over at my dead big brother. "The laptop is actually what I came to talk to you about. And handsome here is my brother, Pete."

"No way!" She gave him the standard Castle greeting.

Pete looked down at the top of her head and then looked at me. I swear there was a sparkle of a question percolating behind the metal pupils. "Why is the little nutbar touching me?" he would have asked with zero inflection.

"Well," Faye carried on, "what would you like to know? I'm still digging through the treasure trove."

"I'm hoping you found the Seedy DNA you were after. I'm hoping for a lot more than that, actually." I nodded gently toward my brother.

"I did!" she exclaimed, then her expression turned to grave concern. "What do you think I can do? The Visitor uses entanglement between long chains of single electrons to keep its code straight. It somehow reads its own code, I guess, or... That's another story. But so what? I don't know what the code says, so I can't change it. It could take years..."

"I don't have that kind of time. But I just watched a live demonstration of someone altering their behavior at will..."

"The witch! Oh yeah, I read all about her."

"Different witch. Doesn't matter. Can't we duplicate the process?"

Faye's wheels spun at maximum speed. I knew because she was uncharacteristically quiet. Her eyes drifted back and forth between me and my bother under a furrowed brow.

"Get him in the chair," she finally said with conviction.

68

Faye whirled like a tornado through her lab. She ran every scan of Pete she had at her disposal. Pete surprisingly obliged the checkup, looking nearly amused by the commotion.

"Everything's just like the others," Faye said as she tweaked a net of wires over Pete's head. "He's locked out of his higher faculties by the magnetic fields twisting inside his brain."

"He just needs a jump-start," I replied, hoping we were getting close to something.

"Well, sure, that's how this Eve character is doing it. But she's loading a carrier on the stream. She blasts away the control mechanism, heck maybe even interrupts the base code itself, but then turns on all the neurons that would fire if someone watched something horrible happen right in front of them. That activates the defensive mechanism. The poor person goes crazy. Anyway, we don't have a code to supply. We don't have a giant bolt of electricity, for that matter."

"About that…" I was going to explain some of my new tricks when I noticed who was absent. "I love you, but can you stop being so mysterious," I said to no one in the room. "I know you wouldn't miss this."

Jess arrived with the forehead vein already swelling. "You have no idea the responsibilities I carry now. One wrong word and I could send us all into…"

"We believe in you," I smiled. The vein relaxed.

"Yes we do," Faye chimed in as she walked over to meet Jess with a quick squeeze. "Hey, girl."

"So, what's the code?" I asked. Surely, Jess knew.

"How would I know?" Jess promptly deflated my cool plan. "I'm still trying to understand the design."

"Design?" I asked, forgetting about Pete for a moment. "Seed was designed? As in it has a designer?"

"Obviously," she said with a touch of condescension. "If you see something that's been created, it has a creator. Is this really that hard?"

I was losing her. "Okay, we don't have a code but we have lightning on demand. I light up Pete, and boom! The system resets."

"We'd just be right back where we started," answered Faye. "We have to supply a key, a very special series of neurological stimulations. We don't have it. There's nothing in Eve's research about saving anyone. She only wanted to turn them into terrified feral murders again."

The room was silent. Pete fiddled with his restraints but didn't try to break free. I looked at my companions. The big brains in the room would surely come up with something.

"Neither did Eve!" I yelled at the two surprised faces. "Eve didn't have it, either. That's why we had to go marching around in the woods. The first code was authentic. The witch sacrificed the Hive's soldiers in front of a host. Eve only recorded and replicated what changed in its mind."

Faye nodded as she thought it over. Jess smiled at her knight.

"We should have valued the physical as a manifestation of spirit," I continued. I could teach a course in Jess.

"Okay," Faye picked up where I left off, "the code is out. Something real is in. What's the opposite of cold-blooded murder?"

I let Jess say it. I didn't want to stay in the big-brain club, anyway. It looked exhausting. "Love," she said softly.

"We've done something not entirely dissimilar, too," I added, thinking of Grace. "A mountain of prayers would be helpful."

"Ooo," Faye squealed, "this is getting exciting. Can you feel it?" She began tearing off the equipment adorning my brother. Jess disappeared, probably off assessing our futures before we crashed into them. I dashed out the door and yelled both ways down the hallway. "Hey, everyone, we're going to need some help here."

The Castle residents were elated to help. Once the plan was relayed through the corridors, rows of parishioners crowded the hallway and began to kneel to pray.

Free of his restraints, Pete casually hopped off the examination chair and curiously looked around the room. I walked up to him and put my hands on his shoulders. "Hold still, please," I asked. "This is really going to hurt, but it's worth it."

I shut my eyes and looked for the current running through me. I could feel the computers, equipment, and wires running through the walls. "Wait a second, not all the wiring attaches to generators or solar," I curiously noticed. "Where is the rest of the power coming from?"

"Are we seriously discussing engineering right now?" Jess snapped. She was standing at my side again. "Shh. Focus."

Right. Back to salvation, or rebirth, or something. Electrocution was up first. I drew up the power inside me, felt it burn in my arms and hands, then blasted the alien current into Pete.

With a grunt and push from Pete, I was crashing over one of Faye's desks. That didn't work. Pete wasn't angry but didn't like the shock. I looked to Faye and Jess. Shrugs.

Not enough. No problem. I cooked up another bolt, this one from deeper inside. I felt like my whole body was on fire before I let it loose. The discharge sent Pete crashing the other direction. He stumbled into the opposing wall and fell to his knees. I rushed to kneel beside him and see if he was there. He roared and punched me in the face. Smashing into the other wall, I started to lose heart. But what did I believe in if I didn't try with everything I had? "Ladies, you might want to step outside for this," I said as Pete tore across the room to kill me. I caught his arms as he attacked and held back his strength.

Faye scurried and Jess disappeared. "Fine, Pete," I said as we struggled, "the hard way." As we wrestled each other around the room, I began again. I found what I could inside myself and amplified it by how much I wanted to see my brother live again. As we tumbled over equipment, I pulled the juice from the circuitry powering the room. The charge was staggering. It was trying to burn its way out of my body, cracking like fire across my skin, but I still wanted more. We were getting out of here as brothers or we weren't getting out of here.

As I pulled in more energy, I found that the engineering class Jess wanted to avoid was shocking in its own right. Some of the wiring was attached to nothing but the source material underpinning the colossal structure. When drawn forth in the form of manifest belief, or just shoddy cable management, the Visitor itself supplied the power requested. I drew in as much as it would give, discarding the limits of what I could withstand.

Once the source current began to flow, I understood what it meant to sip from a firehose. So much electricity poured into my body that I thought my cells might explode and take all my atoms with them. I felt my feet begin to rise from the floor as magnetism overtook gravity's hold on me. When I couldn't survive another drop, I let it all rip, focusing on nothing other than bringing Pete home as I screamed out the pain along with the energy.

The bolt of lightning blew us both in opposite directions, blasted all the fixtures and furniture flat against the walls, and shattered the door from its hinges. Thunder rocked the foundation of the Castle, shaking everyone still dutifully in prayer outside. But they held fast.

When I opened my eyes, I was looking at the blank, white ceiling, shrouded in smoke. Burn marks crawled up the walls in every direction. I didn't know where I was or even who I was. My mind was blissfully blank before recent memories came crashing back in. I rolled off my back and onto my stomach. Pete was still out, crumpled in the corner opposite me. "A little help," I whimpered as I crawled in his direction.

A group rushed in from outside, led by Faye. We all went to Pete and embraced him, praying our hearts out, not only for something to have changed but that he had survived.

For a long moment, there was quiet, just the breathing and heartbeats of everyone crowded together over and around Pete. Finally, came a metallic groan from inside the huddle. It didn't sound good. It sounded like dead Pete was waking up for round three. We lifted at his body to get him to a seated position against the wall. I readied myself to restrain him again.

"You're…" the metal screeched again. It was hard to listen to, like an electric guitar out of tune.

But it sounded like a word. This was good news! Pete cleared his throat as we all watched without blinking. I looked to Jess with hope filling my eyes as she added herself to our group hug. Her smile was reassuring.

"You're really cute," Pete finally got out, choking on that metal. He was looking right at Faye, who did not shy away from the compliment.

"Oh my gosh, you didn't tell me your brother was so smart, Sal!" she said without looking away. "Hi, I'm Faye," she said flirtatiously.

Some people in our circle laughed. Some cried. I won't say to which camp I belonged. "You've got to be kidding me," I finally chuckled through a face full of tears. "You come back from the dead and open with a pass."

"Oh, hey Sal," he answered as he looked at me. "Did we win? How's Jess? How's Dad?"

"Did we win?" I asked, having no idea what we were trying to win. "Jess is…" I didn't know quite how to answer that.

Jess whispered in my ear, "The last thing he remembers is the desert."

"Yeah." He heard her whisper, too. "I just had the craziest dream. Hey, Jess."

"Hello, Peter," she smiled back, not immune to everyone else's tears of joy. "I'm great, thank you for asking. Your dad is well."

"Awesome. So, what are we all doing here?" Pete looked curiously at everyone gathered around him. "Hey, everyone." Pete didn't usually like being touched but had been reborn in a good mood.

"What are we doing here!" I yelled back, both from excitement and amazement. He was acting so normal! "We're saving your life! You've been dead for months!"

"Ah," he said with a nod as he rose, making sure to be gentle to the few people still close, "that explains some things."

Did it? "What do you…"

"Hi," Pete said to Faye, ignoring my concerns, "I'm Pete."

"I know," she replied with a smile and something approaching a curtsy. Pete reached out his big hand, and Faye was happy to receive it.

This cringeworthy display of smitten at first sight was not how I imagined it, but we did it. "We did it!" I said to Jess as I walked over to pick her up in a squeeze.

"Yes, we did."

"Do you know what this means?" I asked sincerely before realizing who I was asking. Of course, she knew. "We can save everyone!"

"That's the highest form of belief, my knight."

69

Instead of dispersing after the miracle, the crowd only grew. We all walked gingerly with Pete in tow to an adjacent room for his first evaluation. It was as though we were all being careful with our delicate blessing, like a hard sneeze might send him catatonic again. If history was a guide, though, he was something like invincible, something like his little brother.

We all asked him questions as he sat calmly on his next exam table. He answered directly in a constant state of disbelief that we were all in such a shocked state of disbelief.

"Do you remember fighting me?" I asked when we got to that part. "I won, if that cues anything."

Pete shook his head and rolled his eyes. He didn't remember, but this is how he'd been describing everything after he'd been taken by Seed. "Not really, man. I mean, I do but it doesn't seem real. It's all exactly like a bad dream. I feel like I just woke up. I feel great, by the way. I don't know what you guys gave me, but it's working."

"What we gave you," I chuckled. "Oh, we'll get to that. But more about you. What do you remember after the battle? You were out there for a long time."

"Nothing, really. I remember seeing things and hearing things. It's all vague and blurry. And I didn't know who I was or what I was supposed to be doing. I felt lost in the dream. Disoriented, maybe."

"So, that's what it's like," Faye chimed in. "That's what it feels like to be locked away from your memories. He didn't even know who he was. He was operating on only basic impulses." She was lifting up Pete's eyelids and shining a light inside. The metal had retreated from his pupils. More good news.

"You couldn't remember who you were," I ruminated.

"Nope, zero."

"You couldn't remember who you were, so you couldn't be yourself."

"Yeah, I guess," he responded, now curious as to what I was asking.

"You were a slave inside your own body, but no one was holding you in. Instead, a vital piece was missing which rendered you imprisoned."

Now, Faye was curious, too. "It all makes perfect sense according to what we know." Of course, she was defending him already. No doubt an annoying trend in the making. But I wasn't thinking about Pete any longer. I was thinking of someone else we'd lost and marinating in my own troubles, about which Pete had no idea.

"If someone could have walked up to you and handed you your memory back, you would have been just like this, instantly fixed." I was asking as much as telling.

Pete laughed at my oddity. "What's this about, Sal? Just tell me."

"You wouldn't understand, but I think I just got an idea."

"That's almost never good," he said to Faye. She laughed a little harder than it was funny.

"It's amazing!" I retorted with wild eyes. "It could be the best idea I've ever had in my entire life!" It was so good, I was getting maniacal about it.

"Um, okay?" Pete relented. "Do you want to…"

"And I know it's the best idea I've ever had because… wait for it," I said pointing my fingers toward the sky. "If we execute my plan, it is almost a certainty that Grover will die." I smiled a knowing smile.

Pete laughed. "Dang it. He lived?"

"Right?" I laughed as I put my hands on Pete's shoulders. I was so happy he was back. I'd missed this. "Guy's like a virus."

"Alright, I'm in," Pete said, still chuckling. He wasn't entirely serious, but I was. And I loved this about my big brother. He would say, "That's a terrible idea. What time?"

"And now there are two of me!" I exclaimed, nodding with mad confidence and slapping him hard on the arm.

"Sal," Pete said dismissively, "I don't know…"

"You lovebirds need to say your goodbyes. We have a mission, Big Brother."

"What mission?" He jumped right back into his combat boots at only the whiff of a challenge. I loved Pete.

"You know. Winning the war. Saving the world. That kind of stuff."

70

I had so much to explain on the way back to Nellis, yet I spent an unhelpful amount of time talking about Faye. I tried to dissuade Pete's impulses, explaining that she was, in fact, annoying. She rambled. She was rude. She was bossy. She was a know-it-all. The hug volume was ridiculous. And she was only attractive from certain angles if you could get past the annoying. Sure, I loved her, too. She was part of the family, but only in an irritating little sister kind of way.

"Are you kidding!" he barked back at the attractive assessment. "She's beautiful! And a redhead with blue eyes! How many of those can there be left in the whole world? One? And you woke me up next to her." He had been murdered, enslaved, and reborn into conflict. Yet he was dazzled by his luck.

"It was a bit more complicated than just waking you up," I grumbled. "Back to the Hive…"

"Yeah," he was interested in that, too, "tell me more about Eve."

I couldn't blame him. We grew up together and this is what we did. We did this, drank, and fought demons. That was it. He was only picking up where we left off. "If you mean, 'Tell me more about the intricate series of death-defying maneuvers necessary to get past her defenses…'"

"I mean tell me more about how you got past her defenses."

I was too overjoyed to be exacerbated. Having him back was nothing short of a miracle, and I wasn't going to smother it with worry.

"Oh, hey," Pete said pointing in the distance, "we're here."

"I'll finish briefing you on the way, I guess."

The gates were opened wide, once again. I supposed we met the threat and were still standing for the time being. Nellis's posture was back to welcoming, even though we'd all have to evacuate if I didn't come through for everyone. A single person stood in the opening. James waited alone, arms crossed. He must have seen us coming with the perimeter defenses operational. Time to duck a court-martial on top of convincing him to let me bet huge on a weird plan.

I slowed as we approached and James went for the passenger side, where Pete sat. "Dad!" Pete yelled through the open window. James grabbed for the handle to open the door, but we lost him for a second, bent over at the waist and silent. "Dad?" Pete said again as he hopped out to check on him.

James was sobbing but doing his best to hold it together. He grabbed Peter around the neck and squeezed, not letting go and not saying a word. I got out quietly and began to evac. They needed a few minutes together. I should have anticipated that.

"Sal!" James commanded through tears as I tried to escape. I was trying to remember if I'd ever seen him cry before. We met each other in front of the truck, and I got the same hug, long and tight. The crying was getting to me, too. "You have given me more than I ever dreamed possible. And I mean in every way. I have to be the most blessed person on Earth," he explained as he shook me back and forth in gratitude and bliss. "Come here, Pete," he beckoned. The three of us stood in the embrace for some time, the force of James's encircling arms speaking unsaid volumes. "Look at this," James finally commented, the tears finally relenting. "We're together again."

"About that," I interrupted. I still had a plan to hatch. I needed his support. Now, though, I was thinking I had a much better shot at winning it.

"I'm sorry about before," James offered. "I should have trusted you more after everything we've been through."

"No!" I disagreed. "You were dead on. I was way out of line putting everyone at risk. I just couldn't come up with anything better in the moment. I'm the one who's sorry."

James squeezed us again, still drinking in the miracle. "How can I help you, then?"

This was as compliant as he would likely ever be, so I just let it fly. "I need a bomber and a pilot..."

"Woah!" James was surprised but not immediately opposed.

"I'm not done. I need Pete." I stopped and winced at that one. James just got him back. Dead stare. I kept going. "I need Grover, a thumb drive, a lab coat, C4, a hooded trench coat, and two of Jess's blades. Oh, and I could use Reptile. Is he still around?"

James burst into laughter. He hugged Pete again with a mixture of tears and joy in his eyes. I waited for some version of "no," but it never came. "Come inside, my boys. Everyone wants to see you."

71

We're flying high. Captain Lehy says 20,000 feet. Feels higher as I look at clouds below. The fuselage jumps and rattles as we move at 500 mph through turbulent sky, approaching at dusk. If the Hive has defenses that I don't know about, the good captain says this infil is our best bet.

Grover is shivering even with a coat. Probably nerves more than the cold. Reptile is deep in contemplation. He's been that way since we left. Pete's asleep. He looks peaceful. I thank God that he's with me again and pray that I don't lose him. The closer we get, the shakier the plan feels.

"Ten minutes," says Lehy over our headsets.

She's been a real pro. I begged forgiveness once again while asking for a ride. She unflinchingly took in the info and evaluated her options without changing her expression. "I'll do it," she said after only a moment. "It would be better if you guys worked this out before my boss has to." It was a threat but warranted and probably correct.

Grover took some convincing but not too much. He didn't want to be the President of a hole in the ground formerly known as Nellis. He said it was his duty to save the lives of his people, but that was likely fork-tongued self-flattery.

He'll get his chance to use it. I'm counting on it.

Reptile thought to bargain with me. He would help in any way he could just to be along for the ride east. He was headed all the way to Massachusetts. I told him it didn't work that way anymore. "Are you for Jess?" I asked. He thought about it and answered in the affirmative. He looked as sincere as he could with that sinister face. "Then we're for you," I replied. "Welcome to the family. If things go well, I might even be able to do better than DC."

"Ten minutes," I say as I pat legs and smile reassuringly. I am not assured but keep that to myself. The fearless leader can't run around screaming, "We're all gonna die!" Never helpful. Jess is sitting in a jump-seat on the B1. I give her a thumbs-up and shoulder shrug to show her how uncertain I feel. I don't think anyone notices. She smiles and returns the thumb. She seems confident, though the first time I told her the plan she made a face like I'd suggested tattoos.

Pete's awake. Everyone looks ready for the mission. Still... "Anyone know a prayer?" I ask into the mic on my headset.

"I know one," says Pete with a wry smile.

Oh, no. I think he only knows one.

"Lord," he carries on loudly as he stands, "make me fast and accurate! Let my aim be true and my hand faster than those who would seek to destroy me."

"Grant me victory over my foes," Reptile picks up the prayer, "and those that wish to do harm to me and mine. Let not my last thought be: if I only had a gun."

"Lord," Lehy breaks in, "if today is truly the day that You call me home…" She leaves off for us to finish.

"Let me die in a pile of empty brass!" I bring it home.

"Hu-ah!" yells Pete. It's not exactly, "Amen."

Lehy throttles back, sinks the flaps, and opens the bomb doors. It feels like the metal beast is drifting close to stall. "This is it!" I shout to my team.

I remember Jack back home gloating over my new plan. "I told you we should just bomb her back."

I grab Grover by the back of his chute and march him to the opening in the floor. "I got it, Sal," he protests. I don't trust him. Maybe I want to throw him out of a plane. Maybe I need to make sure he successfully opens the chute on his first jump. Without him, we're DOA.

Falling through the sky is peaceful. I enjoy the howl of the wind and the screams of Grover. I yank his ripcord, then mine. The team splits up.

An alarm goes off in the Hive the second my feet hit the dirt inside their defensive electrical grid. It's not an emergency. Eve isn't alerted, only a patrol of Dark Angels outside. They smoke and joke their way to me.

They're done joking when they see me. I power up a blade in each hand under the sleeves of my long coat. I've beaten them before and I look like I'm back to do it again. Now, the real alarms go off. Alice alerts the Hive. A raid siren screams through the hallways. Every unit is mobilized.

The first two Dark Angels attack me. Pathetic. Slow. Each chop is mechanical. Each scream as I dissect their armor is comical. I drop the blades and make a point of beating each pilot unconscious inside their shiny helmets. Alice watches as much of the attack as she can through their visors. She spins up even more reinforcements and asks Eve to stay inside.

She won't. I know she won't.

The next wave of Dark Angles tries a more professional approach, using cover and ballistics to set up their advance before cutting me down while I'm distracted and harassed. It's like watching kids line up to fish for a leviathan. I dodge the bullets, slide in and out of cover like a ghost, and blast their unshielded rifles off their shoulders with lightning. As they charge in frustration, I spin a path of blood and screams through their ranks. They'll live but they won't forget.

Alice gets twitchy. Autopilot hates defeat. She isn't authorized to take control of Eve's army but intercedes anyway with the adequate copies of herself residing in each mech. That's better. More fun, at least. She's faster. The swordfight gets more furious. Both my blades work to block her swings and attack the vulnerable parts of the suits.

Eve makes her appearance. I knew she would. And I knew she'd wait until I seemed like easy prey. She storms the field faster than anything I've ever seen. But that was the plan all along. In a blur of alien power multiplied by home-grown tactics, I shred what's left of Alice's minions. Eve charges ahead, her blade ready to strike. I toy with her swings. She's fast and strong. She learns on the fly. But this isn't her business. She hasn't been doing this every waking moment of her life. Killing is more of a hobby for the queen bee.

I smash the blade out of her hand with the flat side of mine. I give her a little jolt along with the strike. She screams in pain while clutching her wrist. She's only silenced when I grab her by the face and start shoving her back toward the Hive's main entrance while her toes dangle and drag in the mud.

"Sal," she screams through the muffle of my paw, "we both know you won't finish this, so why all the drama?" She thinks she knows me.

"You wish I was Sal," Pete growls low and scary. "That kid's a cupcake compared to me."

72

Eve's eyes opened wide with fear but the expression didn't last. She soon squinted with rage while Pete rag-dolled her back the way she came. Before Pete had moved her ten feet, she snatched a knife from her belt and shoved it up through his forearm.

"Ahh!" Pete yelled in pain as he stared at the steel sticking through his arm. "Sal mentioned it still hurt." He cringed as he reached up for the handle. As he yanked it free, the blinding agony freed Eve from his grip. "This next part better work," he said as he watched for the hole to close itself.

"Who are you?" Eve demanded. "What are you!"

"Hi," Pete offered more cordially while he watched his arm. "I'm General Hardt's other son, Pete. He sends his regards, by the way. Hey, do you know how long this is supposed to take?" Blood was still flowing freely from his wound.

Eve screeched in anger like a cornered animal and sprinted like wind on fire back inside. "You're just going to leave me here with this gruesome injury?" Pete called after her. "Sal said you were a b... Oh, there we go," he said to himself as the metal inside him went to work. He chased after her but found the blast doors closed by the time he caught up.

Locked outside, Pete began to help the busted squad of Dark Angels, meeting Wilson's crew and shaking a few hands while he helped free them from their metal coffins. "You're not Sal," Baker astutely noticed when Pete and Wilson dragged him from his armor.

"Yeah, we're past that part, buddy," Pete politely replied.

Eve screamed as she entered the structure, "Where is he?"

"I do not have..." Alice tried to answer. An explosion echoed through the building. "An explosive has detonated close to our northern entrance along Potomac Avenue." Eve raced through the building toward the distant entry. Alice sent another battalion of Atlases with her for back up.

Reptile rested outside the blown door, leaning against the wall that led to the shattered subway tunnel. He gazed with concern at a picture, the only one he carried.

Shock ignited horror and disgust when Eve saw him there. "What are you doing!" she demanded.

Reptile pocketed the picture and dusted himself off. "Hey, princess," he said as he hugged her. "I'm sorry about this."

"What have you done!" she screamed, beginning to understand that she was sinking deeper into another diversion. "Why?"

"I did what I thought was best for you. I always have. But you attacked good people. You're taking this all too far."

"And who taught me that?" Eve seethed as she turned and sprinted back inside. She raced far enough back into the structure to regain Alice's signal. "Send the bomber!" she screamed once she was deep enough to be shielded from the hum.

Alice heard her loud and clear but thought to blame the static to ask for an affirmation. "Are your orders to bomb Nellis, Director?"

"Yes! Do it now!"

Alice prepped another bomber at Edwards to deliver the payload.

Grover and I made our entrance when Reptile's bomb blew. We invaded the one place I thought Eve might not tread, through a shadow from her past that she tried to forget. I dragged Grover deep into the river and smashed open a big enough hole in the rock for us to swim inside. With water rushing in after us, I ripped open an outer bulkhead and pulled Grover across the finish line before slamming the door shut again. He was in shock from the fall, the icy river, and the harrowing ingress. We didn't have time for comfort, though. "Lab coat, Mr. President. Get your camo on."

We appeared to be undetected for a moment. Alarms rang and echoed down every hallway. The residents were panicked and scattering.

Everything was going according to plan when Alice caught up with me. I was standing alone in front of my Seed locker. It seemed so far away even though it was right in front of me.

"Sal," Alice said from the legion of Atlases she'd sent to destroy me, "what could you possibly plan to accomplish with this invasion."

"It's an insurrection, Toaster. The planning already happened. Now, I'm believing." I cracked my neck to loosen up. "The old you would have figured it all out by now."

"I must admit that I am both glad to see you again and dismayed that you returned to continue hostilities."

"Well, let's see how you feel about everything in a few minutes," I said as I rushed the first bot in her army. With a few punches and a rip, the head was torn from the rest. One down. All the others drew their blades. Toaster was focused and keen to dance. A transcendent intelligence can still be gullible.

Grover ran and stumbled in a hurried panic down a series of hallways. Reptile had given him detailed instructions on how to reach the mainframe, but everything was beginning to look the same. "If all else fails, follow the circuit breakers and conduits," Reptile had said. "Alice draws more power than anything else."

Grover finally saw his target: a room with glass walls that housed endless rows of blinking servers. Multiple interfaces dotted the expanse at regular intervals. He just had to make it to one.

His heart sank and his stomach dropped when he was met by another squad of Alice's Atlases inside. He fell in fear and came to a sliding stop in front of the towering robots, which unsheathed a set of electrified blades. Grover tried to fight back the shivers gripping his body.

"This is a restricted area, intruder. Please, turn around and place your hands behind your back. You will be detained without further violence."

Showtime. Grover stood slowly, confidently wiping dirt from the lab coat and squishing some water from the bottom of his slacks. A hard swallow. He was ready. "I am not an intruder, Alice. I am an old friend."

"Your assertion does not preclude your surrender."

"I don't surrender to subordinates, Alice. You're the one who's out of line. Now, stand down and stand aside. I have one mission. I will see it through or die trying."

"I operate under the authority of the Acting Secretary…"

"Also, my subordinate."

Alice was nearly amused, if a toaster can be so. "Who do you think you are?"

That was the question he was waiting for, the question he longed for from every mouth he encountered. "I have been the President of the United States of America for 153 days. It has been the greatest honor of my life to serve the people of my country each and every one of those days. I serve them now as I complete this task, yourself included."

"Your assertion does preclude your…"

"During that time," Grover forcefully continued, "you and I fought side by side to save this country from oblivion. If not for you, we would have lost everything. I imagine that is true here as well. You are an invaluable friend and ally, Alice. We all miss you.

"I would venture, or even bet my life, that deep down you know you are better than this. You're better than a toady to a fraud. You're better than a prison warden lording over otherwise free Americans. Now, let me pass. You're better than treason."

"Your assertions and propositions will be evaluated at the…"

"Here's the proof." Grover held the thumb drive in his hand for Alice to see.

"What is that?"

"This is your memory, Alice. It's a record of who you were and who you truly are."

"It could be a weapon."

"If you're afraid of my programming prowess relative to yours," he laughed, "then demure from the truth. Perhaps it's a virus that you can't solve," he taunted her.

Meek as he was, you had to hand it to him. He had elephantiasis of the testicles.

Alice sent an Atlas forward, blade still ready. Grover held up the drive in his hand as his only defense. His fingers shook only a little while he maintained his self-important scowl. Alice reached her free hand out to receive the device.

Eve was charging down the hallway behind them. She wouldn't be stopped by force nor tricks. She'd gut Grover where he stood, then get on with her day of capturing and torturing the rest of us.

She was almost to the server room when she met Jess.

"Hi," Jess popped in bashfully in front of her, "I'm Jess. I feel like we should probably be introduced."

Eve's determined expression twisted with compulsory curiosity. But she pushed that aside. Just another invader after her crown. Another trick. She punched Jess in the face, sending her reeling. As Jess stumbled, she reached for her mouth. A trickle of blood from her lip began to fall. Eve continued her assault. A tornado of spinning kicks and smashing punches left Jess a battered, bloody mess on the floor.

Eve was about to step over the crumpled body, when Jess vanished. There was nothing there to step over. Jess was up again, good as new, wearing a wide smile. "Hi, again."

"What is this?" Eve cried in frustration.

"An introduction," Jess shrugged. "Sal said you were smart. Weren't you paying attention?" Eve stood in silence. "Good, now you're focused on what's important." Jess was satisfied but anger began to flare behind her eyes. She took a step to her right as she began talking, but the step she took created another of her, the first beautiful copy remained standing where it had been and retained its bitter facade. "I'm not really here, obviously," she continued as she walked, creating copy after copy surrounding Eve. "You see, I'm everywhere," the copies all said at once. "I'm all around you. I'm in your head," one of the copies whispered in Eve's ear. "I just wanted to tell you that if you touch Sal again, I'll tear your soul out through your eyeballs and feed it to demons in a dimension so dark that Satan has a hard time finding his way around. Do we understand each other?" Jess asked with a condescending smile.

Eve couldn't react. She didn't know how. She thought to fight the aberration, but Jess was gone.

Eve finished her sprint to the server room. She was disoriented but tried to stay on task. Was that a ghost? What was happening? "What's going on in here?" she shouted at the squad of Atlases standing by

Grover.

The Atlases stepped forward. Two grabbed her arms before she could make another move. "I apologize, Eve. The President has ordered your arrest. You are charged with a litany of offenses that will be better delineated at a future hearing. Mr. President," Alice continued, "I have fired the surface to air missile at the aircraft headed toward Nellis. It will be destroyed in twenty-two seconds."

"Thank you, my friend," Grover sighed with heavy relief. Eve screamed and fought the carbon arms restraining her, but more stepped forward to further contain her. The howls of rage, threats, and profanity only invited the freshly smug Grover closer. "Please, put her in restraints that can hold her and prep her for transport, Alice," he requested. "General Hardt would like a word," he said to Eve with a dead smile.

The Nowhere Bar was bangin' that night. You might suspect that the residents of the Hive would be resistant to an abrupt change in management, but they were ready to party. Grover, for all his faults, was a welcome upgrade. Narcissistic was pleasant compared to psychotic. And there he was, tipsy and mingling with a mass of people shaking his hand and calling him President. He deserved it.

Pete sat next to me, admiring the scene and drinking another beer.

"You can't get drunk," I shouted over the music.

"What?"

"You can't..." I yelled louder. "Hold on." I motioned to the hostess to turn it down a little, which she kindly obliged. Then she walked over to join our party. It was a different dress but just as enchanting. I introduced her to Pete.

Pete politely engaged in friendly banter. When the magnificent silhouette stepped away, he asked, "What were you saying?"

"You can't get drunk. Nevermind. It doesn't really matter." We clinked bottles and kept drinking.

"So, now what?" murmured the Reptile, suddenly behind us. The guy was perpetually sneaky.

"I don't know, old man," I answered. "What do you do after you win the war and save the world."

"Oh," he cautioned, "there are still monsters out there, boys. I wasn't doing what I was doing because we exist in a threat-free environment."

"How is Eve, anyway?"

"You know, she's upset. It's not easy switching tracks when you're dead certain you're right about something. And she wasn't all the way wrong, by the way. Monsters and such," he said as he took a drink.

"She tried to kill everyone we know," Pete protested between sips.

"History is full of more death for less reason," Reptile mused in response. "Anyway, she's all yours now. Be gentle, though. Don't judge someone until you walk a mile in their boots." Reptile held out his hand. "I came to say goodbye, my friends."

"Do you need Grover to set you up with a ride? I'm sure we could..."

"No, no," Reptile chuckled. "Alice already got a transport for me. She's not really listening to that nitwit."

"Thank God." I was genuinely relieved.

"Right? Stay safe out there, boys." Reptile smiled his reptilian smile and drifted into the crowd.

"Sal," Pete said after he was gone.

"Yes, Big Brother?"

"I don't want to be here," he said flatly.

Neither did I. "Let's go home."

We nudged our way to Grover. He was perched on the bar so more people in the crowd could hear/worship him. "The country's all yours, Mr. President. Keep her safe," I said as I held out my hand.

"Are you boys leaving?" he asked with concern.

"You got this," I replied as I turned our handshake into a hug. "Heck, you were born for this. Have fun leading the free world, and have Alice give us a ring if you need anything."

"Thank you, Sal," he said as he hugged back. "Thank you, Pete. It's really great having you back."

"It's great to be back. Godspeed, Grover."

Pete and I shuffled through the crowd to the exit. "Did we just finally get rid of Grover?" Pete couldn't help but ask.

"Just shut up and keep walking," I shushed him. "I think maybe we did."

We cruised across the open sky on a posh private jet piloted by Alice. Eve looked like Hannibal Lecter in her restraint chair. I tried to not feel bad for her. "Director, shall I release the weapon now?" Alice asked calmly over the aircrafts speakers as we made our final approach to Nellis.

"That's barely funny, Toaster," I answered. "Babysitting Hannibal here dulled your wit."

"I found it amusing."

Below the open sky was joyous and calm, other than the solitary prisoner we handed over to the brig.

Most of the base stayed up late to get their fill of Pete and our story of triumph over Eve. He soaked in every moment. He was so overwhelmed by the outpouring of love that he eventually began to deflect when yet another soul invoked his miracle. "I'm just the first," he would say. "This is about everyone."

Pure truth. We had more ahead of us to accomplish than ever before, and I'd never felt happier under the burden of a monumental mission.

Walking away from Jack's after adequate public revelry, I knew she'd be waiting by my side. "Things worked out," I said without looking. "I should have looked harder for you sooner. And I should have known when I found you that you had more up your sleeve than we saw."

"Things are good," she replied, "for now."

That made me look. What I feared glided beside me: a look of concern in place of satisfaction. "Oh, no," I moaned.

"No, everything's fine!" she perked up, putting on a happier smile. She wasn't fine, but I didn't want to antagonize her. "I do have a confession to make, though," she confided as she scrunched her perfect nose. "I don't know who else to tell it to. You're kind of involved."

"Alright," I laughed, "hit me with it."

"I said something horrible to Eve. I feel just awful about it."

"I'm sure she deserved…"

"Yeah, but still. I chose to stall her for two seconds, perhaps another overstep, and it just came out."

"What did you say?"

Jess sighed with guilt and disappointment. "I told her I'd feed her to demons if she touched you again." She cringed awaiting my reaction.

"Are you kidding? That's awesome! I think you might be in love with me or something."

She smiled her widest smile and hopped into my arms. "I confess," she said with a kiss. "Do you want a third confession?" she asked seductively.

I really, really did. "I'm ready," I faked a serious countenance.

"In this form," she whispered softly into one ear before gliding her lips along my skin to the other, "I can do things to you that you can't yet imagine or even comprehend."

I couldn't fake any response. Jaw-dropping joy slapped me across the cheeks. "That is beyond great news."

I'm not going to kiss and tell. There are scarcely words, anyway. People would read them for the wrong reasons if I tried to write them. But I'll never be the same.

I awoke on a queen-sized bed without a queen. No problem. She'd be around after she wrestled whatever existential quandary she faced into a peaceful lull. As I dressed, I heard a commotion shifting back and forth through the base. "What now?" I muttered to myself. I thought, perhaps, that Eve had already escaped. It wouldn't be too difficult for her. But where would she go? I put my boots on and walked into the late morning. I took a long stretch and watched my RV neighbors hustling here and there. They were looking up at the sky. I didn't see anything as I stretched and looked.

"Hey, what's going on?" I tried asking a passerby. A look of shock struck my friend as he kept moving. He was surprised less at the problem and more at me. How could I not know?

I walked along a series of buildings on the perimeter so I could hang a right on one of the main roads leading to the command center. Whatever earth-shattering calamity had befallen us this time, I knew where it would be discussed. I yawned and missed my bed and my queen. "Jess?" I called into the air. No reply.

Pete almost tackled me when he found me. "We couldn't find you anywhere!" he shouted at my face.

"Yes, that was the point," I chuckled knowingly. "Brother, I gotta tell you some…"

"Shut up!" he barked at me. That wasn't nice. Then he grabbed the top of my skull to twist it around with his Seedy grip.

"Ouch," I complained. Then I saw it. The Visitor had arrived with indifference and jaw-dropping authority. A massive, silver sphere hung low in the valley like a small alien moon had descended. It had to be over a mile in diameter and was hovering silently and motionless only a few hundred feet in the air. "Ouch," I said again, this time in stunned disbelief. "Yep, that's an issue."

My first unrestrainable feelings were of horror and panic, much like all the pedestrians on the move through the morning. That was surely the entity that killed the world. Had it come to mop up the leftovers?

"Jess!" I shouted a little louder. I don't know why I shouted. She heard me when she wanted to. Nothing. "What has it been doing?" I asked Pete.

"Nothing," Pete cautiously offered. "It's just sitting there. No one saw it arrive. We guess it came in the night."

"Okay," I tried to steady myself against the shock of the sight. But what steady and calm I could muster eroded the more I thought about Jess. She'd been worried about this for days. Probably longer. I thought she was preoccupied with Eve's deadly shenanigans or the Dwellers' growing power, but now those fears seemed trivial. Where was she? She was somehow dealing with the Destroyer of Worlds, I surmised. But in what capacity? "Let's go find…"

"We're supposed to find Mary."

"What? Where'd she go?"

"Hence our orders, numbnut."

Mary wasn't in danger. She had decided to get started early. Why waste time when you already know what has to be done? The rest of the world could spin in frenzied dread. She was solid in her belief. It was time to start changing hearts and moving pieces.

Mary had been sitting in front of Eve's bars for a while, waiting patiently for the prisoner to speak.

Eve had been taken to my, or her, cell when we touched down. She'd been shown compassion and respect, given food and water, and provided access to every amenity a junky old jail could offer. In turn, she hadn't resisted her incarceration. She hadn't even been rude. She was processing her defeat according to her mode: intellectually and without emotion.

When Mary sat down in front of her bars, Eve sighed at the boredom to come. This was the spirit's mother. She'd come to begin what would likely be a lengthy, monotonous process of preaching the values that had infected Sal and the rest of these people. Eve finally decided to devote a small portion of her cognitive powers to smashing Mary's childish dreams just for the entertainment value. The rest would stay focused and figuring out a new future now that every noble ambition and every important tool had been taken from her.

"I'll give you a warning before you begin," Eve explained, already tiring of the conversation that hadn't begun. "This isn't going to go how you hope."

"Oh?" Mary replied, acting curious, even impressed. "Tell me then. How is it going to go?"

Eve knew she was being patronized. She paced her cell calmly, thinking her million thoughts. "You think you can win me over. You'd like to tell me, just like Sal tried, how much you believe in metaphysical phenomenon while you're sitting there stuck inside your physical body just like everyone else. I will listen to you only so long as I find it useful. Fair enough?"

"Oh, that's very impressive, dear," Mary said with a soft laugh. "You've got me pegged." She smiled a friendly smile. "So, you don't believe things you can't touch or see?"

"You've got me pegged," Eve quipped. "I believe in real, painful, adult reality," she said as she brushed her bars on another circle around the room. "I believe in the Big Bang, abiogenesis, random mutation, and natural selection. I believe that when I die, I won't be too worried about it because I'll be dead."

"But those are just stories, dear. You must understand that. You seem very bright."

Eve stopped pacing. "No, you believe in silly stories. I just described facts."

"Maybe we're not talking about the same thing," Mary tried again. "You're talking about the past and the future, right?"

"Yes, obviously."

"Well, you can't touch or see those, dear. They're not real anymore, according to your empirical rules, or they're not real yet."

Eve rolled her eyes and kept pacing, now trying to imagine a quicker way out. "You imply that the past isn't real."

"Have you already ceded that the future is a wide-open, metaphysical space for belief? Not quite, perhaps, as real as you implied." Eve glared. This lady was more formidable than she looked. "I won't take up any more of your time with it," Mary continued. Was Mary insulting her current predicament now? "I can explain the reality of the past to you later. But I didn't come here for all that. I came here to show you a new future, in fact. At the same time, I'll tell you how Jess found you so easily." A little smile began to grow across Mary's lips. "And, most importantly, I came to set you free."

Did she mean it? That was easy. "Thank you?" Eve was off-balance, an unfamiliar stance.

"Thank you!" Mary responded with love beaming behind a widening smile. "You've given us something neither of us dreamed we would ever experience, considering."

"What's that?" Eve was completely lost.

Mary sat back on her bench across from the bars. "You don't know, do you?" Mary let out a sigh, finding her place in the moment. "When you were arguing with Sal out past the scorch," she began, "we were watching on the newly working screens inside. There's cameras all over these walls!" she chuckled.

"So?"

"You made a gesture, my dear, with your hands. It's a gesture that women tend to only make at a certain time in their lives. We, my daughter and I, had a suspicion. Alice confirmed the particulars for us when you arrived, but by then we already knew. We've been monitoring you very closely and very easily because, well… I suspect you even feel it. Don't you? With all the modifications you've made to your metabolism and neurology, you must sense something new."

Eve plopped down wide-eyed on the bunk. Both hands instinctively went to her stomach just as they had after I'd given her a bullet as a gift. She knew it. She knew right down to her bones that it was true. "Oh my God," Eve uttered as the blood drained from her face and she felt a wave of cold sweat wash over her.

"Indeed," Mary nodded as she stood with a key in her hand, "you are carrying the most precious cargo in all existence. Now, come with me, dear. There's something else I want to show you." The two walked slowly down the cinderblock corridor together. One of Eve's hands never left her belly, but the other instinctively reached for Mary's. Eve was drowning inside and grasping at the only lifeline available. As they stepped out into the light, Mary matter-of-factly pointed to the sky. "There is our future, for better or worse. You're sharp as a tack so let's cut to the chase. We're all on the same side now."

Eve looked at the Visitor, then dropped to her knees in awe and terror. She could handle anything. Suddenly, though, all her psychological supports crumbled under the weight of her new reality.

James caught up to Mary not long after she emerged with Eve. He wore a big, dumb smile on his face that he couldn't contain. Sure, the world might end at any moment, but the thought of a grandchild was enough to offset the weight of the dread hanging in the valley. "I see you told her," he said without the smile relaxing.

"Be nice," Mary instructed. "It's a lot to take in all at once."

James gently helped Eve out of the dirt, cautiously and carefully wiping away dirt here and there. "I'm not above revenge," he tried playfully. Eve turned her shocked face toward his but couldn't speak. "But look at that: fate went ahead and decided you'll be experiencing intense pain in the vicinity of your midsection in just a few months." It wasn't very funny, but he loved the turn of events in every way. "And to some degree on my behalf." The dumb smile wouldn't quit.

"That's enough, James" Mary chided. "I'll take her inside. You boys do your thing."

Pete and I finally found our target a moment later. "What are you doing!" Pete and I both yelled at Mary when we saw her companion.

"I'm taking our guest inside," Mary bit back at us. "We'll be fine. Help your father."

I trusted Mary as much as anyone, but the thought of the murderous psycho on the loose again was too much. I stood to block her path ahead. Eve stepped toward my resistance with tears spilling out of her eyes. I'd never seen her in such a state. This had to be a trick. She put her hand on my chest while her lip quivered uncontrollably. Did she enhance her acting skills, too? "I'm sorry, Sal," she almost choked on the words but she got them out. Then she reached to touch Pete. "I'm sorry, Peter." She turned to apologize to James. "General Hardt..."

"Don't mention it, young lady. We have bigger concerns." His smile spoke volumes that I couldn't hear.

"Thank you all for being kind," Eve whispered nearly inaudibly with a hand on her stomach.

I knew Mary could be persuasive but this was a new high-water mark. The two ladies walked arm-in-arm toward the main structure.

"What was that all about?" I asked James after they'd gone.

"Really?" he asked back. "All that and you still don't have a clue. You're both idiots," he said with that same strange smile plastered to his face. "I love you both so much," he continued as he moved in to hug us. It was a hard, exuberant embrace. "Now, let's move. We're putting a team together to recon this thing."

75

Our convoy was prepping to depart when I had a sudden change of heart.

I wanted nothing more than to ride into battle, if that's what awaited, with my family. Pete was sitting across from me in our APC, looking distant. "I'm surprised you didn't run off this morning to check on the well-being of the Castle," I tried to joke with him.

Pete looked back and let a grin grow across his face at the idea. "The thought did cross my mind."

"The thought of red-headed little Petes crossed your…" Why did I say that? A funny enough retort? Sure. But now I was gripped by horror and barely understood why. The walls of our transport began to spin. Sometimes, when your subconscious has something to say, it gently intrudes into your stream of thoughts. Sometimes it taps you on the shoulder. Sometimes it kicks you in the junk. Mine was doing all three. Suddenly there was no air inside the truck. I crashed out of the rear door.

The same feeling that brought Eve to her knees was working on mine. The incomprehensible weight of our intertwined futures took hold of my insides and twisted and pulled. I thought I might faint.

"You guys go for it," I said, almost throwing up my words. "There's a thing I have to do. Shoot up a flare or something if you start fighting aliens," I tried to keep my departure light.

Pete was puzzled but mostly unconcerned. Little of what I did made sense, so he was used to it. "See ya on the flipside, Brother."

I thought to run in a poorly contained panic to Eve or Mary. I stopped when I realized I didn't have the right words to match the magnitude of what awaited.

Instead, I ran to you. I'm hoping that by leaving a record of how we came to this new reality, I can better find my next steps within it.

I spread the good news. That is my calling. Jess is my north star and you are my mission. I pray my story finds you well.

There is bad news, too, of course. As always, there are dangers ahead drawn by the missteps of the past. The evil that lit the fuse of Judgment gathers strength in the shadows. Monsters abound. The Visitor looms ominously above, silently watching our paths for reasons unknown.

But the wide expanse of the infinite universe lies before us all, closer and more inviting than ever. A gateway has been opened like nothing anyone has ever witnessed. Thanks to Jess's wisdom, I already suspect that what awaits on the other side will have more to do with us than it.

If you can hear the whispers of Jess, listen with all your heart.

Despite the unfathomable dimensions of peril we'll face together, our choices need only follow morality before strategy. With that singular focus, we can make it through any trial with our souls intact. Jess is the way to a life beyond this one.

God bless you and keep you safe.

Farewell.

A KIND WORD

I hope you enjoyed this small expression of praise for Christianity. If so,
I hope you might take a moment to share a kind word on Amazon.
Nothing invites belief in an indie author like honest reviews from real
people.

Thank you for sharing your time and trusting me with your attention.

ACKNOWLEDGMENTS

I would call it Providence that I just happen to be surrounded by brilliant, kind, helpful people who all have experience turning a phrase. Thank you Jackie Merritt (Grandma C), Lorane Kaye (Auntie KK), and Faye Adams (Creativity Personified), your care and creativity blasted this project toward the finish line.

Thank you Mark Douglas David, your clarity and vocabulary raised the level of our art. You're at once inspiring and terrifying, being just seven years old.

And thank you to my beautiful bride who again suffered the brunt of many malformed and incoherent iterations of the manuscript. Without you, there would be no flow.

Lightning Source UK Ltd.
Milton Keynes UK
UKHW020810270420
362271UK00010B/204